"As anyone who has studied New Testament chronology knows, the dates frequently presented to unsuspecting undergraduates as settled 'facts' are often anything but. In *Rethinking the Dates of the New Testament*, Bernier presents a synthetic, comprehensive, and rigorously reasoned case for earlier composition. This book is a major contribution to the study of Christian origins. It not only needs to be read; it needs to be reckoned with."

—**Brant Pitre**, Augustine Institute Graduate School of Theology

"Bernier has written the go-to book on dating the collection of texts now known as the New Testament (and some of the Apostolic Fathers). Bernier provides the first dedicated work on New Testament chronology for the twenty-first century, and it is a resource that I desperately wished for in my earlier years as a student. He combines critical analysis with balanced judgments and communicates technical issues and problems in an easy-to-read, jargon-free way. I found myself surprised, challenged, and better informed. Anyone interested in the emergence of Jesus-movement literature and history must consult this book."

—**Isaac T. Soon**, Crandall University

"Chronology provides us with a window into the history of the earliest followers of Jesus and can help to establish an important piece of the contexts in which the books of the New Testament were written. In this rigorous yet accessible book, Bernier presents a compelling case for relatively early dates for the New Testament texts. *Rethinking the Dates of the New Testament* provides readable, fair, and concise presentations of the central questions, passages, arguments, and debates pertaining to the chronology of the composition of each book of the New Testament. This makes it a fantastic introduction to a key scholarly issue. At the same time, Bernier's arguments are methodologically grounded and careful, resulting in evidence-based conclusions that are reasonable and responsible. The book is engaging and clear, making it a good resource for students, but it is also the sort of historically and logically rigorous work that will make it a must-read for anyone interested in historical approaches to the New Testament or early Christianity."

—**Jordan J. Ryan**, Wheaton College

"In this carefully argued study, New Testament scholar Jonathan Bernier addresses the deceptively simple but exceedingly complex question of when

T0284874

the texts included in the New Testament—as well as 1 Clement, the Didache, the Epistle of Barnabas, and the Shepherd of Hermas—were written. Most scholars routinely accept what has become the majority view regarding these dates without themselves engaging the multiple problems that lurk below the surface. Here we find, for the first time in fifty years, a full monograph dedicated to offering the reader a synthetic treatment of the issues involved. Regardless of whether one accepts Bernier's conclusions, this book is the new must-read volume for anyone who wants to examine the dates of these ancient compositions."

—**Anders Runesson**, University of Oslo

"Bernier offers a much-needed corrective to the tendency for dates assigned to New Testament works to drift further in opposite directions due more to ideological preferences than to evidence, or to be placed in the middle of a possible range as though that were the best way to respond to our uncertainty. With careful attention to the evidence for each work, Bernier makes a strong case for dates that are often earlier than the scholarly consensus. He takes seriously our inability to be certain and precise about dates, never shying away from providing a range that starts astonishingly early or continues well into the second century when the evidence supports it. At the same time he never allows the range of possibilities to hinder arguing for what is *likely*. Whether by gaining wide acceptance or by prompting well-argued responses, Bernier's book promises to shake up the scholarly study of the New Testament and some extracanonical Christian works. What Bernier has provided will undoubtedly serve as an impetus to refreshing scholarly conversations for decades to come."

—**James F. McGrath**, Butler University, Indianapolis

RETHINKING THE DATES OF THE NEW TESTAMENT

RETHINKING THE DATES OF THE NEW TESTAMENT

The Evidence for Early Composition

Jonathan Bernier

Baker Academic
a division of Baker Publishing Group
Grand Rapids, Michigan

© 2022 by Jonathan Bernier

Published by Baker Academic
a division of Baker Publishing Group
PO Box 6287, Grand Rapids, MI 49516-6287
www.bakeracademic.com

Printed in the United States of America

Library of Congress Cataloging-in-Publication Data
Names: Bernier, Jonathan, author.
Title: Rethinking the dates of the New Testament : the evidence for early composition / Jonathan
    Bernier.
Description: Grand Rapids, Michigan : Baker Academic, a division of Baker Publishing Group,
    [2022] | Includes bibliographical references and index.
Identifiers: LCCN 2021047692 | ISBN 9781540961808 (paperback) | ISBN 9781540965264
    (casebound) | ISBN 9781493434671 (ebook) | ISBN 9781493434688 (pdf)
Subjects: LCSH: Bible. New Testament—Authorship—Date of authorship. | Manuscript dating.
Classification: LCC BS2315.5 .B47 2022 | DDC 225.6/6—dc23/eng/20211006
LC record available at https://lccn.loc.gov/2021047692

Baker Publishing Group publications use paper produced from sustainable forestry practices and post-consumer waste whenever possible.

22   23   24   25   26   27   28   8   7   6   5   4   3   2

In memory of Sascha Kokott (1977–2019)
And in honor of Heidi Kokott

Contents

PART 5 Early Extracanonical Writings

Acknowledgments

As is inevitable in a study of this size, I owe greater debts to a greater number of people than I could ever hope to repay or even mention. This problem is magnified by the fact that this project was fifteen years in the making, having begun during my doctoral studies as notes for my comprehensive examinations. What I expected to be an afternoon's labor soon developed into a private obsession and eventually grew into a monograph. Nonetheless, I will here try to thank as many people as I can.

As always, I thank my parents, Anne and Alan Bernier, for their numerous forms of support over the years and my oldest and dearest friends, Jamie and Debra Lediet, and their children, Nicholas and Madison, for decades of friendship. Jamie in particular witnessed the roots of this study; no doubt the interests that led to this work were sown when we were children sitting in church together. And I thank our Sunday school teachers, Alwyn Conquest and his late wife, Elizabeth, for humoring our antics and inflaming our imaginations. More recently, Alwyn audited my course on Revelation at Regis College in Toronto, which was an honor since I first studied the book with any earnestness in his Sunday school class.

I thank William Acres, of Huron University College at the University of Western Ontario, for being my first academic mentor; my *Doktorvater*, Anders Runesson, then of McMaster University and now of the University of Oslo, not just for almost twenty years of friendship and mentorship but more concretely for being the first to raise the possibility that someone somewhere might actually be interested in reading my thoughts on the dates of the New Testament; Eileen Schuller and Stephen Westerholm, professors emeriti from the Department of Religious Studies at McMaster University, whose collective wisdom continues to inform both my teaching and my writing; my former doctoral classmates at McMaster University, John G. Bolton and Jordan Ryan, for probably hundreds of hours of conversations about the matters discussed within these pages; the many other wonderful staff, classmates, students, and faculty at McMaster University who over the years supported me and my work in so many ways, most notably Stephanie Balkwill, Kimberly Beek, Miriam DeCock, Caleb De Jong, Abigail MacBain, the late Camilla Mryglod, and Alisha Pomazon; Wally Cirafesi and Greg Fewster, for our incredibly fruitful group reading of John A. T. Robinson's *Redating the New Testament* almost a decade ago now; Bill Heroman, whose unflagging support for my work in general and this study in particular has been a constant source of encouragement; and my former students and colleagues at St. Francis Xavier University, especially Ronald Charles, Ken Penner, and Adela Sandness.

This project might never have reached completion if I had not relocated in the summer of 2018 to Regis College (Toronto), where I was granted the privilege not only of teaching New Testament but also of serving as the executive director of the Lonergan Research Institute (LRI). The warmth and support of the Regis community combined with the resources available at the broader Toronto School of Theology (TST) and University of Toronto have been a godsend, as has the opportunity to find gainful academic employment within a two-hour train ride of my hometown. Arnel Aquino, Julie Cachia, Elaine Chu, John Dadosky, Teresa Helik, Scott Lewis, Mary Reynolds, Gordon Rixon, Colleen Shantz, Jerry Skira, and Scott Vaincourt were particularly helpful during my transition to and first years at Regis and the TST; and I cannot speak highly enough of Susan Wood, who joined Regis as academic dean when I entered my second year at the college. I must also express my gratitude to the many students and scholastics here at the TST who have taught me at least as much as I have taught them. I would single out for mention Andrea Nicole Carandang, Kyu-Hong Cho, Christopher Kellerman, Adam Lalonde, Virginia Mervar, Sam Needham, Robert Revington, and Ashley Tran.

Words cannot adequately express my gratitude to the board of the LRI, as well as to members of the broader Lonergan community, for their generous support as I transitioned into the role of executive director. In addition to names already mentioned above, Brian Bajzek, Darren Dias, Joseph Gordon, Greg Lauzon, Fred Lawrence, Reid Locklin, Eric Mabry, Kenneth Melchin, Gilles Mongeau, Mark Morelli, Neil Ormerod, Justin Schwartz, Michael Vertin, and Jeremy Wilkins all deserve special mention. I would also like to especially recognize the support of Robert M. Doran, who passed away just a few weeks before I submitted this manuscript to the publisher. I cannot praise or thank highly enough the past and present graduate assistants who have honored the LRI with their remarkable skills during my tenure, including Robyn Boeré, Meghan Bowen, Hannah Ferguson, Erica Lee, Fiona Li, Patrick Nolin, and Matthew Thollander. Now-doctor Boeré and soon-to-be-doctor Li deserve special mention: Robyn for her work leading and organizing the graduate assistants as well as helping me settle into my new role during my first year as director, and Fiona for seamlessly taking over Robyn's responsibilities in my second.

The Canadian Jesuits have been beyond generous in their support. I am humbled daily that they have entrusted me not only to teach the study of Sacred Scripture but also to direct an apostolate devoted to preserving, promoting, developing, and implementing the thought of one of their own. In addition to those whom I have already mentioned, I would thank Peter Bisson, who was serving as provincial of the former Jesuits in English Canada when I was hired and began working at Regis and the LRI; Erik Oland, the current provincial of the Jesuits of Canada; Joseph Schner, past president of Regis College, who was instrumental in the process that brought me to Regis and the LRI; and Thomas Worcester of the New England province, current president of Regis College. The Society of Jesus has for almost five centuries labored to elevate and enrich our collective intellectual life, and I am honored and grateful for the opportunity to help support in even the smallest way their ongoing labors in this regard.

Friends on social media have no doubt heard about The Cat, a.k.a. Cupid. I would thank her, but she needs no further inflation of her ego.

I began working on these acknowledgments two years before the manuscript was due because I knew my own memory well enough to be painfully aware that no amount of time would ensure that I properly thanked all whom I should. I have revisited it periodically with the hope that this would minimize the likelihood of forgetting those whose names ought not be forgotten. Please do not judge me too harshly if your name is absent when it ought not to be. Such failure speaks entirely to the imperfection of my memory, and not at all to the depth of my gratitude. All of you named here and many more should expect to find some part of yourselves in this book: your contributions to my life and thought have cumulatively made it a far better work than it could have otherwise been.

I owe so much to so many. Nonetheless, there was no question that I must dedicate this book to one of my oldest and dearest friends, who tragically passed away on December 12, 2019. As such, this book is dedicated to Sascha and Heidi Kokott. Sascha, thank you for almost thirty years of ridiculous antics, inside jokes, and most importantly, steadfast friendship through all seasons. You truly were the best of us, and I am far better for having known you. And Heidi, I will never truly understand your grief over Sascha's passing, but I do know that you have every reason to be proud of your son. Please accept this dedication as a humble testament to how much he touched my life and that of so many others.

Abbreviations

General

§(§)	section marker(s)
BCE	before the Common Era
ca.	*circa*, approximately
CE	of the Common Era
cf.	*confer*, compare
chap(s).	chapter(s)
d.	died
ed(s).	editor(s), edited by, edition
esp.	especially
et al.	*et alii*, and others
Gk.	Greek
i.e.	*id est*, that is
km	kilometer(s)
Lat.	Latin
n.s.	new series
NSDAP	Nationalsozialistische Deutsche Arbeiterpartei, Nazi Party
NT	New Testament
OT	Old Testament
p(p).	page(s)
Praef.	*praefatio*, preface
r.	reigned
SBL	Society of Biblical Literature
trans.	translator(s), translated by, translation

Old Testament

Gen.	Genesis
Exod.	Exodus
Lev.	Leviticus
Num.	Numbers
Deut.	Deuteronomy
Josh.	Joshua
Judg.	Judges
Ruth	Ruth
1 Sam.	1 Samuel
2 Sam.	2 Samuel
1 Kings	1 Kings
2 Kings	2 Kings
1 Chron.	1 Chronicles
2 Chron.	2 Chronicles
Ezra	Ezra
Neh.	Nehemiah
Esther	Esther
Job	Job
Ps(s).	Psalm(s)
Prov.	Proverbs
Eccles.	Ecclesiastes
Song	Song of Songs
Isa.	Isaiah
Jer.	Jeremiah
Lam.	Lamentations
Ezek.	Ezekiel
Dan.	Daniel
Hosea	Hosea
Joel	Joel

Amos   Amos
Obad.   Obadiah
Jon.   Jonah
Mic.   Micah
Nah.   Nahum
Hab.   Habakkuk
Zeph.   Zephaniah
Hag.   Haggai
Zech.   Zechariah
Mal.   Malachi

New Testament

Matt.   Matthew
Mark   Mark
Luke   Luke
John   John
Acts   Acts
Rom.   Romans
1 Cor.   1 Corinthians
2 Cor.   2 Corinthians
Gal.   Galatians
Eph.   Ephesians
Phil.   Philippians
Col.   Colossians
1 Thess.   1 Thessalonians
2 Thess.   2 Thessalonians
1 Tim.   1 Timothy
2 Tim.   2 Timothy
Titus   Titus
Philem.   Philemon
Heb.   Hebrews
James   James
1 Pet.   1 Peter
2 Pet.   2 Peter
1 John   1 John
2 John   2 John
3 John   3 John
Jude   Jude
Rev.   Revelation

Old Testament Apocrypha

1 Macc.   1 Maccabees
Sir.   Sirach
Wis.   Wisdom of Solomon

Old Testament Pseudepigrapha

2 Bar.   2 Baruch
4 Ezra   4 Ezra
Sib. Or.   Sibylline Oracles

Dead Sea Scrolls and Papyri

4QFlor   Florilegium, also Midrash on Eschatology[a]
H   Codex Hierosolymitanus
𝔓   papyrus
P.Oxy.XV 1782 The Oxyrhynchus Papyri. Series 18. Edited by B. P. Grenfell and A. S. Hunt. London: Egypt Exploration Society in Graeco-Roman Memoirs, 1922

Josephus

Ant.   *Jewish Antiquities*
J.W.   *Jewish War*

Rabbinic Works

b. Ber.   Babylonian Talmud, Berakhot

Apostolic Fathers

Barn.   Barnabas
1–2 Clem.   1–2 Clement
Did.   Didache
Herm. Mand. Shepherd of Hermas, Mandate(s)
Herm. Sim. Shepherd of Hermas, Similitude(s)
Herm. Vis. Shepherd of Hermas, Vision(s)
Ign. *Eph.*   Ignatius, *To the Ephesians*
Ign. *Magn.* Ignatius, *To the Magnesians*
Ign. *Phld.* Ignatius, *To the Philadelphians*
Ign. *Pol.*   Ignatius, *To Polycarp*
Ign. *Smyrn.* Ignatius, *To the Smyrnaeans*

Ign. *Trall.* Ignatius, *To the Trallians*
Pol. *Phil.* Polycarp, *To the Philippians*

New Testament Apocrypha and Pseudepigrapha

Acts Pet. Acts of Peter
Gos. Thom. Gospel of Thomas

Classical Authors
Dio Cassius

Hist. rom. *Historiae romanae* (*Roman History*)

Dio Chrysostom

Pulchr. *De pulchritudine* (*Or.* 21) (*Oration on Beauty*)

Homer

Il. *Ilias* (*Iliad*)

Pliny the Younger

Ep. *Epistulae*

Suetonius

Claud. *Divus Claudius*
Dom. *Domitianus*

Tacitus

Ann. *Annales*
Hist. *Historiae*

Patristic Writings
Athanasius

Ep. fest. *Epistulae festales* (*Festal Letters*)

Clement of Alexandria

Paed. *Paedagogus* (*Christ the Educator*)
Strom. *Stromateis* (*Miscellanies*)

Epiphanius

Pan. *Panarion* (*Adversus haereses*) (*Refutation of All Heresies*)

Eusebius

Hist. eccl. *Historia ecclesiastica* (*Ecclesiastical History*)

Irenaeus

Haer. *Adversus haereses* (*Elenchos*) (*Against Heresies*)

Jerome

Chron. *Chronicon Eusebii a Graeco Latine redditum et continuatum*
Vir. ill. *De viris illustribus*

Justin Martyr

Dial. *Dialogus cum Tryphone* (*Dialogue with Trypho*)

Tertullian

Cult. fem. *De cultu feminarum* (*The Apparel of Women*)

Bibliographic Sources

BRANE Bible and Religions of the Ancient Near East Collective
LCL Loeb Classical Library
NA[28] *Nestle-Aland Novum Testamentum Graece.* Edited by Barbara and Kurt Aland, Johannes Karavidopoulos, Carlo M. Martini, and Bruce M. Metzger. 28th ed. Stuttgart: Deutsche Bibelgesellschaft, 2012.
SBLHS *The SBL Handbook of Style.* 2nd ed. Atlanta: SBL Press, 2014.

Introduction

This study asks when each of the twenty-seven books that are now collected in the corpus known as the New Testament were written. It will additionally ask when four extracanonical texts (1 Clement, Didache, Epistle of Barnabas, and Shepherd of Hermas) were written. It will conclude that, with the notable exception of the undisputed Pauline Epistles, the majority of the texts that were eventually incorporated into the New Testament corpus were likely written twenty to thirty years earlier than is typically supposed by contemporary biblical scholars. If chronology is the proverbial backbone of history, then the study of Christian origins has developed a scoliosis.

Only a synthetic treatment will be fully adequate to the task of investigating the dates of the New Testament texts. A synthetic treatment considers judgments on a disparate range of distinct yet densely interconnected matters and seeks to integrate them into a complex but unified synthesis. Concretely, such synthetic treatment is necessary because truly serious consideration of the date of any given New Testament text will tend to spiderweb into a need to treat one or more of the other twenty-six. The instance of 1 Timothy 5:18 can readily illustrate this spiderwebbing effect and consequent need for synthesis. First Timothy 5:18 reads as follows: "For the scripture says, 'You shall not muzzle an ox while it is treading out the grain,' and 'The laborer deserves to be paid.'" Here 1 Timothy 5:18 cites first a passage from Deuteronomy (namely, 25:4), followed by a passage found verbatim in Luke 10:7 (with a close parallel in Matt. 10:10). One's judgment regarding the literary relationship between 1 Timothy 5:18 and Luke 10:7 will have significant implications for how one dates these texts, and vice versa. If one judges that 1 Timothy 5:18 is quoting Luke's Gospel, then one must also judge that 1 Timothy postdates Luke's

Gospel. Alternatively, if one judges Luke's Gospel to be later than 1 Timothy 5:18, then one must judge that the latter does not quote Luke 10:7. Yet this does not begin to consider other possibilities—for instance, that 1 Timothy is quoting hypothetical source material such as Q or oral tradition.[1] The relationship between Luke's Gospel and 1 Timothy 5:18 will moreover relate to questions about the Pauline authorship of the epistle. If 1 Timothy 5:18 is judged to be Pauline, then we know that this piece of Jesus tradition existed in its specifically Lukan form by no later than Paul's death, which more likely than not occurred sometime between 62 and 68. Conversely, if one judges that Luke's Gospel must be a post-70 composition and that 1 Timothy 5:18 does indeed quote Luke 10:7, then unless one decides that Paul died later than 68, one must judge that 1 Timothy 5:18 is pseudo-Pauline. Further, questions about the date of Luke's Gospel inevitably intersect with questions about those of Mark's, Matthew's, and Acts. As such, the judgments one makes regarding 1 Timothy 5:18 are mutually entailed with judgments regarding the authenticity of the letter and not only Luke's Gospel but also the broader synoptic tradition. "Disturb the position of one major piece and the pattern starts disconcertingly to dissolve," wrote John A. T. Robinson when he considered the density and interrelationship of the judgments necessary in studying the dates of the New Testament texts.[2] If anything, Robinson was guilty of understatement. Only a synthetic treatment allows us to organize the relevant material in such a way as to fully appreciate its empirical significance for determining when the books of the New Testament corpus were written.

A synthetic treatment of the dates of the New Testament texts, if done properly, will inevitably be of monograph length. We have discussed the limitations that judgments about 1 Timothy 5:18 place upon judgments about the synoptic tradition, and vice versa. When we multiply such examples across the twenty-seven books of the New Testament and other potentially relevant early Christian texts, we begin to get a sense of the task's complexity. Such complexity cannot be adequately managed in an article-length contribution, or even in a series of such contributions. Yet despite (or perhaps because of) this complexity, we have remarkably few monograph-length critical studies completed by professional biblical scholars and dedicated to establishing the compositional dates of the entire New Testament corpus. Indeed, John

---

1. "Q" is the name frequently given to a hypothetical text that the majority of New Testament scholars considers to have been a common source for the Gospels of Matthew and Luke.
2. Robinson, *Redating*, 9.

Robinson's *Redating the New Testament* was the only one to appear in the twentieth century, and the present study represents the first in the twenty-first. This dearth of adequate-length monographs should not be taken as evidence that the dates of the New Testament are so solidly established as to be immune to significant revision but rather as reason to suspect that the dates so frequently affirmed have not been quite so solidly established as we might want to think. Indeed, for such a basic historical matter, there is a somewhat disconcerting multiplicity of irreconcilable views.

The History of Scholarship

The current state of academic discourse regarding the compositional dates of the New Testament texts can be summarized much as follows. We might heuristically distinguish between three broad chronological frameworks, which may be designated "lower," "middle," and "higher" chronologies. All three of these frameworks agree that the undisputed Pauline Epistles should be dated to around the 50s of the first century.[3] Lower chronologies date much of the balance of the New Testament corpus prior to 70; middle chronologies date much of the balance to the period between 70 and 100; and higher chronologies date much of the balance of the New Testament to the second century. Comparable tripartite divisions often use the terms "early," "middle," or "late," for what I here call "lower," "middle," and "higher," respectively. The respective terms can be used more or less interchangeably and are largely a matter of personal taste. Most New Testament scholars would today affirm the middle chronology as most probable, such that it can also be described as the "majority" chronology.

A comparative representation of these three frameworks might look something as follows:

Book	Lower*	Middle (Majority)[†]	Higher[‡]
Matthew	50	70–75	130
Mark	45	65–73	80
Luke	60	80–95	110
John	65	80–110	140
Acts	62	80–95	130

3. As almost all dates given in this study are CE, I will only note when they are BCE. As such, a year without a CE or BCE notation should be read as CE.

Book	Lower*	Middle (Majority)†	Higher‡
Romans	57	56–57	50
1 Corinthians	55	56	50
2 Corinthians	56	56	50
Galatians	56	53	50
Ephesians	58	57–59	100
Philippians	58	57–59	50
Colossians	58	57–59	80
1 Thessalonians	50	48–49	40
2 Thessalonians	50–51	48–49	120
1 Timothy	55	90–110	140
2 Timothy	58	90–110	140
Titus	57	90–110	140
Philemon	58	57–62	50
Hebrews	67	81–96	110
James	47–48	70–90	130
1 Peter	65	81–96	110
2 Peter	61–62	110–120	150
1 John	60–65	80–110	140
2 John	60–65	80–110	140
3 John	60–65	80–110	140
Jude	61–62	100–130	130
Revelation	68	93–96	150
1 Clement	70	93–97	130
Didache	60	120	150
Epistle of Barnabas	75	130	140
Shepherd of Hermas	prior to 85	140	150

*Following Robinson, *Redating*, 352, with some modification. Robinson is followed here since (apart from the present study) *Redating* represents the most recent monograph-length synthetic defense of a lower chronology. Modifications are made in interest of resolving ambiguities in Robinson's own summary of his position.

†Following Harnack, *Chronologie*, 717–22, with some modification. Harnack is followed here since his *Chronologie* represents the most recent monograph-length synthetic defense of something close to a middle chronology. Modifications are made in the interest of best representing the middle chronology as it stands ca. 2022. Unfortunately, to the best of this author's knowledge, Harnack's *Chronologie* has never been translated into English.

‡Following Sturdy, *Redrawing the Boundaries*, 83–86. Sturdy is followed here since *Redrawing* (though incomplete at the time of his passing) represents the most recent effort to mount a monograph-length synthetic defense of a higher chronology.

Of course, in practice each framework will acknowledge variations among actual working biblical scholars, and the boundaries between them will at times be quite porous. Nonetheless, this threefold heuristic typology allows us to begin talking meaningfully about the history of dating the New Testament texts.

For most of Christian history, it was generally supposed that the New Testament texts were written by the authors to which they were traditionally attributed. These traditional authors were contemporaries of Jesus and Paul (in some cases, such as with Mark and perhaps Luke, younger contemporaries). As such, most scholars supposed that the New Testament had been written within just a few decades of Jesus's crucifixion. In the terms articulated above, the traditional time line for the composition of the New Testament was a lower chronology. With the emergence of modern biblical criticism over the course of the nineteenth century, scholars queried whether a traditional time line is consistent with the relevant data. The first major chronological scheme of the modern era was formulated in the mid-nineteenth century by Ferdinand Christian Baur. Baur's chronological framework is the highest that has attracted wide support among New Testament scholars. Baur argued that the latest New Testament text written was John's Gospel, which he dated to the time of the Quartodeciman controversy in the last third of the second century.[4] He allowed that Paul wrote only Romans, 1 and 2 Corinthians, and Galatians, judging that the rest of the Pauline corpus were post-Pauline compositions.[5]

New Testament scholarship was right to question the traditional time line. Our convictions regarding the origins of the New Testament should be grounded in historical investigation, not unquestioned acceptance of tradition. The fact that the traditional chronology assigns earlier dates is not sufficient reason to affirm a lower chronology. Conversely, the fact that an early pioneer such as Baur argued for later years of composition is not sufficient reason to affirm a higher chronology. As such, it was also right for scholars to question the Baurian chronology. This occurred at length in the generation following Baur. J. B. Lightfoot argued that John's Gospel could not have been written much later than 100, approximately three-quarters of a century earlier than Baur had dated the text.[6] Subsequent papyrological discoveries

4. Cf. esp. Baur, *First Three Centuries*, 131–32. For this and the following discussion, cf. also Robinson's treatment of the history of the study of the compositional dates of the New Testament in *Redating*, 4–9.

5. Baur, *Paul, the Apostle*, 1:255–381, 2:1–105.

6. Cf. Lightfoot, *Gospel of St. John*, 41–78, 205–325. Although the core of this volume is Lightfoot's once-lost commentary on John's Gospel, discovered by Ben Witherington in 2013,

appeared to confirm Lightfoot's conclusion, although this confirmation has been contested.[7] Insofar as John's Gospel was still considered to be the latest written among the canonical Gospels, Lightfoot's work contributed to a tendency to date the Synoptic Gospels earlier than 100. Moving to the balance of the New Testament, Lightfoot held that Paul wrote all thirteen letters attributed to him, thus necessitating the judgment that none of these could postdate his death.[8] Although contemporary scholars would grant that only Romans, 1 and 2 Corinthians, Galatians, Philippians, 1 Thessalonians, and Philemon are indisputably Pauline, with Lightfoot we nonetheless see the emergence of a tendency to lower the overall dates of the New Testament texts from those proposed at the outset of modern historical-critical scholarship.

Standing near the turn of the twentieth century, Adolf von Harnack's *Die Chronologie der Litteratur bis Irenaeus*, published in 1897, followed this tendency to date the New Testament texts substantially earlier than did Baur. In many but not all cases, Harnack opted for dates not far from those of Lightfoot. Harnack would later come to date Luke's Gospel and Acts prior to 70, such that by the end of his career he came to straddle the line between a lower and a middle chronology.[9] The inter- and postwar years saw a shift away from a focus upon basic historical matters such as chronology and toward the concerns of form and redaction criticism. As such, Harnack's *Chronologie* constituted the last synthetic, monograph-length study of the dates of the New Testament completed by a professional biblical scholar until Robinson published his *Redating the New Testament* almost exactly eighty years later. Robinson in turn continued the "Lightfootian" tendency toward lowering the dates of the New Testament, (in)famously arguing that the entirety of the corpus was written prior to 70. The present volume constitutes the first such study since Robinson's *Redating the New Testament*, which is itself now the better part of fifty years old.

At the time of his death, J. V. M. Sturdy was working on a monograph-length response to Robinson's *Redating the New Testament*, which would have constituted a synthetic argument for a higher chronology. Unfortunately, Sturdy

---

the pages cited here contain material Lightfoot previously published in Lightfoot, *Biblical Essays*, 1–198.

7. Cf. the discussion of these matters in chap. 3.

8. Cf. Lightfoot, *Biblical Essays*, 213–33, 397–418; Lightfoot, *2 Corinthians and 1 Peter*, 1–21.

9. Cf. Harnack, *Date of the Acts*, 99–133.

was unable to complete the volume before his death. What he did manage to produce has now been made available posthumously as *Redrawing the Boundaries*. Certainly, it is better to have access to this material than it would be to not have access. Nonetheless, the arguments contained therein are in many instances significantly underdeveloped. Indeed, Jonathan Knight, in his preface to *Redrawing the Boundaries*, suggests that it "should be regarded as the outline of an argument and not a finished text in itself."[10] Presumably Sturdy intended to develop his arguments more fully, but we do not know how he would have elected to do so. We also do not know where the work of developing those arguments might have led him to revise or even abandon positions adopted in the incomplete work, and whether such revision would have resulted in lower or higher estimates for any given date of composition. As such, through no fault of its author, Sturdy's *Redrawing the Boundaries* does not stand as an adequate reply to Robinson's *Redating the New Testament*.[11] Moreover, given the incomplete state of *Redrawing the Boundaries*, it would be uncharitable to consider it the best possible argument for a higher chronology. There has been no comparable synthetic effort to articulate and defend a middle chronology in response to Robinson, perhaps because as the majority position it is not seen as something requiring defense. Cumulatively, although Robinson's chronology has not been widely adopted, neither has it been systematically refuted. Rather, it has suffered what we might describe as benign neglect.

Given the current state of the question, three volumes seem to be necessary at this juncture. One would be a rearticulated argument for a lower chronology, comparable in depth and breadth of research and quality of argumentation to Robinson's. This study aims to be that volume. A second volume would argue for a middle chronology, and a third for a higher one. With all three volumes produced, we could let the individual reader decide which presents the strongest overall case. I am not the scholar to produce all three volumes. The discipline of New Testament studies deserves for each of these volumes to be argued as effectively as possible, and that is best achieved when they are written by persons firmly and enthusiastically convinced that their preferred chronological framework best accounts for the data. I only believe that to be the case with lower chronology and thus lack the requisite qualifications to argue most effectively for middle and higher chronologies. Nonetheless, I would be most

10. Knight, preface to Sturdy, *Redrawing the Boundaries*, vii.
11. But see also Sturdy, review of *Redating*. Sturdy's review is remarkably balanced and fair, especially given that he fundamentally disagrees with Robinson's conclusion.

gratified if this volume serves as impetus and aid for the necessary, comparable volumes arguing for middle and higher chronologies. Until such volumes are produced, lower chronology will occupy an intellectually privileged position, insofar as it will remain the only broad framework for the dates of the New Testament texts to have received the requisite, monograph-length, synthetic defense since the Victorian era. Indeed, it will have received two such defenses during that time, while middle and higher chronologies will have received none.

On Going beyond Robinson

As discussed above, this study seeks to present a renewed case for a lower chronology of the New Testament compositions. As such, it will frequently suggest dates for the composition of the New Testament texts that are in many (but far from all) cases similar to those advanced in Robinson's *Redating the New Testament*. Given that Robinson made the requisite monograph-length case for a lower chronology, the reader might legitimately wonder why a renewed case is necessary at all. This is best explicated by identifying certain limitations in Robinson's work.

Robinson's *Redating the New Testament* attracted a great deal of attention from his fellow biblical scholars as well as church historians. This is hardly surprising. Robinson was already a well-established name within New Testament studies and the broader theological world. His 1963 monograph, *Honest to God*, had previously been a deeply influential work. And since *Redating the New Testament* was the first work of its sort since Harnack's *Chronologie* eighty years earlier, New Testament scholars could ill afford to ignore its arguments. But it was probably the central thesis—namely, that all the New Testament was written prior to 70—that attracted most attention. Some responses were positive.[12] Many were fair.[13] A few were neither.[14] Here, I identify what I consider to be the three most significant problems with Robinson's argumentation in *Redating the New Testament*: Robinson's tendency to approach the events of 70 through arguments from silence; what I term his

12. In this category we include Ellis, "Dating the New Testament"; Moody, review of *Redating*. Ellis describes his own *Making of the New Testament* (xv–xvi) as a "supplement to Robinson's investigations."

13. In this category we include reviews of Robinson's *Redating* by the following: Donahue, Hardy, Murphy, Sloyan, Snyder, and Sturdy.

14. In this category we include Fitzmyer, "Two Views"; Grant, review of *Redating*.

"Neronian error"; and his less-than-adequate attention to the method and organization of his study.

The Events of 70 and Arguing from Silence

From 66 through 73, Jewish rebel groups within the land of Israel engaged in open revolt against Roman rule. Particularly crucial for purposes of this study are the events of 70. In that year, the Romans besieged and eventually razed Jerusalem. The temple was destroyed. Here, Josephus's account may help us understand the extent of the destruction.

> The army now having no victims either for slaughter or plunder, through lack of all objects on which to vent their rage—for they would assuredly never have desisted through a desire to spare anything so long as there was work to be done—Caesar ordered the whole city and the temple to be razed to the ground, leaving only the loftiest of the towers, Phasael, Hippicus, and Mariamme, and the portion of the wall enclosing the city on the west: the latter as an encampment for the garrison that was to remain, and the towers to indicate to posterity the nature of the city and of the strong defences which had yet yielded to Roman prowess. All the rest of the wall encompassing the city was so completely levelled to the ground as to leave future visitors to the spot no ground for believing that it had ever been inhabited. Such was the end to which the frenzy of revolutionaries brought Jerusalem, that splendid city of world-wide renown.[15]

Of the fall of Jerusalem and the destruction of the temple, Robinson writes,

> One of the oddest facts about the New Testament is that what on any showing appears to be the single most datable and climatic event of the period—the fall of Jerusalem in AD 70, and with it the collapse of institutional Judaism based on the temple—is never once mentioned as a past fact. It is, of course, predicted; and these predictions are, in some cases at least, assumed to be written (or written up) after the event. But the silence is nevertheless as significant as the silence for Sherlock Holmes of the dog that did not bark.[16]

Since Robinson's writing, scholars have challenged whether the events of 70 were as traumatic a turning point for Jewish life and religion as he seems to

15. Josephus, *J.W.* 7.1.1 §§1–4 (Thackeray).
16. Robinson, *Redating*, 13.

suppose.[17] Although such challenges are relevant to Robinson's observation, of greater immediate interest is his invocation of the argument from silence. It is of course quite true that the New Testament never refers to the fall of Jerusalem as a past fact. It does not necessarily follow, however, that this silence in and of itself is particularly significant for establishing the dates of the New Testament. Indeed, I argue that in most cases it is not.

John Lange has considered the historiographical issues surrounding arguments from silence at length.[18] He identifies two conditions for affirming arguments from silence that seem particularly relevant for our work: (1) "There is a document, D, extant, in which the event, E, is not mentioned"; and (2) "E must be such that, if it had occurred, the author of D could not have overlooked it."[19] These are not the only conditions that Lange discusses, but they are the most relevant for our present purposes. In order to more fully account for the probabilistic nature of historiography, I would soften the second of these conditions, such that it reads, "E must be such that, if it had occurred, the author of D is not likely to have overlooked it." Even granted this softer articulation, it is far from evident that the above conditions are both met in the case of the New Testament's treatment of events of 70. Regarding the first condition, it is indeed the case that the New Testament corpus fails to mention the destruction of the temple as a past event. Nonetheless, regarding the second condition, it is not self-evident to me that we should expect the New Testament authors to have done so if writing after 70.

The matter of 70, however, cannot be ignored since a writing's knowledge of either the current state of the temple or of its eventual fate can constitute crucial data. Concretely, when considering the matter of 70 regarding any given New Testament book, we must ask two questions: (1) Is there material in the book that is most fully intelligible only if written prior to 70? (2) Is there material in the book that is most fully intelligible only if written after 70? If there is material in the book that is most fully intelligible only if it was written prior to 70, *and* other material in the book that is most fully intelligible only if it was written after 70, then the book likely postdates 70 but preserves pre-70 material. If there is material that is most fully intelligible only if written prior to 70, and if there is no material in the book that is most fully intelligible only

---

17. Cf. the discussions in Schwartz and Weiss, *Was 70 CE a Watershed?*
18. Lange, "Argument from Silence." Lange is engaging the work of Langlois and Seignobos, *Study of History.*
19. Lange, "Argument from Silence," 290.

if written subsequent to 70, then the book most likely predates 70. If there is no material that is most fully intelligible only if written prior to 70, and no material that is most fully intelligible only if written subsequent to 70, then the probability that the book predates 70 is equal to the probability that it post-dates it. If there is no material in the book that is most fully intelligible only if written prior to 70, and if there is material that is most fully intelligible only if written subsequent to 70, then the book most likely postdates 70 (although one cannot exclude the possibility that it contains material which predates 70). The above possibilities might well be summarized in the following diagram:

		Is there material that is most fully intelligible only if written prior to 70?	
		Yes	No
Is there material that is most fully intelligible only if written after 70?	Yes	The book most likely post-dates 70, while preserving material that predates 70.	The book most likely post-dates 70, although it might also preserve material that predates 70.
	No	The book most likely pre-dates 70.	There is equal probability that the book predates or post-dates 70.

It is the contention of this study that while there are New Testament books that contain material most fully intelligible only if written prior to 70, there are no New Testament books that contain material most fully intelligible only if written after 70. By focusing on what the texts say rather than on what they do not say, we can come to this conclusion without falling into a fallacious argument from silence.

The Domitianic and Neronian Errors

Robinson is deeply and rightly skeptical about what we might call the "Domitianic Error."[20] Said error has two limbs: first, that in his later years the emperor Domitian (r. 81–96) actively and significantly persecuted the early Christians; second, that many of the unspecified references to persecution scattered throughout the New Testament are references to this putative Domitianic persecution. From these limbs, scholars often conclude that

20. Cf. esp. Robinson, *Redating*, 230–33.

a given New Testament text must postdate the beginning of the supposed Domitianic persecution. The difficulty with the first limb is that Domitian might not have actively and significantly persecuted the early Christians. The problem with the second limb is that even if he did, many if not most of the references to persecution throughout the New Testament might refer instead to another persecution. As noted above, Robinson rightly rejects this Domitianic error, but then in turn he adopts what we might call a "Neronian error," which replicates both limbs noted above but with regard to the emperor Nero (r. 54–68).

In modern scholarship, the first of the limbs enumerated above is closely associated with no less a name than Lightfoot.[21] In the ancient world, the first notice of a possible Domitianic persecution appears in the late second century, when Melito of Sardis singles out Nero and Domitian as active persecutors of the Christian faith.[22] Melito's testimony at least raises the possibility that Christians suffered as a result of actions associated with Domitian. Yet already a century ago, the classicist E. T. Merrill argued that this Domitianic persecution never happened.[23] Only careful attention to the data can resolve the matter.

Suetonius reports that Domitian had Flavius Clemens put to death in 95 and describes the latter as lacking energy.[24] Lightfoot interprets Flavius Clemens's supposed lack of energy as the consequence of the equivocal situation in which a Christian holding high office would have found himself.[25] At best we can say of Lightfoot's reading that it is not impossible, but it hardly rises to the level of probability. Writing somewhat later than Suetonius, Dio Cassius also reports that "Domitian slew, along with many others, Flavius Clemens the consul, although he was a cousin and had to wife Flavia Domitilla, who was also a relative of the emperor's. The charge brought against them both was that of atheism, a charge on which many others who drifted into Jewish ways were condemned. Some of these were put to death, and the rest were at least deprived of their property. Domitilla was merely banished to Pandateria."[26] Lightfoot argues that this combination of "atheism" and "Jewish practices" renders it virtually certain that Flavius Clemens and

---

21. Cf. the discussion in Lightfoot, *Apostolic Fathers*, pt. 1, 1:33–42.
22. According to Eusebius, *Hist. eccl.* 4.26.8–9.
23. Merrill, *Essays in Early Christian History*, 148–73.
24. Suetonius, *Dom.* 15.
25. Lightfoot, *Apostolic Fathers*, pt. 1, 1:35.
26. Dio Cassius, *Hist. rom.* 67.14.1–2 (Cary).

Flavia Domitilla were Christians.[27] More recently, Peter Lampe has argued that Flavius Clemens was not a Christian but that Flavia Domitilla was.[28] For our purposes, even if Flavius Clemens or Flavia Domitilla was Christian, the execution of one member of the imperial family and the banishment of another hardly suffice to demonstrate any wider anti-Christian activity during Domitian's reign.

In his discussion of such supposed wider anti-Christian activity, Eusebius reports that Domitian banished many Christians, singling out by name John the Evangelist and Flavia Domitilla.[29] Eusebius then reports that Domitian ordered the execution of the family of David, which led to the grandsons of Jude, brother of Jesus, being brought before the emperor.[30] Yet, as Eusebius himself relates the incident, Domitian had Jude's grandsons released without any punishment and then ordered that the persecution of Christians cease.[31] Indeed, leaving aside questions regarding the veracity of Eusebius's account, whether Domitian's purported interrogation of the family of David was motivated by anti-Christian sentiment or policy is not clear. The incident is at least equally if not more intelligible as resulting from measures aimed at preventing messianic uprisings in the decades following the first revolt. While there is some reason to think that Domitian's reign was not a high-water mark in Christian-imperial relations, there is little evidence for widespread persecution.

We have not yet addressed the second limb of the Domitianic error—namely, that many of the unspecified references to persecution in the New Testament are to the supposed Domitianic persecution. Let us grant for the sake of argument that the occurrence of a Domitianic persecution was more widespread than the evidence necessarily warrants. Certainly, many of the references to persecution in the New Testament might be to this supposed Domitianic persecution. In many cases, however, they could potentially be references to other persecutions, ones that have nothing to do with Domitian. They need to be determined on a case-by-case basis. The relevant passages will be considered throughout this study.

Although Robinson recognizes the dangers of the Domitianic error, he unfortunately tends to lapse into a comparable "Neronian error." This Neronian

27. As argued by Lightfoot, *Apostolic Fathers*, pt. 1, 1:34.
28. Lampe, *From Paul to Valentinus*, 198–205.
29. Eusebius, *Hist. eccl.* 3.17–18.
30. Eusebius, *Hist. eccl.* 3.19.1–3.20.7.
31. Eusebius, *Hist. eccl.* 3.20.5.

error shares limbs quite similar to those of the Domitianic error: first, that
Nero actively and significantly persecuted the church; second, that many of
the unspecified references to persecution scattered throughout the New Testament are references to this putative Neronian persecution. Admittedly, the
first limb of the Neronian error holds up to empirical scrutiny better than
its Domitianic counterpart, in that we have greater reason to suppose that
Christians experienced what they considered to be persecution under Nero
rather than under Domitian. Suetonius and Tacitus both report such measures, with Tacitus identifying these anti-Christian measures as a response to
the Great Fire of Rome in July 64.[32] Yet Brent Shaw has recently called into
question whether there was ever such a Neronian persecution.[33] Though Shaw
judges it improbable that Nero arrested persons already known as Christians
in connection with the fire, he also leaves open the possibility that "some
persons labelled *Chrestiani* were caught up in the dragnet of 64 and suffered
punishment, [and] Christians later (mistakenly or deliberately) interpreted
these actions as the Roman state having persecuted them *as Christians*."[34]
This latter possibility would suffice for us to at least consider that certain
unspecified references to persecution in the New Testament literature might
refer in retrospect to these events. Such persons need not have already been
labeled "Christians" at this time but rather merely belonged to groups that
Tacitus knew by this term in retrospect.

It is on its second limb, however, that Robinson's Neronian error is most
evident. While it is altogether possible that certain unspecified references to
persecution within the New Testament corpus do indeed have the events of
the 60s in mind, most such references are sufficiently vague that they could
refer to any persecutory experience over the first few Christian decades. In
some cases, these need not even reference any specific or actual experience
of persecution. Just as New Testament scholarship tends to see Domitian's
presence more frequently than the data permit, Robinson tends to do the same
with Nero's rule. A sterling example of this is the treatment of 1 Clement. A
tradition going back to Lightfoot associates the references to hardships within
1 Clement 1–7 with Domitian.[35] Robinson instead associates these references

32. Suetonius, *Nero* 16.2; Tacitus, *Ann.* 15.44.
33. Shaw, "Myth of the Neronian Persecution." Cf. also Jones, "Historicity of the Neronian
Persecution"; Shaw, "Response to Christopher Jones."
34. Shaw, "Response to Christopher Jones," 241–42 (emphasis original).
35. Lightfoot, *Apostolic Fathers*, pt. 1, 1:350–52.

with the Neronian persecution.[36] Unfortunately, as we will see in chapter 9, these references could very well be to any other persecution. Alternatively, they might be to persecution in general rather than to a specific event. This study thus aims to bring much the same skepticism that Robinson quite appropriately brought to Domitianic explanations and apply it to Neronian ones as well. Indeed, it will conclude that only one New Testament book—namely, Revelation—betrays likely knowledge of the Neronian persecution.

Method and Organization

We earlier saw Robinson quote Sherlock Holmes. Personally, I prefer Hercule Poirot, who regularly lectures those around him on the need for method in any investigation. The typical New Testament scholar working today would fully agree with Poirot. Indeed, from the perspective of current New Testament studies, one of the significant limitations of Robinson's *Redating the New Testament* is a failure to explicitly address the matter of method. Such lack of explicit attention to method allows Robinson's critics to misunderstand or misrepresent his historical methods. By way of example, Robert Grant writes, "Robinson's arguments are based essentially on authority, sometimes that of 19th-century English scholars (Zahn and Harnack)."[37] This is not altogether accurate. Certainly, Robinson cites secondary scholarship, as is de rigueur in New Testament studies, and since it is difficult to please everyone, Donald J. Murphy criticizes him for not citing enough sources.[38] With Grant, I certainly acknowledge that Robinson too quickly affirms the rather problematic argumentation at times put forward in George Edmundson's *The Church in Rome in the First Century*.[39] But Robinson consistently surveys the relevant data from the ancient world carefully, and it is this data, not appeal to authority, that is the basis of his judgments. Indeed, Grant demonstrates very well how Robinson is appealing to data, not to authority. Grant argues that "another authority, not really any more weighty, is Eusebius, whose comments Robinson uses from the *Chronicles* and the *Church History* when they please him; often they do not."[40] Then Grant goes on to note that "Robinson himself does a fine job of demolishing

36. Cf. Robinson, *Redating*, 144, 330.
37. Grant, review of *Redating*, 295.
38. Murphy, review of *Redating*, 564.
39. Grant, review of *Redating*, 295.
40. Grant, review of *Redating*, 295.

a Eusebian date when he wants to."[41] Grant also notes correctly that Robinson rejects Irenaeus's statement that Revelation was written under Domitian and cites the various ancient sources that Robinson uses in making his decision.[42] Yet Grant's criticism fails to distinguish between three distinct operations: citing the secondary literature with which a scholar has interacted; the work of determining the relevance of ancient data to the task of historical reconstruction; and the fallacious appeal to authority. Robinson does the first and second of these at length, but rarely, if ever, the third.

Grant's criticism, however, does lead us to ask two important questions: What constitutes evidence, and how should the historical work handle it? Robinson's method is quite close to that developed by the British philosopher of history R. G. Collingwood.[43] Such method is defined broadly as "inferential." Any or all statements by ancient writers, along with any or all artifacts or features uncovered by archaeologists, can be theoretically integrated into what Collingwood terms the historian's "web of imaginative construction."[44] When evaluating any given argument regarding what happened in the past, it is the quality of this "web" that is evaluated. Such a conception of the historian's work leads Collingwood to write,

> The web of imaginative construction is something far more solid and powerful than we have hitherto realized. So far from relying for its validity upon the support of given facts, it actually serves as the touchstone by which we decide whether alleged facts are genuine. Suetonius tells me that Nero at one time intended to evacuate Britain. I reject his statement, not because any better authority flatly contradicts it, for of course none does; but because my reconstruction of Nero's policy based on Tacitus will not allow me to think that Suetonius is right. And if I am told that this is merely to say I prefer Tacitus to Suetonius, I confess that I do: but I do so just because I find myself able to incorporate what Tacitus tells me into a coherent and continuous picture of my own, and cannot do this for Suetonius.[45]

Robinson is engaged in much the same sort of procedure when he concludes that Eusebius (or Irenaeus) is more or less accurate on this point but

41. Grant, review of *Redating*, 295.
42. Grant, review of *Redating*, 295.
43. Cf. Collingwood, *Idea of History*.
44. Cf. Collingwood, *Idea of History*, 242–44.
45. Collingwood, *Idea of History*, 244.

must be rejected on another. This is really unobjectionable, as far as it goes. Where Robinson gets into difficulties is that he never explicates how he goes about building his web of imaginative construction. This leads not only to a lack of clarity but also to positions that at times border on the fantastic.[46] Perhaps most problematic, having failed to attend carefully to the matter of method, Robinson ends up presenting the relevant data and argumentation in a somewhat haphazard fashion. Why this datum is presented before that one, why a certain datum receives greater significance than another one, and so on, is often less than clear. At times *Redating the New Testament* reads like a stream of consciousness that has something to do with the compositional dates of the New Testament. This poses some difficulty for navigating *Redating the New Testament* and for evaluating the quality of its argumentation. By way of concrete example, while writing of Robinson's argumentation regarding the date of Luke-Acts, Joseph Fitzmyer wryly states that "it is difficult to respond to a writer who likes to shift the burden of proof to others and characterizes as 'dogmatic' (an adjective very dear to Robinson) any view that he opposes."[47] Although I might quibble with Fitzmyer's characterization of Robinson's argumentation, it is certainly true that Robinson's language is at times infelicitous. *Redating the New Testament* would be easier to follow and thus frankly more persuasive had Robinson taken care to be more systematic in presenting his argumentation. This study thus aims to be much more explicit about how it arrives at its conclusions, why a given argument is important, and where it fits into the larger structure of the work. We turn to this explicatory task in the next section.

Defining the Question

Much like Robinson, my own methodological inclinations can be described as inferential, drawing heavily upon the work of Collingwood but also the mediating work of Bernard Lonergan and Ben F. Meyer.[48] In my understanding,

---

46. Cf., for instance, his argument that the author of Hebrews knew and was responding to the *Quo Vadis?* myth, and that this supports a pre-70 date for the letter—even though the *Quo Vadis?* myth itself is unattested prior to the second century (Robinson, *Redating*, 214). Cf. more on this matter in chap. 7 below.

47. Fitzmyer, *Luke*, 1:55.

48. For my fuller engagement with the thought of Lonergan and Meyer as it relates to NT historiography, cf. Bernier, *Quest*, esp. 1–70. For examples of Collingwood's influence on Lonergan and Meyer, cf. esp. Lonergan, *Method in Theology*, 164–219; Meyer, *Aims of Jesus*, 81–92;

historical method consists of three fundamental steps: identify and *define* the research question, *generate* hypotheses that might answer the question, and *adjudicate* between competing hypotheses in order to determine the best answer. This and the following sections discuss each of these steps in turn. In this section, we identify and define our research question. This study seeks to answer a single overarching question: When were those texts that were later collected into the Christian New Testament composed? What follows will explicate the significant terms in this carefully formulated question.

Date of Composition

By "when were . . . composed," or what we might more grammatically designate "the date of composition," I refer to the time at which the author or authors *completed* the text in question. I emphasize completion because Robinson recurrently fails to make clear whether he is interested primarily in when the works in question were more or less finished or the time span over which they were being written. This recurrent failure leads to ambiguities in his discussion of the data and his own argumentation. That having been said, it goes without saying that many of the texts under discussion in this work were surely the product of extended compositional processes. Moreover, all the texts under discussion evince some degree of variation after the date of completion suggested here.

My aim is always for absolute rather than relative dates, although relative dates will often be indispensable in the effort to define absolute ones. Absolute dates, in the context of this study, are those defined by reference to the Gregorian calendar for months and days, and the BCE/CE system for years. Relative dates are those defined by reference to other events, usually by defining the order in which they occurred and, if possible, the temporal interval between their occurrences. For instance, to state that Paul set out for Rome in 59 is to state an absolute date, but to state that this occurred two years after he was arrested in Jerusalem is to state a relative date. Although I aim to define absolute dates with as much precision as possible, in most cases a difference of a couple years or sometimes more in either direction would not substantially alter the framework being developed.

Meyer, *Critical Realism*, 157–72. Cf. also the recent discussion of Collingwood's relevance for NT scholarship in Ryan, "Jesus at the Crossroads." Meyer's own project was in large part an effort to mediate Lonergan's thought for NT studies; cf. esp. Meyer, *Critical Realism*; and Meyer, *Reality and Illusion*.

Texts

By the term "texts" I mean objects that we would recognize as versions of the biblical books under discussion. In seeking to determine more precisely the content of these texts, I depend upon the work of the editors of the *Novum Testamentum Graece*, 28th edition (typically abbreviated as NA[28]). For the purposes of this study, textual criticism of the New Testament is sufficiently developed that unless one can demonstrate positively that a passage found in NA[28] and adduced as evidence for a text's date of composition is a secondary addition, one should assume that it is of relevance for our purposes. Any other procedure risks descent into an unworkable morass wherein one must demonstrate that every single word in a text, perhaps even every single letter, is coeval with every other. Such a tedious procedure forecloses any real possibility for historical inquiry. In truth, there are relatively few instances in which a given chronological argument is affected by a significantly contested textual tradition. These instances will be considered on a case-by-case basis.

The fact and development of early Christian textuality have often been studied as objects in their own rights. This has potential implications for establishing the compositional dates of the New Testament texts. It has been fashionable throughout the modern period to suppose that it took some time for early Christians to have either the capacity or the inclination to write texts, especially extended narratives such as the Gospels.[49] If indeed we can establish that there was a date before which Christians either were unable or unwilling to write texts, then we would be forced to conclude that all extant Christian texts postdate that time. Such a date would be altogether welcome: it would serve to narrow the chronological range within which our texts might have been produced. Let us then examine the evidence for this putative early Christian inability or reluctance to write.

We begin with the question of ability.[50] Unless we suppose that the entirety of the Pauline corpus is spurious and late, we know that early Christians were writing as early as 50. Indeed, the most recently proposed significant revision of Pauline chronology—that of Douglas Campbell—argues that 1 and 2 Thessalonians were written sometime in 40 through 42, almost a decade

49. Cf. the relatively recent overview of this supposition and related issues in Eve, *Behind the Gospels*, 15–158.
50. Cf. the earlier treatment of this matter in Bernier, *Quest*, 136–37. On the *status quaestionis* regarding Jewish literacy in the mid-first century, cf. the succinct overview of "Scribal Culture in the Time of Jesus" provided by Keith, *Jesus' Literacy*, 71–123.

earlier than most other chronologies place the earliest Pauline texts.[51] We will see in chapter 6 that there is reason not to date 1 and 2 Thessalonians as early as 40. Nonetheless, there is an undeniable insight operative within Douglas Campbell's work; namely, that if—as virtually no New Testament scholar would dispute—Paul could have been writing as early as 50, then there is little reason to doubt that he could have been writing ca. 40. And if Paul could have been writing ca. 40, then there is little reason to doubt that there were other Christians who could have been doing the same. Moreover, if Paul could have composed texts such as Romans by the end of the 50s, then it is unclear why other Christians could not have composed texts such as the canonical Gospels just as early.

Further confidence regarding the existence of literate Christians prior to 50 is to be found in the limited statistical and demographical evidence available to us. It has become conventional wisdom to say that 5 to 15 percent of persons in the ancient world were literate.[52] More recent work has suggested that the range was more likely 2.5 to 5 percent for the adult population of Roman Judea.[53] Properly speaking, both the presence within early Christian communities of persons from the diaspora and the spread of the new movement into the broader eastern Mediterranean limits the propriety of utilizing statistics specific to Judea, but our argument is only strengthened if we use the numbers that are least favorable rather than those most favorable. For the sake of argument, let us suppose that 2.5 percent most closely approximates the literacy rate among early Christian communities. When we are told, then, that three thousand joined the church during the first Christian Pentecost (Acts 2:41), we have reason to think that seventy-five of these were literate; when we are told that five hundred brothers and sisters saw the risen Jesus (1 Cor. 15:6), we have reason to think that twelve of these were literate; and when we are told that 120 persons were present when Matthias was chosen to succeed Judas (Acts 1:15), we have reason to think that three of these were literate. Even allowing for the possibilities that these demographics are exaggerated and that the early Christians likely came disproportionately from lower social classes and thus might have had a lower rate of literacy than the general population, there is good reason to think that already within the first decade of Christianity there were dozens if not hundreds of literate persons within the new movement. This is apart from the possibility

51. Cf. D. Campbell, *Framing Paul*, 190–253.
52. Cf. the classic study in Harris, *Ancient Literacy*, 323–37.
53. Wise, *Language and Literacy*, 350.

that members of the movement could have potentially hired scribes to assist them in composing documents of various sorts.

On the matter of willingness to write, we should take note of early Christian respect for written texts, particularly those of the Jewish scriptural tradition.[54] Although certainly there was much in the Jewish religious tradition beyond its writings, nonetheless it is in no small part by reference to those writings that the earliest Christian literature articulates the movement's emerging understanding of itself and its world. Such a reality should hardly come as a surprise since the Judaism of the first century was very much a religion of the book. By ca. 30, it was well understood that the God of Israel communicated through written texts, even if there was not yet a definitive list of the texts through which that God communicated the most fully. The content of the New Testament books themselves show that early Christians were heavily invested in Jewish written texts and thus can be expected to have been not only reading but also writing.

It might be objected that the earliest Christians would not have written much because they expected this world to end soon. This, of course, is not an argument but a hypothesis, one that must be tested against the data. Once again, the undisputed Pauline Epistles put the lie to this hypothesis. Few New Testament writers anticipate an imminent eschaton as clearly as does Paul.[55] Nonetheless, this did not stop Paul from being one of the most prolific writers of whom we are aware from the first Christian century. We also find anticipations of a relatively swift end to this world throughout the balance of the New Testament corpus. Indeed, if this anticipated end had been a significant barrier to writing, then we would have few if any texts that evince such an anticipation. We would not even know that the eschaton was a widespread anticipation. Cumulatively, it does not seem that early Christian eschatology constituted a barrier to early Christian writing. This conclusion stands even without the example of Qumran, which scholars such as Earle Ellis and Harry Gamble have quite appropriately cited as another verifiable instance wherein the anticipated end of this world constituted not a barrier but arguably an impetus to writing.[56] The development of Christian literacy is nonprobative for purposes of establishing the date of any New Testament or other early Christian text.

54. Cf. the earlier treatment of this matter in Bernier, *Quest*, 141–42.
55. Cf. 1 Thess. 4:14, 17, where Paul speaks in the first-person plural when discussing those who are still alive when the Lord returns.
56. Ellis, *Prophecy and Hermeneutic*, 242–43; Gamble, *Books and Readers*, 19–20.

The New Testament

I am concerned not with any or all texts but specifically with those that were later collected into the Christian New Testament. The decision to limit the investigation to such texts is driven not by some sort of canonical bias but by a practical need to limit the scope of investigation combined with a recognition of my own expertise. On the one hand, the canon provides a ready delimitation; on the other, I am by primary training a New Testament scholar and thus most fully equipped to consider the texts grouped within that corpus. Nevertheless, this study considers the compositional dates of four early Christian texts in addition to those collected in the New Testament: 1 Clement, the Didache, the Epistle of Barnabas, and the Shepherd of Hermas. In large part, these texts are selected because each of them might be reckoned as roughly coeval with the Christian New Testament. As such, any complete, synthetic work on the matter should address them. These are also the four extracanonical texts considered by Robinson in *Redating the New Testament*, so this present study would be woefully incomplete if they were not addressed.[57]

It should also be noted that I do not seek to define the date for hypothetical source-texts, such as Q. Matters related to such hypothetical sources will be addressed as they become incidentally relevant to the investigation, but the dates at which they might have been composed are not treated as objects of study in their own right. This is done primarily as a matter of economy. A study of this sort threatens to become unwieldy in dealing with just the extant texts, whose existence is beyond reasonable dispute, much less nonextant and contestable ones. No judgment regarding the existence of these texts is implied by this decision.

Generating Hypotheses

The previous section defined this study's overarching research question. We must now consider how we will go about answering it. As discussed above, we can distinguish heuristically between a step in which we generate possible hypotheses, and another in which we determine which of these is most likely the correct answer. In this section we consider the former step, identifying three basic procedures designed to generate hypotheses regarding the dates

57. See *Redating*, 312–35.

of the New Testament texts: synchronization, contextualization, and authorial biography.

Synchronization

Synchronization encompasses the classic work of establishing the text's temporal relationship to other events or situations, including the composition of other texts. We have already seen this in practice with the matter of 70. Here we can adapt that earlier discussion so that it is more widely applicable. The following chart, adapted and generalized from our earlier discussion of 70, helps summarize the above:

		Is there material in the book that is most fully intelligible only if written prior to a given event or situation?	
		Yes	No
Is there material in the book that is most fully intelligible only if written after a given event or situation?	Yes	The book most likely postdates the given event or situation, while preserving material that predates it.	The book most likely postdates the given event or situation and might preserve material that predates it.
	No	The book most likely predates the given event or situation.	There is equal probability that the book predates or postdates a given event or situation.

The above rubric will function as our basic heuristic for thinking about synchronization.

In addition to synchronizing our texts with events such as the crucifixion or the destruction of the temple, we can potentially also synchronize by utilizing certain classic criticisms employed by New Testament scholars. Insofar as they are of relevance, insights from textual, reception, source, and redaction criticisms will tend to represent instances of synchronization. Unfortunately, such insights tend to be of limited relevance for establishing when the New Testament texts were composed. No doubt we can judge with a high degree of confidence that a text was composed before the earliest time that it is clearly attested in the data relevant for the work of textual or reception criticism. Most texts, however, were written sometime earlier than their earliest attestation, often much earlier. $\mathfrak{P}^{46}$—the earliest extant manuscript of Paul's Letters—is perhaps the classic cautionary tale here. Young Kyu Kim argues that $\mathfrak{P}^{46}$ dates prior to the beginning of Domitian's reign in 81.[58] Even this would allow for dates notably later than those likely for at least the undisputed Pauline Epistles. Yet Philip Comfort and David Barrett—who are notorious for dating New Testament fragments earlier than most—reject this very early date and assign $\mathfrak{P}^{46}$ to the early second century.[59] Most textual critics would probably date $\mathfrak{P}^{46}$ later even than Comfort and Barrett, and as such, unless we were to affirm Kim's quite early date, we are left with the earliest manuscript witness to the Pauline corpus dating up to a half century or more later than the texts contained therein were likely first written. For its part, reception criticism's relevance for our work is likewise vitiated by the time between composition and attestation and also by uncertainties regarding what in fact constitutes evidence of reception. Nonetheless, these matters will be considered throughout this study, under the common heading of "external attestation."

Source criticism can likewise at times yield helpful although typically imprecise data regarding the compositional dates of the New Testament texts. It is a given that if text A constitutes a source for text B, then A must predate B, and B must postdate A. This would yield a relative chronology for the texts in question. If we already have an absolute date for text A, then we know that text B was written later than said date; alternatively, if we already have an absolute date for text B, then we know that text A was written earlier than said date. Unfortunately, due primarily to the nature of the data, source-critical judgments tend to be more contestable than we prefer for purposes of establishing when a text was written. Only rarely will they permit a high degree of confidence in chronological decision-making. Nonetheless, source-critical data will at times allow us to favor certain relative chronologies over others.

For its part, redaction criticism is typically relevant only insofar as it grapples with the reality that some texts might well have been written over an extended period. For instance, most New Testament scholars likely agree that John 21 is a secondary addition to the Fourth Gospel, or at least was composed later than the rest of the text. If that is indeed the case, and if John 21:19 also indicates that Peter passed away before this chapter was written, then we must be open to the possibility that while the Fourth Gospel

58. Kim, "Dating of P[46]."
59. Cf. Comfort and Barrett, *Earliest New Testament Greek Manuscripts*, 1:183–87.

in toto postdates Peter's death, the majority of the text predates his death.[60] Instances wherein we must consider such matters will be discussed where appropriate.

Despite the above limitations, synchronization can narrow down the range of possible compositional dates to a century or less for almost every text considered in this study. This is not insignificant. By contrast, some texts in the Hebrew Bible have a range of possible compositional dates that are upward of a millennium. For instance, most biblical scholars hold that the Pentateuch took on its definitive shape only in the late preexilic or early postexilic periods. Yet just in the five years before this book was published, at least two projects have appeared that argue that the core of Deuteronomy should be dated several centuries earlier. In the first of these projects, Sandra Richter holds that the core of Deuteronomy likely dates from ca. 1000 BCE.[61] In the second, Josef Schubert argues that Deuteronomy must have been more or less complete by no later than the division of the United Monarchy, ca. 930 BCE.[62] In earlier but still relatively recent scholarship, Kenneth Kitchen has maintained that the forms of the various pentateuchal covenants find their strongest analogies in Late Bronze Age (ca. 1400–1200 BCE) treaties, and Pekka Pitkänen has argued that at least the core of Deuteronomy was in existence by ca. 1050 BCE.[63] My concern here is not to evaluate these claims.[64] Rather, I observe only that the data permit scholars to entertain a chronological range encompassing several centuries for much of the pentateuchal material. Given this reality faced by those in pentateuchal studies, we already have reason to celebrate our capacity to narrow down, via synchronization, the range of compositional dates for the New Testament texts to within a century or less.

As a procedural matter, it is assumed without argument that each of the texts we seek to date in this volume were written after Jesus's death. Against the older consensus, which dated the crucifixion to either 30 or 33, we must now reckon with the possibility that any year from 29 through 34 is a candidate.[65] As such, if I state that a given early Christian text was written before

60. Cf. the fuller discussion in chap. 3 below.
61. Richter, "Question of Provenance"; Richter, "Neo-Babylonian and Persian Periods." Cf. the response by Berge et al., "Are Economics a Key?"
62. Schubert, *Dating Deuteronomy*.
63. Cf. Kitchen, *Reliability of the Old Testament*, 283–94; Pitkänen, *Central Sanctuary and Centralization*.
64. But cf. the appendix to Bernier, "Re-visioning Social Values," 18–20.
65. Cf. Bond, "Dating the Death of Jesus"; Pitre, *Jesus and the Last Supper*, 251–373.

70 (for instance), then it should always be taken for granted that I mean no earlier than 29 and no later than 70. It seems unnecessarily pedantic to spell this out in every instance, however, and I avoid doing so.

Contextualization

Alongside synchronization is the work of contextualization, which seeks to establish the text's probable relationship to the general course of early Christian development in areas such as ecclesiology, Christology, gentile inclusion, and so on. Baur's effort to situate the New Testament documents within his own understanding of early Christian development is an exemplar of contextualization.[66] In principle, form- and genre-critical data are of relevance for the work of contextualization. If it can be shown that a given literary form or genre flourished at a given time, then we have some warrant to argue that texts displaying that form or genre likely date to around that time. Likewise, the work of the history of religions schools could potentially be of use. Such work sought to situate the development of especially Christology in relation to broader patterns of religious imagery, thought, and practice.[67]

In studying the ancient world, however, contextualization tends to work on a temporal scale larger than the one with which we are concerned. This is perhaps best demonstrated by reference to recent work in Hebrew Bible studies. As already alluded to above, Richter argues that the historical core of Deuteronomy—the so-called *Urdeuteronomium*, which she defines as Deuteronomy 4:44–27:26—most fully reflects the economic realities present in Palestine ca. 1000 BCE; thus she concludes that it likely dates from around this time.[68] For their part, Ronald Hendel and Jan Joosten have recently argued that the language of the Torah represents a form of Hebrew best attested from (but potentially in existence before) the eighth through the sixth centuries BCE.[69] Such arguments are of relevance only because the possible date range for the texts of the Pentateuch are measured in centuries. In a study such as this, where we are concerned with texts that can be dated to within a century or less, the utility of contextualization will tend to be limited.

---

66. Cf. esp. his grand synthesis in Baur, *First Three Centuries*, 41–137.

67. Cf. Bauckham, *Jesus and the God of Israel*; Bousset, *Kyrios Christos*; Dunn, *Christology in the Making*; Hurtado, *Lord Jesus Christ*; Hurtado, *One God, One Lord*.

68. Richter, "Question of Provenance."

69. Hendel and Joosten, *How Old Is the Hebrew Bible?*, 60–72. Note that in 2020 Joosten pled guilty to possession of child pornography.

Further, arguments from contextualization need to be utilized with extreme care lest we fall into the trap of circular reasoning, in which a given developmental scheme is used to generate a chronological one, and then the chronological one is used to defend the original developmental scheme. In practice, the best we can usually say is that a probable developmental scheme will tend to favor a lower, middle, or higher range of dates permitted via synchronization. Often we cannot say even that.

Authorial Biography

By contrast to the relative vagaries of contextualization, no procedure in principle permits greater precision than that of authorial biography, which proceeds from what we know about the author and prompts us to ask when in her or his life a given text is best situated. For instance, in Galatians 1:18 Paul tells us that he went up to Jerusalem three years after his conversion, and in Galatians 2:1 that he went again after fourteen years. Thus Galatians can date no earlier than the second of these visits. But perhaps the single most effective use of authorial biography comes in the case of Romans. As will be argued in chapter 6, Romans was most likely written during the three months that Paul spent in Achaia, according to Acts 20:3a. These three months can be dated with confidence to the winter of 56/57. As intimated by these examples, authorial biography will be particularly useful with regard to the Pauline Epistles.

Authorial biography forces us to confront the unavoidable question of authenticity. To minimize space devoted to antecedent issues and instead focus upon determining compositional dates, I have opted not to dedicate significant space to rehashing the arguments for or against the authenticity of disputed texts. Those arguments exist, but they are simply not reproduced here at length. I do not ignore them, however. They will be considered as we move through the relevant texts. In four cases—1 and 2 Timothy, Titus, and 2 Peter—this will lead us to propose two possible date ranges: one if they are authentic compositions, and a second if they are pseudonymous.

Conclusion

This section has identified a threefold rubric by which to generate hypotheses: *Synchronization* seeks to establish the text's temporal relationship to other events or situations, including the composition of other texts. *Contextualization* seeks to establish the text's probable relationship to the general course of early Christian development. *Authorial biography* proceeds from what we know about the author and seeks to establish when in her or his life a given text is best situated.

This rubric serves largely to organize and coordinate the relevant data. In and of itself, it does not provide us with the means by which to adjudicate between hypotheses.

Adjudicating Answers

Above we considered how to go about generating hypotheses regarding the compositional dates of New Testament (and other early Christian) texts. The work of hypothesis generation, however, frequently results in more than one possible answer to our questions. In such situations, we need a means by which to adjudicate between such possibilities. I suggest that, in any given case, the hypothesis to be preferred is the one that (1) employs the fewest number of logical fallacies, (2) can account for the greatest quantity of relevant data, and (3) can do so with the highest degree of parsimony.

Freedom from Fallacy

"Freedom from fallacy" represents the most significant advance beyond my earlier published discussions of historical method.[70] It is introduced in order to exercise greater control over hypotheses that might well explain a great deal of evidence in a parsimonious manner but that are clearly absurd. In principle, even one logical fallacy tends to be too many; freedom from fallacy becomes a desideratum. Of course, we must avoid the fallacy fallacy, which supposes that if an argument contains a fallacy, then its conclusion must be false. A hypothesis can be altogether true, even if the reasons given for its affirmation are utterly fallacious. Nonetheless, until the hypothesis can be articulated in such a way as to exclude fallacious argumentation, we should be wary of affirming it as true.

Evidentiary Scope

Compared to freedom from fallacies, we can be more forgiving in regard to the quantity of data—or what we might also call evidentiary scope—for which

70. Cf. esp. Bernier, *Quest*, 68–69.

the hypothesis can account. The world is a messy place, and our knowledge of it is always partial. Rarely can we expect to fully explain all the data relevant to a given matter. Still, all things being equal, a fallacy-free hypothesis that can account for 90 percent of the data is to be preferred over a fallacy-free hypothesis that can account for only 45 percent of the data. Of course, all things are not always equal. Certain data will be of greater relevance than others; a failure to account for these data will pose a greater barrier to affirming the hypothesis than a failure to account for other, less relevant data. Still, quantity of data explained is a helpful criterion.

Parsimony

For its part, parsimony tends to be a tiebreaker. It is what one considers when one has two or more hypotheses that are free of fallacies and that can account for a roughly comparable quantity of data. If our respective hypotheses are equally free of fallacies and can account for the same data but your account requires three entities whereas mine requires five, then your account is probably to be preferred. Again, the criterion of parsimony cannot be used slavishly, but it does tend to separate stronger hypotheses from weaker ones.

Conclusion

The above is a heuristic description of the work of adjudication. Adjudication aims to determine which among competing hypotheses employs the fewest number of logical fallacies while accounting for the greatest quantity of relevant data with the highest degree of parsimony.

Adjudication, of course, tends to be notably messier in practice than the above account suggests. It is not a calculus. It cannot be reduced to number grubbing. Moreover, the work is not as linear as the heuristic description suggests. Insights achieved through the process of hypothesis generation might lead one to redefine the question, and insights achieved through the process of adjudicating hypotheses might lead one to not only redefine the question but also generate new hypotheses or new articulations of old ones. Nonetheless, the heuristic description helps us to think about what we are doing when we formulate history; it also provides the reader with insight regarding how the author is making judgments throughout the study.

Treatment of Primary and Secondary Literature

My previously published work is characterized by a style perhaps best exemplified by Martin Hengel's *Judaism and Hellenism*, which notoriously
required a second volume just for endnotes and indexes. By comparison,
the notations within this study are relatively light. This is not the result of
failure or refusal to engage with the thoughts of other scholars but rather
a conscious decision to limit the scope of a study that could easily become
unwieldy. New Testament scholarship often ends up constituting tertiary
literature written on secondary literature. There is, of course, a place for
such work. Nonetheless, this study is meant to be secondary literature on
primary literature. My central aim throughout is to show the reader how I
have made use of the texts and other relevant data from the ancient world
to build my arguments. More concretely, rather than glutting my text with
constant references to the commentaries that have aided my work, I will, in
a single footnote at the outset of each chapter, indicate those I have found
the most useful for my purposes. The majority of these are from the Anchor
Bible, Hermeneia, International Critical Commentary, and Word Biblical
Commentary series; I find that judicious reading of the relevant commentaries in these series tends to bring most of the relevant critical issues to
one's attention. More specific citations will typically be reserved for direct
engagement with a given scholar's arguments. Not surprisingly, I engage
with Robinson's *Redating the New Testament* more frequently than any
other single work. This engagement will be the most intense when I register
disagreements with Robinson. In recognition that many readers will likely
not be professional biblical scholars, I cite works that are available in English
whenever possible.

Regarding primary literature, it is my aim that even those who disagree
with my conclusions will find that the way in which I organize and present the
relevant evidence facilitates their own thinking about the dates at which the
New Testament texts were composed. When presenting such evidence in this
study, I will generally present biblical quotations first from the New Revised
Standard Version (NRSV) and then discuss the Greek text as needed. This
is done to balance the needs of interested persons who might have little if
any training in Greek with the needs of those who have a legitimate interest
in seeing how I handle the Greek text. I follow a comparable practice when

quoting the Apostolic Fathers, except I will cite the English translation and Greek text as given in Michael Holmes's edition.[71]

One final word is required regarding what we might call the ethics of citation. There have been recent conversations among biblical scholars regarding how to best handle the scholarly legacy both of persons who belonged to the NSDAP (the Germany National Socialist Party; i.e., the Nazis), and of persons credibly accused of (and even more those who have confessed to or been convicted of) sexual assault, harassment, or exploitation. I have spent much time reflecting upon and conversing with colleagues over this matter and greatly appreciate their insights.[72] In recognition of the very real ethical questions raised through these conversations, I have decided to engage with the work of such persons as infrequently as possible. I have three primary aims in adopting this practice. The first is to stand in solidarity with victims and survivors. The second is to help foster practices and discourses that foreground the rights and well-being of persons minoritized by a discipline that has notably and unacceptably excluded persons of color and women, as well as to pursue a concrete zero tolerance policy toward racism, sexual abuse, harassment, and exploitation. The third is to concretely contribute, in even the smallest way, to the ongoing effort of coming to terms with a disciplinary history that includes persons of dubious character. There was one instance in which I considered it unavoidable to cite an individual whom I know to have been credibly accused (in this case convicted) of sexual misconduct; in my judgment, not to cite this person in this case would introduce an unacceptable lacuna into the present work. There is another instance (earlier in this introduction) in which I have cited a work coauthored by someone convicted of sexual misconduct. I decided that it was unfair to the other author to ignore this contribution. In both cases I report the respective convictions since I think it important to inform readers and allow them to make their own judgment on the matter of what to do with the work of such persons. I have cited no scholar whom I know to have been an NSDAP member. If I have inadvertently cited any NSDAP member or any other scholar credibly accused of sexual misconduct, then please accept my humblest apologies for the oversight.

71. Holmes, *Apostolic Fathers*.
72. I express great gratitude to the organizers and members of the BRANE Collective: their work in facilitating such discourses has greatly enriched my own thinking on these matters. Eva Mroczek and Jacqueline Vayntrub are especially to be commended for their work in moving these conversations forward.

Overview of This Study

This introduction aims to give the reader an initial orientation to this study. By this point she or he should have a sense of the central question being asked, the answer this study will offer to that question, and the method by which the answer will be generated. The central question is when the texts later collected into the Christian New Testament were composed. The answer is *primarily between the years 40 and 70 of the first century*. The method is inferential: through (1) defining the research questions; (2) generating hypotheses through the work of synchronization, contextualization, and authorial biography; and (3) adjudicating hypotheses by utilizing the criteria identified as freedom from fallacy, evidentiary scope, and parsimony. The balance of this study is taken up with elaborating this question, answer, and method through close engagement with the data.

The study overall is organized in loose adherence to the canonical ordering of the New Testament. That order, however, is broken as needed to best facilitate the presentation of the arguments. There are five parts to this study, each containing two chapters. Part 1 considers the compositional dates of the Synoptic Gospels and Acts, with chapter 1 exploring the work of synchronization and chapter 2 the work of contextualization and authorial biography. Part 2 considers the compositional dates of the Johannine literature, with chapter 3 discussing the Gospel of John and chapter 4 the Letters of John and the book of Revelation. Part 3 considers the compositional dates of the canonical Pauline Epistles, with chapter 5 analyzing the role of Acts in the study of Pauline chronology and chapter 6 when the Letters were written. Part 4 considers the compositional date of Hebrews and the Catholic Epistles (less the Johannine Epistles, which were treated in part 2), with chapter 7 discussing Hebrews and the Epistle of James and chapter 8 discussing 1 and 2 Peter and Jude. Part 5 considers the compositional dates of select extracanonical writings, with chapter 9 focusing on 1 Clement and the Didache and chapter 10 the Epistle of Barnabas and the Shepherd of Hermas. A conclusion will follow, summarizing—as any conclusion should—the arguments of the study.

The Synoptic Gospels and Acts

I

Synchronization

The aim of part 1 is to establish the probable dates for the Gospels of Matthew, Mark, and Luke, as well as the Acts of the Apostles.[1] Due to the densely interconnected nature of these texts, they will be treated together. We begin in chapter 1 by considering matters of synchronization in relation to all four of these texts, then continue in chapter 2 with matters of contextualization and authorial biography. Although most scholars date Mark's Gospel to ca. 70, Matthew's Gospel to ca. 80, and Luke-Acts to ca. 85 through 90, this chapter argues that Acts was written ca. 62 and the Synoptic Gospels before that date, with Matthew's Gospel likely written prior to Luke's Gospel, and Mark's Gospel prior to Matthew's Gospel.

Synchronization

This chapter will consider (1) external attestation of the Synoptic Gospels and Acts, (2) the Synoptic problem, (3) the Synoptic Gospels' respective

---

1. In developing chap. 1, I found the following particularly useful: Bovon, *Luke*; Conzelmann, *Acts*; Crossley, *Date of Mark's Gospel*; Davies and Allison, *Matthew*; Donahue and Harrington, *Mark*; Evans, *Mark 8:27–16:20*; Fitzmyer, *Acts*; Fitzmyer, *Luke*; Guelich, *Mark 1–8:26*; Gundry, *Mark*; Gundry, *Matthew*; Hagner, *Matthew*; D. Harrington, *Matthew*; Hemer, *Book of Acts*; Hengel, *Four Gospels*; Hengel, *Gospel of Mark*; Hooker, *Mark*; Johnson, *Luke*; Keener, *Acts*; Luz, *Matthew*; Marcus, *Mark 1–8*; Marcus, *Mark 8–16*; Nolland, *Luke*; Wenham, *Redating Matthew, Mark and Luke*; Yarbro Collins, *Mark*.

relationships to the events of the Jewish War and especially the destruction of the temple in 70, and (4) chronological concerns specific to Luke and Acts, such as the unity of Luke-Acts, the relationship of Luke-Acts to the writings of Josephus, Marcion, and Paul, and the end of Acts. Through the work of synchronization, we conclude it is probable that the Gospels of Matthew, Mark, and Luke, as well as the Acts of the Apostles, were in each case composed no later than ca. 62.

External Attestation

It is likely that Papias was aware of Mark's Gospel and with less probability also Matthew's Gospel.[2] It is also likely that Ignatius of Antioch was aware of Matthew's Gospel.[3] Given that these writers were most likely active during the reign of Trajan (r. 98–117), we should be wary of dating either of these Gospels much later than 120. In his definitive and careful study of the relevant material, Andrew Gregory concludes that there is no certain evidence that Luke's Gospel and Acts were being read before, respectively, ca. 150 and ca. 170.[4] On the basis of attestation, we thus cannot exclude a date for Luke-Acts as late as the mid-second century.

The Synoptic Problem

Few questions have vexed modern New Testament scholarship more fully than that of the interrelationships among the Gospels of Matthew, Mark, and Luke.[5] That these three texts are related is beyond any reasonable doubt, and a definitive account of their interrelationship would greatly advance the cause of Synoptic chronology. Here is a concrete example: one of the earliest proposals to explain the interrelatedness of the Synoptic Gospels was the so-called Augustinian Hypothesis, which in its modern form argues that Matthew wrote first, then Mark used Matthew's Gospel as a source, and then Luke used both.[6] If this were to be affirmed, then we would have established a relative

2. Cf. Eusebius, *Hist. eccl.* 3.39.15–16, as well as the discussion of this passage in chap. 2 on authorial biography below.
3. Cf. esp. the parallel between Ign. *Smyrn.* 1.1 and Matt. 3:15.
4. Gregory, *Reception of Luke and Acts*, 293–98, 350–51.
5. For a general history of efforts to solve the synoptic problem, cf. Dungan, *History of the Synoptic Problem*.
6. Probably the most current, extensive defense of the Augustinian hypothesis is to be found in Wenham, *Redating Matthew, Mark and Luke*.

chronology for the Synoptic Gospels: Matthew's Gospel would predate both Mark's and Luke's; Mark's Gospel would postdate Matthew's and predate Luke's; and Luke's Gospel would postdate both Matthew's and Mark's. This would not itself establish absolute dates, but if we were to build upon this relative chronology by dating any one Synoptic Gospel absolutely, then we would have also identified at least some temporal limits for the other two.

Unfortunately, Synoptic source criticism has not yet reached a place of consensus. In *Redating the New Testament*, John Robinson makes too much of the disagreements among Synoptic source critics. He ultimately opts for a somewhat idiosyncratic approach to the Synoptic problem, which focuses too much on the development of the Synoptic Gospels and consequently becomes mired in tangentially relevant considerations.[7] In reality, Synoptic source criticism is not as divided as a casual glance might suggest. Among Synoptic source critics working today we find a strong preference for Markan priority—that is, the supposition that Mark wrote first, with Matthew and Luke utilizing his Gospel as a source text. Contemporary proponents of Markan priority are further divided between those who affirm the Two Document Hypothesis and those who affirm the Farrer-Goulder Hypothesis.[8] This division has to do with the so-called double tradition—that is, the material that Matthew and Luke have in common but that is not in Mark. Proponents of the Two Document Hypothesis (Markan priority with Q) argue that, for the double tradition, Matthew and Luke each independently used a third, nonextant source dubbed "Q"; and proponents of the Farrer-Goulder Hypothesis (Markan priority without Q) argue that Luke's source for this double-tradition material was simply Matthew's Gospel.

From the above, it is evident that both solutions to the Synoptic problem preferred by specialists affirm that, among the Synoptic Gospels, Mark's Gospel was written first; they either do not exclude (in the case of the Two Document Hypothesis) or affirm (in the case of the Farrer-Goulder view) the hypothesis that Luke was written last. Thus we can reasonably operate on the working supposition that the chronologies placing Mark's Gospel first and Luke's last are those least likely to run into source-critical difficulties. Yet it must be emphasized that our preferences for Markan priority and even more so for Lukan posteriority are not immune to revision. If there is compelling

---

7. Robinson, *Redating*, 92–94.

8. The most accessible accounts and strongest defenses of these respective hypotheses remain, respectively, Kloppenborg Verbin, *Excavating Q*; Goodacre, *Case Against Q*.

reason on other grounds to date Luke's Gospel earlier than either Matthew's or Mark's, then we must consider the possibility.[9] Still, the data appear to be such that we can reasonably and provisionally operate on a preference for chronologies in which the date of Luke's Gospel is later than the date of Matthew's, which is in turn later than the date of Mark's.

The Matter of 70

Many New Testament scholars consider it a given that the Synoptic Gospels—or at least Matthew's and Luke's Gospels—betray knowledge of the events of the Jewish War (66–73), and more specifically the destruction of the Jerusalem temple in 70.[10] Speaking specifically regarding the Gospel of Matthew, Donald Hagner refers to "the dogmatism of critical orthodoxy concerning a post-70 date."[11] This is unfair. Scholars who hold that one or more of the Synoptic Gospels are post-70 compositions do so because they believe that the evidence best supports this position. Indeed, it goes without saying that any text betraying knowledge of the second temple's destruction as a past event must postdate 70. Nonetheless, whether the Synoptic Gospels do betray such knowledge is not as self-evident as often supposed. For his part, Robinson rightly observes that the Synoptic Gospels, and indeed the entirety of the New Testament, never refer to the destruction of the temple as a past event; this observation is indeed foundational for his development of a lower chronology.[12] As discussed in the introduction to this study, however, Robinson

9. Cf. the arguments for Lukan priority over Matthew's Gospel in Hengel, *Four Gospels*, 169–207; MacEwen, *Matthean Posteriority*.

10. Recent commentators who suppose a post-70 date for Matthew's Gospel as well as Luke's, on the basis of the events of 70, include Fitzmyer, *Luke*, 1:53–57; D. Harrington, *Matthew*, 8; Luz, *Matthew*, 1:58. Davies and Allison date Matthew's Gospel after 70, but more due to their assumption that Mark's dates to around the time of the Jewish War (*Matthew*, 1:131). Hagner is open to but does not insist upon a pre-70 date for Matthew's Gospel (*Matthew*, 1:lxxiii–lxxv). Gundry is an outlier among recent commentators in insisting upon a pre-70 date for Matthew's Gospel (*Matthew*, 599–608). There is a marked preference to date Mark's Gospel after the beginning of the Jewish War in 66, with scholars divided regarding whether Mark's Gospel should date before or after 70. Those who date Mark's Gospel after 66 but before 70 include Guelich, *Mark 1–8:26*, xxxi–xxxii; Yarbro Collins, *Mark*, 11–14. Alternatively, those who date Mark's Gospel after 66 but allow for the possibility of a post-70 composition include Donahue and Harrington, *Mark*, 44; Hooker, *Mark*, 8; Marcus, *Mark 1–8*, 38. Once again, Gundry is an outlier, arguing that Mark's Gospel likely predates not only the events of 70 but the outbreak of the Jewish War in 66 (Gundry, *Mark*, 1041–42).

11. Hagner, *Matthew*, 1:lxxv.

12. Robinson, *Redating*, 13–30.

so emphasizes this point that he risks lapsing into a fallacious argument from silence. Fortunately for proponents of the lower chronology, arguments from silence are not required. Rather, attentive readings of the relevant material in the Synoptic Gospels are such that Luke's Gospel might reasonably be thought to predate 70, while Matthew's and Mark's Gospels almost certainly do. In what follows in this section, we first consider relevant passages that are *least* probative for purposes of establishing the compositional dates of the Synoptic Gospels and then move toward those which are *most* probative.

The Torn Curtain (Matt. 27:51; Mark 15:38; Luke 23:45)

Perhaps the weakest argument for post-70 dates for any of the Synoptic Gospels involve the traditions of the torn curtain. They read as follows.

> At that moment the curtain of the temple was torn in two, from top to bottom. The earth shook, and the rocks were split. (Matt. 27:51)

> And the curtain of the temple was torn in two, from top to bottom. (Mark 15:38)

> And the curtain of the temple was torn in two. (Luke 23:45b)

Robinson fails to discuss these verses, probably because none of them reports the temple's destruction. Indeed, the fact that these verses do not report the temple's destruction does somewhat vitiate the hypothesis that these verses suppose the temple's destruction. Nonetheless, a scholarly tradition holds that these passages—especially the Matthean and Lukan variants—suppose the destruction of the temple as background.[13] Frequently they are read as portents of the destruction, written after it had occurred. This is hardly impossible. Josephus, after all, writes about such portents. Here we quote the relevant passage at length:

> Thus it was that the wretched people were deluded at that time by charlatans and pretended messengers of the deity; while they neither heeded nor believed in the manifest portents that foretold the coming desolation, but, as if thunderstruck and bereft of eyes and mind, disregarded the plain warnings of God. So it was when a star, resembling a sword, stood over the city, and a comet which continued for a year. So again when, before the revolt and the commotion

13. Cf. discussions in Davies and Allison, *Matthew*, 3:630–32; Evans, *Mark 8:27–16:20*, 508–10; D. Harrington, *Matthew*, 400; Nolland, *Luke*, 3:1157–58; Yarbro Collins, *Mark*, 759–63.

that led to war, at the time when the people were assembling for the feast of unleavened bread, on the eighth of the month Xanthicus, at the ninth hour of the night, so brilliant a light shone round the altar and the sanctuary that it seemed to be broad daylight; and this continued for half an hour. By the inexperienced this was regarded as a good omen, but by the sacred scribes it was at once interpreted in accordance with after events. At that same feast a cow that had been brought by some one for sacrifice gave birth to a lamb in the midst of the court of the temple; moreover, the eastern gate of the inner court—it was of brass and very massive, and, when closed towards evening, could scarcely be moved by twenty men; fastened with iron-bound bars, it had bolts which were sunk to a great depth into a threshold consisting of a solid block of stone—this gate was observed at the sixth hour of the night to have opened of its own accord. The watchmen of the temple ran and reported the matter to the captain, and he came up and with difficulty succeeded in shutting it. This again to the uninitiated seemed the best of omens, as they supposed that God had opened to them the gate of blessings; but the learned understood that the security of the temple was dissolving of its own accord and that the opening of the gate meant a present to the enemy, interpreting the portent in their own minds as indicative of coming desolation. Again, not many days after the festival, on the twenty-first of the month Artemisium, there appeared a miraculous phenomenon, passing belief. Indeed, what I am about to relate would, I imagine, have been deemed a fable, were it not for the narratives of eyewitnesses and for the subsequent calamities which deserved to be so signalized. For before sunset throughout all parts of the country chariots were seen in the air and armed battalions hurtling through the clouds and encompassing the cities. Moreover, at the feast which is called Pentecost, the priests on entering the inner court of the temple by night, as their custom was in the discharge of their ministrations, reported that they were conscious, first of a commotion and a din, and after that of a voice as of a host, "We are departing hence."[14]

The parallel with Josephus is imprecise. We know that he is writing post-70, not because he reports such portents but because he explicitly narrates the events of that year retrospectively; this is what we do not find in the Synoptic Gospels. Nonetheless, it is plausible that Matthew 27:51, Mark 15:38, and Luke 23:45 narrate portents of the events of 70 retrospectively.

Still, it is conceivable that the tradition of the torn curtain emerged pre-70, perhaps to thematize the growing Christian openness to gentile inclusion or

14. Cf. Josephus, *J.W.* 6.5.3 §§288–99 (Thackeray).

alternatively out of a growing ambivalence toward the temple cult. Cumulatively, the lack of clear reference to the destruction of the temple and the passages' intelligibility in a pre-70 context are not such that one must read these passages as portents written after the fact. They seem at least as intelligible before 70 as after 70.

The Wedding Banquet (Matt. 22:7)

Robinson suggests that Matthew 22:7 is more likely than any other verse in the New Testament to have the events of 70 in mind.[15] This somewhat overstates its relevance to the present discussion. Matthew 22:7 adds to the parable of the wedding banquet the notice that "the king was enraged. He sent his troops, destroyed those murderers, and burned their city."[16] As Robinson intimates, it is frequently supposed that Matthew 22:7 was written with the events of 70 in mind. Taken on its own, this is a plausible interpretation. Whether it is a necessary or even the best interpretation is far from self-evident. First, the parabolic nature of this passage opens questions about whether the passage intends to reference concrete historical events. Second, whether the city in question is meant to be Jerusalem is not clear. Third, even if we grant that the passage intends to reference concrete historical events and that the city in question is meant to be Jerusalem, it is again subject to debate whether the events in question are those of 70.

Matthew 22:7 contains imagery found elsewhere in the ancient Near East and indeed in the Jewish Scriptures.[17] It particularly resonates with Judith 1:7–15, which reports that Nebuchadnezzar waged destructive war against nations that refused to heed his messengers' call to join him, as well as 2 Chronicles 36:15–19, which depicts the destruction of the first temple as a consequence of Israel's failure to accept God's prophets. Such material suffices to demonstrate that a scenario much like that found in Matthew 22:1–7 was intelligible prior to 70.

The above considerations do not prove fatal to the hypothesis that Matthew 22:7 refers to the destruction of the temple after the fact, but neither are they particularly friendly to that hypothesis. They do create a scenario in which

---

15. Robinson, *Redating*, 20.
16. Cf. the larger parable as found respectively in Matt. 22:1–10; Luke 14:16–24; Gos. Thom. 64.
17. Cf. Josh. 6:21–24; Judg. 1:8; 18:27; 20:48; and 1 Macc. 5:28, 35. Frequently cited as an authority on this matter is Rengstorf, "Der Stadt der Mörder."

Matthew 22:7 is at least as intelligible before 70 as after. The passage is best considered to be nonprobative for establishing the date of Matthew's Gospel.

Not One Stone (Matt. 24:1-2; Mark 13:1-2; Luke 21:5-6)

We now turn to the passages in which Jesus most explicitly predicts the destruction of the temple.

> As Jesus came out of the temple and was going away, his disciples came to point out to him the buildings of the temple. Then he asked them, "You see all these, do you not? Truly I tell you, not one stone will be left here upon another; all will be thrown down." (Matt. 24:1–2)

> As he came out of the temple, one of his disciples said to him, "Look, Teacher, what large stones and what large buildings!" Then Jesus asked him, "Do you see these great buildings? Not one stone will be left upon another; all will be thrown down." (Mark 13:1–2)

> When some were speaking about the temple, how it was adorned with beautiful stones and gifts dedicated to God, he said, "As for these things that you see, the days will come when not one stone will be left upon another; all will be thrown down." (Luke 21:5–6)

With these passages we confront the crux of the matter of 70 as it relates to the Synoptic Gospels—namely, whether it is reasonable to suppose that anyone prior to 70 could have anticipated the destruction of the temple. Certainly, if such anticipation was impossible before 70, then the Synoptic Gospels cannot predate the destruction. As always, we should welcome such a conclusion because it decisively narrows down the range of possible compositional dates.

The data is such, however, that it is conceivable persons might have anticipated the destruction of the temple before 70. Josephus informs us of a prophet ("one Jesus, son of Ananias") who predicted the temple's destruction several years prior to the outbreak of the war. Here it is again worth quoting at length.

> Four years before the war, when the city was enjoying profound peace and prosperity, there came to the feast at which it is the custom of all Jews to erect tabernacles to God, one Jesus, son of Ananias, a rude peasant, who, standing

in the temple, suddenly began to cry out, "A voice from the east, a voice from the west, a voice from the four winds; a voice against Jerusalem and the sanctuary, a voice against the bridegroom and the bride, a voice against all the people." Day and night he went about all the alleys with this cry on his lips. Some of the leading citizens, incensed at these ill-omened words, arrested the fellow and severely chastised him. But he, without a word on his own behalf or for the private ear of those who smote him, only continued his cries as before. Thereupon, the magistrates, supposing, as was indeed the case, that the man was under some supernatural impulse, brought him before the Roman governor; there, although flayed to the bone with scourges, he neither sued for mercy nor shed a tear, but, merely introducing the most mournful of variations into his ejaculation, responded to each stroke with "Woe to Jerusalem!" When Albinus, the governor, asked him who and whence he was and why he uttered these cries, he answered him never a word, but unceasingly reiterated his dirge over the city, until Albinus pronounced him a maniac and let him go. During the whole period up to the outbreak of war he neither approached nor was seen talking to any of the citizens, but daily, like a prayer that he had conned, repeated his lament, "Woe to Jerusalem!" He neither cursed any of those who beat him from day to day, nor blessed those who offered him food: to all men that melancholy presage was his one reply. His cries were loudest at the festivals. So for seven years and five months he continued his wail, his voice never flagging nor his strength exhausted, until in the siege, having seen his presage verified, he found his rest. For, while going his round and shouting in piercing tones from the wall, "Woe once more to the city and to the people and to the temple," as he added a last word, "and woe to me also," a stone hurled from the *ballista* struck and killed him on the spot. So with those ominous words still upon his lips he passed away.[18]

From this passage, Robinson rightly concludes, "That Jesus could have predicted the doom of Jerusalem and its sanctuary is no more inherently improbable than that another Jesus, the son of Ananias, should have done so in the autumn of 62."[19] Mark Goodacre has recently contested Robinson on this matter, writing, "The problem for this perspective is that Jesus ben Ananias's prophecy occurs in a literary work that postdates 70."[20] Certainly, Josephus's account of Jesus ben Ananias's prophecy establishes that such prophecies could be reported in texts that postdate 70, but that hardly excludes the

18. Josephus, *J.W.* 6.5.3 §§300–309 (Thackeray).
19. Robinson, *Redating*, 15.
20. Goodacre, *Thomas and the Gospels*, 166.

possibility that they could also be reported in pre-70 texts. The issue is not when Josephus is writing, but rather whether his account of Jesus ben Ananias is sufficiently plausible as to establish a precedent for pre-70 prophecies of the temple's destruction. Because the temple had been destroyed before, nothing seems particularly incredible about the possibility that in the decades prior to the Jewish War someone might have anticipated such destruction in their own time.

Given the above considerations, Matthew 24:1–2, Mark 13:1–2, and Luke 21:5–6 appear to be intelligible if interpreted as pre-70 compositions. Indeed, proponents of middle chronologies frequently concede this fact and often date Mark's Gospel after the outbreak of war in 66 but before the destruction of the temple in 70. If Mark 13:1 can permit a pre-70 dating, then it is unclear why either Matthew 24:1 or Luke 21:5 must mandate a post-70 one.[21] Indeed, the data are such that if any of these passages necessitate a post-70 date, then all must—but none of these passages do. Yet they hardly exclude a post-70 date for any of the Synoptic Gospels; indeed, it is reasonable to read these passages as prophecies after the fact. Once again, these passages should be considered nonprobative for purposes of establishing the dates of the Synoptic Gospels.

False Testimony (Matt. 26:59–61; 27:39–40; Mark 14:57–58)

Nowhere in *Redating the New Testament* does Robinson address Matthew 26:59–61, Matthew 27:39–40, and Mark 14:57–58 in relation to the destruction of the temple. This is unfortunate and somewhat surprising, given their obvious relevance to the question of what the Synoptic Evangelists might have known about 70. Turning to the passages in question, they read as follows.

> Now the chief priests and the whole council were looking for false testimony against Jesus so that they might put him to death, but they found none, though many false witnesses came forward. At last two came forward and said, "This fellow said, 'I am able to destroy the temple of God and to build it in three days.'" (Matt. 26:59–61)

> Those who passed by derided him, shaking their heads and saying, "You who would destroy the temple and build it in three days, save yourself! If you are the Son of God, come down from the cross." (Matt. 27:39–40)

21. Cf. the similar observation in Robinson, *Redating*, 14–15.

> Some stood up and gave false testimony against him, saying, "We heard him say, 'I will destroy this temple that is made with hands, and in three days I will build another, not made with hands.'" (Mark 14:57–58)

Beginning with Matthew 26:59–61 and 27:39–40, it seems equally plausible that the passage predates 70 or at least in part postdates it. Jesus elsewhere predicts that he will die and then rise again in three days.[22] John 2:19–22 not only explicitly presents Jesus's prophecy that he would destroy and rebuild the temple as an allegorical reference to his own death and resurrection but also states that his contemporaries wrongly understood him to be speaking literally about the temple.[23] Indeed, the language of "three days" should lead us to at least consider the possibility that each of these passages is related to predictions of Jesus's death and resurrection. Given this three-day tradition, we can argue that Jesus did literally say he would destroy and rebuild the temple in three days, that (rightly or wrongly) this was interpreted in a literal sense during his lifetime, that after the events of Easter the early Christians (rightly or wrongly) reinterpreted it as an allegorical reference to his body, and that they viewed as false any allegations that he claimed he would destroy and rebuild the Jerusalem temple in three days. In other words, it is possible that the references predate 70 and that early Christians then sought to repudiate this as false testimony only after it became obvious that the Jerusalem temple would not be rebuilt in relatively short order. We should probably, in the cases of both Matthew 26:59–61 and 27:39–40, consider the arguments for a pre-70 and a post-70 date to be roughly balanced.

Mark 14:57–58 is more complicated. Not only is the report presented explicitly as false testimony, but the predicted reconstruction is of a temple "not made with hands." This might lead us to suspect that the passage has in view a metaphorical or eschatological building. Anticipations of a coming eschatological temple are documented prior to 70.[24] Once again, reference to passion and resurrection cannot be ruled out. Nonetheless, the denial that Jesus uttered such a prediction as well as the potential metaphorical or eschatological meaning implicit in the phrase "not made with hands" are both plausible responses

22. Cf. Matt. 12:40; 16:21; 17:23; 20:19; 27:63–64; Mark 8:31; 9:31; 10:34; Luke 9:22; 18:33; 24:7, 46.

23. Cf. the discussion in chap. 3.

24. Cf. the discussion in Marcus, *Mark 8–16*, 1015, about the eschatological temple anticipated by 4QFlor, a text that certainly predates 70.

to the events of 70. Thus, while this passage might well be intelligible if it was composed prior to 70, it seems equally intelligible if composed after 70.

Cumulatively, the prophecies of destruction and reconstruction found in Matthew 26:59–61, 27:39–40, and Mark 14:57–58 are equally intelligible before and after the destruction. They thus should be reckoned as nonprobative for purposes of establishing the compositional date of Matthew's Gospel.

The Desolating Sacrifice (Matt. 24:15–31; Mark 13:14–27)

Nothing thus far considered regarding the matter of 70 can be said to favor any specific chronology, whether lower, middle, or higher. Careful attention to the "texts of desolation" found in Matthew 24:25–31 and Mark 13:14–27, however, should incline us strongly toward a pre-70 date for the Matthean and Markan Gospels.

So when you see the desolating sacrilege standing in the holy place, as was spoken of by the prophet Daniel (let the reader understand), then those in Judea must flee to the mountains; the one on the housetop must not go down to take what is in the house; the one in the field must not turn back to get a coat. Woe to those who are pregnant and to those who are nursing infants in those days! Pray that your flight may not be in winter or on a sabbath. For at that time there will be great suffering, such as has not been from the beginning of the world until now, no, and never will be. And if those days had not been cut short, no one would be saved; but for the sake of the elect those days will be cut short. Then if anyone says to you, "Look! Here is the Messiah!" or "There he is!"—do not believe it. For false messiahs and false prophets will appear and produce great signs and omens, to lead astray, if possible, even the elect. Take note, I have told you beforehand. So, if they say to you, "Look! He is in the wilderness," do not go out. If they say, "Look! He is in the inner rooms," do not believe it. For as the lightning comes from the east and flashes as far as the west, so will be the coming of the Son of Man. Wherever the corpse is, there the vultures will gather. Immediately after the suffering of those days the sun will be darkened, and the moon will not give its light; the stars will fall from heaven, and the powers of heaven will be shaken. Then the sign of the Son of Man will appear in heaven, and then all the tribes of the earth will mourn, and they will see "the Son of Man coming on the clouds of heaven" with power and great glory. And he will send out his angels with a loud trumpet call, and they will gather his elect from the four winds, from one end of heaven to the other. (Matt. 24:15–31)

But when you see the desolating sacrilege set up where it ought not to be (let the reader understand), then those in Judea must flee to the mountains; the one on the housetop must not go down or enter the house to take anything away; the one in the field must not turn back to get a coat. Woe to those who are pregnant and to those who are nursing infants in those days! Pray that it may not be in winter. For in those days there will be suffering, such as has not been from the beginning of the creation that God created until now, no, and never will be. And if the Lord had not cut short those days, no one would be saved; but for the sake of the elect, whom he chose, he has cut short those days. And if anyone says to you at that time, "Look! Here is the Messiah!" or "Look! There he is!"—do not believe it. False messiahs and false prophets will appear and produce signs and omens, to lead astray, if possible, the elect. But be alert; I have already told you everything. But in those days, after that suffering, the sun will be darkened, and the moon will not give its light, and the stars will be falling from heaven, and the powers in the heavens will be shaken. Then they will see "the Son of Man coming in clouds" with great power and glory. Then he will send out the angels, and gather his elect from the four winds, from the ends of the earth to the ends of heaven. (Mark 13:14–27)

Robinson very much emphasizes the significance of these passages.[25] Indeed, they provide the strongest positive argument that he advances for dating the Gospels of Matthew and Mark prior to 70. In the absence of material that indubitably postdates the destruction of the temple, I am persuaded that these passages virtually exclude a post-70 date for either the Matthean or Markan Gospels. As such, much of what follows in this section rehearses Robinson's arguments, although I will register some disagreements as we proceed.

Both Matthew 24:15 and Mark 13:14 refer to a desolating sacrilege. Although neither specifies the temple as the place where that sacrilege will be set up, the Old Testament background renders it virtually certain that the temple is in view here. It is worth citing the relevant passages.

Now on the fifteenth day of Chislev, in the one hundred forty-fifth year, they erected a desolating sacrilege on the altar of burnt offering. They also built altars in the surrounding towns of Judah. (1 Macc. 1:54)

After the sixty-two weeks, an anointed one shall be cut off and shall have nothing, and the troops of the prince who is to come shall destroy the city and the

25. Cf. Robinson, *Redating*, 16–19, 22–25.

sanctuary. Its end shall come with a flood, and to the end there shall be war. Desolations are decreed. He shall make a strong covenant with many for one week, and for half of the week he shall make sacrifice and offering cease; and in their place shall be an abomination that desolates, until the decreed end is poured out upon the desolator. (Dan. 9:26–27)

Forces sent by him shall occupy and profane the temple and fortress. They shall abolish the regular burnt offering and set up the abomination that makes desolate. (Dan. 11:31)

From the time that the regular burnt offering is taken away and the abomination that desolates is set up, there shall be one thousand two hundred ninety days. (Dan. 12:11)

First Maccabees 1:54 and Daniel 9:26–27, 11:31, and 12:11 all speak of some sort of desolation associated with the Jerusalem temple. Given such scriptural precedent, it seems likely that Matthew's and Mark's Gospels likewise locate the "desolating sacrilege" within the Jerusalem temple.

Robinson makes much of the tradition that during the Jewish War the Jerusalem Christians fled not to the mountains—as advised in Matthew 24:16 and Mark 13:14—but rather to the city of Pella in the Decapolis.[26] Given this contradiction between the Pella tradition on the one hand and Mark 13:14 on the other, Robinson argues that the latter cannot be referring to the events of the Jewish War. Frankly, this assumes too much about the reliability of the Pella tradition.[27] An urgent question nonetheless presents itself to those who argue that these passages were written post-70, with the destruction of the temple in view: Why warn people of an event that has already happened?[28] Partially in response to this question, it is often argued that the warning—or at least its Markan variant—originated early in the war, *before* the temple was destroyed.[29] Once such an argument is affirmed in the case of the Markan parallel, it cannot be excluded in the case of the Matthean. If little specifically distinguishes the Markan and Matthean parallels, then

26. Robinson, *Redating*, 16–17. Cf. Eusebius, *Hist. eccl.* 3.5.3; also Epiphanius, *De mensuris et ponderibus* 15; Epiphanius, *Pan.* 29.7.7–9 and 30.2.7.

27. On the Pella tradition, cf. more recent scholars such as Balabanski, *Eschatology in the Making*, 101–34; Murphy-O'Connor, *Keys to Jerusalem*, 169–72.

28. A matter emphasized by Robinson, *Redating*, 25.

29. As famously argued by Hengel, *Gospel of Mark*, 16–28.

it is in principle at least as probable that both postdate 70 as it is that they predate 70.

Nonetheless, it is far from clear that either Matthew 24:15–31 or Mark 13:14–27 have the destruction of the temple in view. Although Daniel 9:26 does speak of a prince who comes to destroy the city and sanctuary, there is nothing in the language of desolation itself that necessarily implies destruction. Indeed, though this could be an argument from silence, that Daniel 9:26 refers to the destruction of the sanctuary makes it all the more notable that Matthew 24:15–31 and Mark 13:14–27 never speak of the same. The language was there in their source material, yet they chose not to use it. More concretely, it has been argued that the Matthean and Markan language of a desolating sacrilege could describe the installation of Caligula's statue in the temple in 40.[30] Crucially, this language of a desolating sacrilege and the surrounding narrative could have emerged at any time in the Palestinian church's experience between the 30s and 70.[31] Indeed, although hardly necessary for the present argument, it is difficult to see why this apocalyptic language could not have originated already during Jesus's ministry.[32]

Matthew 24:15–31 and Mark 13:14–27 present yet further and more pressing difficulties on a post-70 reading. Both Mark and Matthew associate the temple's fate with the parousia and the eschaton (Matt. 24:30–31; Mark 13:26–27). How plausible is it that this association emerged post-70 when we know that the temple's fate did not coincide with either the parousia or the eschaton? We must attend carefully to detail here, beginning with Matthew's Gospel. In Matthew 24:15–29, Jesus warns of the great danger that will ensue once the desolating sacrifice stands where it ought not. Then, in Matthew 24:29, we are told that a series of ominous prodigies will appear "immediately [*eutheōs*] after the suffering of those days." In Matthew 24:30, we are told that "then" (*tote*) the Son of Man will appear and send out his angels to gather in the elect (v. 31). Certainly, Matthew supposes that the prodigies will appear immediately following the suffering associated with the desolating sacrifice. It is possible that when we read "and then" (*kai tote*) in Matthew 24:30, the author means "and then [after some time]," but there is nothing in the text requiring this. Moreover, the prodigies of Matthew 24:29 seem intended as an immediate herald for the Son of Man's coming. Indeed, it is

---

30. Cf. the discussion in Crossley, *Date of Mark's Gospel*, 29–37.
31. Cf. the discussion in Crossley, *Date of Mark's Gospel*, 37–43.
32. As argued by Wright, *Jesus and the Victory*, 339–68.

difficult to see why one would think that the *kai tote* of verse 30 implies any significant time interval. Insofar as we can be confident that the Son of Man did not come on a cloud shortly after the destruction of the temple nor send his angels to gather the elect from the four winds, we can also be reasonably confident that neither did someone in the post-70 period suggest that he had by use of a retroactive prophecy.

In Mark 13:14–23, much as in the Matthean text, we hear of the suffering that will ensue following the advent of the desolating sacrilege. Then in Mark 13:24, we are told that a series of ominous prodigies will appear "in those days, after that suffering" (*en ekeinais tais hēmerais meta tēn thlipsin ekeinēn*). In Mark 13:27–28, again as in the Matthean text, we are told that "then" (*tote*) the Son of Man will appear and send out his angels to gather in the elect. Notably, where Matthew 24:29 states that the prodigies heralding the Son of Man will come immediately after the suffering, Mark 13:24 states that they will occur "in those days, after that suffering." "After that suffering" could more readily allow for some sort of temporal interval than does Matthew 24:30. Nonetheless, that these prodigies will appear "in those days" does not easily permit us to think the interval to be of particularly significant length. Thus we should think it probable that Mark envisions the events of Mark 13:24–27 occurring in close succession. This is less precise than the language of immediacy that we find in Matthew 24:29, but nonetheless that the Son of Man will appear "in those days" probably does not permit a significant temporal interval between the desolating sacrilege and the parousia. Moreover, insofar as we operate on the supposition of Markan priority, then anything that favors a pre-70 date for Matthew's Gospel also favors a pre-70 date for Mark's.

N. T. Wright has argued that the language of the Son of Man coming in clouds speaks metaphorically of Christ's vindication in the events of 70.[33] He sums up this argument by stating, "When Jerusalem is destroyed, and Jesus' people escape from the ruin just in time, *that will be* YHWH becoming king, bringing about the liberation of his true covenant people, the true return from exile, the beginning of the new world order."[34] Admittedly, we can grant that Wright's reading is possible, but at the same time it seems improbable. First, James Crossley has shown that there is no warrant to think that a first-century

---

33. Wright, *Jesus and the Victory*, 360–65.
34. Wright, *Jesus and the Victory*, 363 (emphasis original).

Jewish writer using such language would mean anything but what the text literally says.[35] Second, it is difficult to imagine how fleeing Jerusalem in the face of Roman destruction could be experienced as a particularly triumphant and liberative moment. It is especially hard to see how a flight from Jerusalem could be understood as a return from exile. Cumulatively, it seems better to let Matthew 24:15–31 and Mark 13:14–27 say what they say and to recognize that they were likely written before the events of 70.

While the above considerations do not exclude a post-70 provenance for either the Matthean or the Markan Gospel, they are sufficient to render both Gospels significantly more intelligible in a pre-70 context. Absent other considerations, we should be strongly inclined to situate both Matthew's and Mark's Gospels prior to 70.

This Generation Will Not Pass Away (Matt. 24:34; Mark 13:30; Luke 21:32)

In Matthew 24:34 // Mark 13:30 Jesus tells his hearers, "Truly I tell you, this generation will not pass away until all these things have taken place." "These things" refers to the apocalyptic discourse in Matthew 24:15–31 and Mark 13:14–27.[36] Luke 21:32 is nearly identical: "Truly I tell you, this generation will not pass away until all things have taken place." The implication is that the Synoptic Evangelists expected the eschaton to occur within the lifetime of Jesus's contemporaries.[37] Robinson argues that it is "incredible" that on a post-70 date no effort was made to explain why "this generation" had passed before the eschaton.[38] This rather overstates the matter. A baby born in 30 would be forty years old by 70, and an adult in 30 would be sixty or older. By 100, this baby would be seventy and the adults ninety or older. We also have reports of at least one of Jesus's followers living to the time of Trajan (r. 98–117).[39] Thus, while Matthew 24:34 // Mark 13:30 // Luke 21:32 perhaps incline us toward lower and middle dates for these Gospels, they cannot rule out a date after 100.

35. Crossley, *Date of Mark's Gospel*, 23–25.
36. Cf. the discussion above.
37. On alternate readings of "this generation" (*hē genea autē*), cf. Davies and Allison, *Matthew*, 3:366–68; Luz, *Matthew*, 3:208–9.
38. Cf. Robinson, *Redating*, 24–25.
39. Irenaeus, *Haer.* 2.22.5; 3.3.4. Irenaeus identifies this follower as "John." On the difficulties associated with identifying disciples named "John," cf. chap. 3.

Some Standing Here (Matt. 16:28; Mark 9:1; Luke 9:27)

Jesus tells his followers in Matthew 16:28, "Truly I tell you, there are some standing here who will not taste death before they see the Son of Man coming in his kingdom"; in Mark 9:1, "Truly I tell you, there are some standing here who will not taste death until they see that the kingdom of God has come with power"; and in Luke 9:27, "But truly I tell you, there are some standing here who will not taste death before they see the kingdom of God." Robinson wants to see these as a piece with Matthew 24:34 // Mark 13:30 // Luke 21:32, representing anticipations that Jesus would return within the lifetime of those who followed him during his earthly life.[40] Although I am sympathetic to such a reading, Matthew 16:28, Mark 9:1, and Luke 9:27 are not as clearly related to the eschaton and the parousia. While they support a lower or middle date most strongly, they cannot rule out a higher one.

The Temple Destroyed (Luke 19:41-44; 21:20-28)

Let us now turn to the Lukan counterpart to the Matthean and Markan texts of desolation: Luke 21:20–28, which should also be read alongside Luke 19:41–44.

> As he came near and saw the city, he wept over it, saying, "If you, even you, had only recognized on this day the things that make for peace! But now they are hidden from your eyes. Indeed, the days will come upon you, when your enemies will set up ramparts around you and surround you, and hem you in on every side. They will crush you to the ground, you and your children within you, and they will not leave within you one stone upon another; because you did not recognize the time of your visitation from God." (Luke 19:41–44)

> When you see Jerusalem surrounded by armies, then know that its desolation has come near. Then those in Judea must flee to the mountains, and those inside the city must leave it, and those out in the country must not enter it; for these are days of vengeance, as a fulfillment of all that is written. Woe to those who are pregnant and to those who are nursing infants in those days! For there will be great distress on the earth and wrath against this people; they will fall by the edge of the sword and be taken away as captives among all nations; and Jerusalem will be trampled on by the Gentiles, until the times of the Gentiles are fulfilled. There will be signs in the sun, the moon, and the stars, and on the

---

40. Discussed in Robinson, *Redating*, 24–25.

earth distress among nations confused by the roaring of the sea and the waves. People will faint from fear and foreboding of what is coming upon the world, for the powers of the heavens will be shaken. Then they will see "the Son of Man coming in a cloud" with power and great glory. Now when these things begin to take place, stand up and raise your heads, because your redemption is drawing near. (Luke 21:20–28)

Compared to its Matthean and Markan parallels, Luke 21:20–28 emphasizes the threat of war and violence against Jerusalem; Luke 19:41–44 demonstrates that this Lukan emphasis upon war and violence is not limited to 21:20–28. Certainly, the dominant interpretation among modern scholars is that both Luke 19:41–44 and 21:20–28 have in view the events of the first Jewish War (66–70), and perhaps even more precisely the siege and fall of Jerusalem.[41] Perhaps most relevant are Luke 21:20, which replaces the Matthean and Markan references to a desolating sacrilege with an explicit statement that Jerusalem will be surrounded by armies, and 21:24, where Luke introduces the prophecy that the gentiles will trample the holy city.

As has been a recurrent theme throughout our discussion, there is nothing in the Lukan text that could not have been imagined before 70. As argued by C. H. Dodd and emphasized by Robinson, the Lukan material appears to have been influenced more by scriptural traditions that detail the destruction of the first temple in 586 BCE than by the Maccabean-era texts that influenced the Matthean and Markan parallels and concern the desecration of the second temple.[42] Moreover, as Robinson notes, the warning in Luke 21:21 to either leave or not enter the city once it is surrounded by armies does not necessarily fit well within the context of the siege of Jerusalem.[43] This is not sufficient to establish a pre-70 origin for this passage, but it should give us pause before we confidently assume a post-70 one.

Yet Luke 21:24b allows for the possibility that Luke has moved the events of the eschaton and parousia from the fall of the temple to a future fulfillment of the "times of the Gentiles." Thus, while the eschatological content of the Matthean and Markan parallels militates against reading these as post-70

41. Cf. Fitzmyer, *Luke*, 2:1323; Johnson, *Luke*, 326; Bovon, *Luke*, 3:115. Nolland argues that Luke 19:41–44 and 21:20–28 need not be post-70 compositions but rather could have originated pre-70 in response to Jewish polemic regarding Christian commitment to the temple establishment (*Luke*, 1:xxxviii–xxxix; 3:999–1004).

42. Cf. Dodd, "Fall of Jerusalem," quoted by Robinson, *Redating*, 27.

43. Robinson, *Redating*, 28–29.

compositions, the Lukan parallel can much more plausibly be read as an attempt to come to terms with the fact that the temple was destroyed without the parousia coming to pass. Therefore, we must acknowledge that given the evidence considered thus far, Luke's Gospel is more intelligibly a post-70 work than are either Matthew's or Mark's. Indeed, given what we have considered thus far, the evidence for a pre-70 Gospel of Luke seems equally balanced with the evidence for a post-70 one. Our discussion of synchronization will thus focus upon those arguments that might lead us to favor either a pre- or post-70 provenance for Luke's Gospel as well as for Acts.

Specific Lukan Concerns

In discussing the matter of 70, we judged that while it is probable that both Matthew's and Mark's Gospels predate 70, it is merely possible that Luke's does. In this section we turn to questions of synchronization specific to Luke-Acts.[44]

The Unity of Luke-Acts

That Luke's Gospel and the Acts of the Apostles should be read as a two-volume work has become a scholarly commonplace, although not one without challenges.[45] For our purposes, such challenges are largely beside the point. If we were to reject the literary unity of the two texts or even common authorship, Luke 1:1–4 and Acts 1:1–2 render it virtually certain that the author of Acts has Luke's Gospel in mind. These texts read as follows:

> Since many have undertaken to set down an orderly account of the events that have been fulfilled among us, just as they were handed on to us by those who from the beginning were eyewitnesses and servants of the word, I too decided, after investigating everything carefully from the very first, to write an orderly account for you, most excellent Theophilus, so that you may know the truth concerning the things about which you have been instructed. (Luke 1:1–4)

> In the first book, Theophilus, I wrote about all that Jesus did and taught from the beginning until the day when he was taken up to heaven, after giving instructions through the Holy Spirit to the apostles whom he had chosen. (Acts 1:1–2)

---

44. I would like to thank Karl Armstrong for early access to his *Dating Acts*. Although I was unable to engage with it as much as I would like, I cannot strongly enough recommend this volume to those interested specifically in the date of Acts.

45. Cf. the discussion in Rowe, "Unity of Luke-Acts."

Given the references in each to Theophilus and the explicit reference in Acts to "the first book," which tells the story of Jesus's life, it is likely that Luke's Gospel and Acts were intended to form a two-volume work—or perhaps the latter is an intentional sequel to the former (whether by the same author or another). In either case, Luke's Gospel was almost certainly composed before Acts.

Building upon our previous discussion regarding the Synoptic problem, we should prefer chronologies that date Luke's Gospel prior to Acts; Matthew's and Mark's Gospels before Luke's; and Mark's prior to Matthew's. As it is however possible that Matthew used Luke's Gospel, we must also be mindful of the possibility that Matthew's Gospel dates later than even Acts.

Did Luke Know Josephus?

It has been argued that Luke-Acts evinces knowledge of Josephus's works, and more specifically, his *Antiquities*, written ca. 93. Robinson deals with Lukan knowledge of Josephus in one sentence, dismissing it with the suggestion that it had been largely abandoned by then-contemporary scholarship.[46] Such dismissal is not sufficient for our purposes, in no small part because more recent scholarship has sought to resuscitate the argument that Luke knew Josephus.[47] Nonetheless, this section argues that a negative judgment on the matter of Lukan use of Josephus remains most fully warranted by the relevant data.

Insofar as the subject matter covered by Josephus partially overlaps with that covered by Luke, we should hardly be surprised to see some coincidences between their respective texts. The question is whether these coincidences suffice to affirm Lukan knowledge of Josephus. Only two areas of possible contact between Luke-Acts and Josephus merit an extended discussion: (1) the treatment of Quirinius and the census and (2) the accounts of Judas the Galilean, Theudas, and "the Egyptian."[48] Both Luke and Josephus report that Quirinius

46. Robinson, *Redating*, 88. Cf. the similar judgment in Hemer, *Book of Acts*, 95n104, who argues that while Lukan use of Josephus was a popular position in the Victorian era, it was "forcibly rebutted" at the turn of the twentieth century by Plummer, *St. Luke*, xxix–xxx. Cf. the significantly more substantive but ultimately still negative discussion of Lukan knowledge of Josephus in Armstrong, *Dating Acts*, 84–94.

47. Cf. most notably, Mason, *Josephus and the New Testament*, 251–95.

48. On the census, cf. Luke 2:2; Josephus, *Ant.* 17.13.5 §354; 18.1.1 §§1–2; 18.2.1 §26. On Judas the Galilean, cf. Acts 5:37; Josephus, *Ant.* 18.1.6 §23; 20.5.1 §§97–99; Josephus, *J.W.* 2.4.1 §56; 2.8.1 §118; 2.17.8 §433; 7.8.1 §253. On Theudas, cf. Acts 5:36; Josephus, *Ant.* 18.1.1 §§4–10. Cf. also the discussion in Mason, *Josephus and the New Testament*, 277–82.

undertook a census. Luke situates it during the reign of Herod the Great (d. 4 BCE), but Josephus places it following the deposition of Herod Archelaus in 6 CE. We need not determine which of these reports might be accurate and which might be inaccurate. For our purposes it is sufficient to note that to the extent that Luke's account is fundamentally irreconcilable with Josephus's, we have reason to doubt that either one stands as a source for the other.

This doubt only increases the closer we look at the data. Josephus and Acts mention only three—and precisely the same three—rebel leaders who operated in the decades before the Jewish War: Judas the Galilean, Theudas, and the anonymous figure known only as "the Egyptian." The question before us is whether this convergence is best accounted for by Luke's use of Josephus's writings. The logical alternatives to Lukan dependence upon Josephus are that Josephus used Luke-Acts, or that Josephus and Luke-Acts each had independent reason to single out these three figures. The data alone can aid us in determining which among these alternatives is most likely. Much as with the case of the Quirinus data, the most obvious barrier to affirming either that Luke is dependent upon Josephus or Josephus upon Luke comes from the famous contradiction between the two authors. In Acts 5:36–37, Luke's Gamaliel I places Theudas's revolt before that of Judas the Galilean, but Josephus reports that Judas's revolt predated Theudas's by about forty years. It has been argued that this contradiction actually demonstrates that Luke knew Josephus, because at one point Josephus discusses Theudas shortly before discussing Judas's sons.[49] The argument is that Luke was confused: he read about Theudas, saw a reference to Judas, and concluded that Theudas must have preceded Judas. Although this is possible, it does not seem probable. Turning to a place where Luke clearly diverges from Josephus in order to demonstrate that Luke knew Josephus only demonstrates how weak the hypothesis is.[50] For the same reason, we should be wary of affirming Josephus's dependence upon Luke-Acts. Indeed, the divergence gives us reason to suspect that Luke and Josephus are independently reporting upon the same course of events, possibly using some sources in common.

Such suspicion of independence only increases when one asks a crucial empirical question: Why the Egyptian? For the sake of argument, if we

49. Pervo, *Dating Acts*, 152–60. Note that in 2001, Pervo confessed to and was convicted of possessing significant amounts of child pornography. I beg the reader's forgiveness in citing the work of someone convicted for exploiting children. Yet I felt that this argument for Luke's knowledge of Josephus is too significant to pass over in silence, and I could not see how to engage it without citing Pervo.

50. Cf. the engagement with Pervo's argument in Armstrong, *Dating Acts*, 86–93.

suppose Josephus's independence or priority, why did he single out the Egyptian? Why, if there were innumerable rebel figures, did Josephus choose a figure whose name he did not know? The most intelligible answer is that the Egyptian's operations were remembered as in some way significant. These operations loomed large in the memories of those who lived through the period, even though his name did not. Josephus singled out this figure because his sources, oral or written, did so before him; he may have selected Judas and Theudas for much the same reason. This raises the possibility that Luke, too, emphasizes these three figures on the basis of his own sources. Indeed, given their precise combination of similarities and differences, it is likely that both Luke and Josephus drew upon different sources from the decades leading up to the Jewish War that nonetheless emphasized Judas, Theudas, and the Egyptian. Certainly, the crucial differences between Luke and Josephus in the treatment of these figures should make us wary of positing that either is directly dependent upon the other. Such wariness is likewise well warranted regarding the relationship between Luke-Acts and Josephus more generally.

Cumulatively, while we cannot exclude Lukan knowledge of Josephus, neither is such knowledge more than a possibility. The relationship between Luke-Acts and Josephus's writings should be considered nonprobative for establishing the compositional date of the former.

Marcion's Gospel

According to late second- and early third-century fathers, Marcion (who was active in Rome in probably the 140s) produced a version of Luke's Gospel shorn of material that he found to be doctrinally unacceptable.[51] For the most part, modern critical scholarship has been content to affirm these patristic reports. Even Adolf von Harnack—for whom Marcion stood as a sort of spiritual hero—was willing to grant that Marcion's Gospel was a redacted Luke.[52] Nonetheless, dissenters have argued that Marcion's Gospel was in fact a proto-Luke and that our canonical Luke-Acts was in part an orthodox response to Marcionism.[53] Robinson does not address this issue in *Redating*

---

51. Cf. esp. Irenaeus's report that Marcion "mutilates" Luke's Gospel (*Haer.* 1.27.2).

52. Harnack, *Marcion*, 25–29.

53. This theory is most strongly linked with Knox, *Marcion and the New Testament*. It has recently been revived by esp. Klinghardt, "Marcionite Gospel"; Tyson, *Marcion and Luke-Acts*. Cf. the history of scholarship in Roth, "Marcion's Gospel and Luke." For efforts to determine

the New Testament, but as with Luke's use of Josephus, there is enough recent support for this hypothesis that it needs to be addressed.[54]

I have found Judith Lieu's assessment of the matter to be most compelling.[55] Lieu argues that Marcion used a text very close to our Lukan Gospel as the basis for his Gospel, albeit one that perhaps lacked certain passages. Lieu also argues that Marcion did not simply utilize this version of the Lukan text but rather modified it to suit his theological interests. Lieu further suggests that as such our canonical Luke's Gospel must postdate Marcion. I am not convinced that this need be the case. Given the diversity of second-century texts, it seems altogether possible that Marcion's core text lacked passages found in coeval variants of the Lukan text. Indeed, one might be very surprised to discover that Marcion had a copy of Luke's Gospel identical to what we find in NA[28]. Regardless, apart from this qualification, Lieu's position seems the best balance between the reality of textual diversity in the second century and Marcion's apparent interest in producing a Gospel shorn of material he deemed to be inappropriate.

Luke's (Non)Use of Paul's Letters

Given that Acts narrates at least some of Paul's career, the question of its relationship to the Pauline corpus is sometimes raised.[56] In recent scholarship Richard Pervo in particular has urged that Acts demonstrates knowledge of Paul's Letters and thus must date later than 100. One specific quote epitomizes the difficulties with Pervo's argument: "Luke made use of canonical 2 Corinthians, which is not attested before ca. 120–130 (Marcion, possibly Polycarp) and was not available before 100."[57] For our purposes, two relevant claims are made here. First, that Luke used 2 Corinthians; second, that Luke would not have had access to 2 Corinthians before 100. Regarding the first claim, Pervo's evidence for Luke's knowledge of 2 Corinthians consists of the parallels he identifies between Acts 9:23–25 and 2 Corinthians 11:32–33.[58]

---

the contents of Marcion's Gospel, cf. Harnack, *Marcion*, 25–53; Lieu, *Marcion*, 209–33; Moll, *Arch-Heretic Marcion*, 89–102.

54. Cf. the engagement with the recently renewed arguments that Acts was in part a response to Marcion, in Armstrong, *Dating Acts*, 18–19.

55. Lieu, *Marcion*, 209.

56. Cf. the recent engagement with this matter in Armstrong, *Dating Acts*, 75–84.

57. Pervo, *Dating Acts*, 62.

58. Pervo, *Dating Acts*, 60–64.

After some time had passed, the Jews plotted to kill him [in Damascus], but their plot became known to Saul. They were watching the gates day and night so that they might kill him; but his disciples took him by night and let him down through an opening in the wall, lowering him in a basket. (Acts 9:23–25)

In Damascus, the governor under King Aretas guarded the city of Damascus in order to seize me, but I was let down in a basket through a window in the wall, and escaped from his hands. (2 Cor. 11:32–33)

It is certainly possible that in composing Acts 9:23–25, Luke had access to 2 Corinthians 11:32–33. Both narrate what is likely the same event—namely, Paul's flight from Damascus under some sort of threat. Nonetheless, there is little verbal agreement between the two texts. Indeed, the only verbal similarity that Pervo can identify is that both refer to Paul being let down in a basket. The reported details differ significantly between the two accounts. In Acts, Paul fears being killed by "the Jews"; in 2 Corinthians, he fears being arrested by the ethnarch of King Aretas. Pervo must resort to arguing that "Luke has taken up and transformed an item from Paul's correspondence," thus speaking about an "inversion of fact represented in the appropriation of 2 Corinthians to Acts 9."[59] Given that there is little verbal agreement between the two passages and significant differences between them, it seems at least as probable, if not more so, that Luke simply is not making use of 2 Corinthians.

For the sake of argument, however, let us suppose that Acts 9:23–25 does demonstrate knowledge of 2 Corinthians 11:32–33. What should we make of Pervo's claim that Luke would not have had access to 2 Corinthians before 100? Pervo's primary argument for this claim is that while 1 Clement makes use of Romans and 1 Corinthians, it does not make use of 2 Corinthians.[60] He more fully argues that 2 Corinthians "would have been manna from heaven for the composer(s) of *1 Clement*, because it presents the founding apostle, Paul, vigorously chastising the Corinthian believers for rebelling against lawful ("apostolic") authority—and that is the very subject of *1 Clement* itself."[61] As always, we must be wary of any argument from silence. The composer(s) of 1 Clement might not have had access to 2 Corinthians, true; it is also possible that, for whatever reason, they decided not

59. Pervo, *Dating Acts*, 61.
60. Pervo, *Dating Acts*, 62.
61. Pervo, *Dating Acts*, 62.

to make use of it. Further, if we do grant that the composer(s) of 1 Clement did not have access to 2 Corinthians, it does not follow that no one did. It is entirely possible that 2 Corinthians was unknown in Rome when 1 Clement was written from that locale, yet was already available elsewhere.[62] Indeed, virtually all scholars agree that 2 Corinthians was written in the 50s.[63] Thus, unless we imagine that 2 Corinthians disappeared as soon as it left Paul's hands only to be rediscovered ca. 100, we should imagine that it had at least some circulation from the late 50s through to the end of the century.

Pervo further argues that Acts must postdate not only the composition of certain Pauline Epistles but also the first collection of Paul's Letters.[64] This does not follow, as the letters could have circulated independently as soon as they were first sent to their destination churches. Moreover, the existence of such a collection is conceivable as early as the 60s.[65] David Trobisch has argued that Paul himself approved a collection that included Romans, 1 and 2 Corinthians, and Galatians.[66] F. B. A. Asiedu has recently tried to prove that the work of collecting Paul's Letters began while—according to Romans 16:23—he was staying in Gaius's house.[67] What matters for our purposes is not whether Trobisch is correct in identifying an early collection of the letters approved by Paul himself, or whether Asiedu is correct in identifying Gaius's house as the place where the writings began to be collected. Rather, what is important is that such scenarios are at least as plausible as any that would date the first collection of Paul's writings later in the century.

We will see below that Acts (and by implication Luke's Gospel) cannot postdate 62. Given the above discussion and our purposes, the question becomes not whether it is likely that Luke knew any Pauline Letters but whether he knew any Pauline Letters that postdate 62. Only then would Luke's possible knowledge of the Pauline corpus have any relevance for purposes of establishing the date of Luke-Acts. Of the eight Pauline Letters that Pervo thinks Luke to have most likely known, six (Romans, 1 and 2 Corinthians, Galatians, Philippians, and 1 Thessalonians) are among the undisputed letters—that is, those that virtually all New Testament scholars agree were written at least in part by Paul. Moreover, virtually no scholars would date these letters later

62. On the date of 1 Clement, cf. chap. 9.
63. On the date of 2 Corinthians, cf. chap. 6.
64. Pervo, *Dating Acts*, 138.
65. Cf. the discussion in Armstrong, *Dating Acts*, 77.
66. Trobisch, *Paul's Letter Collection*, 54–97.
67. Asiedu, *Paul and His Letters*, 306–22.

than 62.[68] These texts have little bearing, then, on the date of Luke-Acts, regardless of whether they were known to Luke. Yet Pervo also argues that Luke likely used Ephesians and Colossians. If Luke did use Ephesians and Colossians, if these are pseudo-Pauline letters, and if they date after 62, then Luke-Acts must date likewise.[69] Yet as we saw with Acts 9:23–25 and 2 Corinthians 11:32–33 above, Pervo is unable to produce the level of verbal agreement that we would normally expect when trying to establish that one text demonstrates knowledge of another.

Luke's use of Paul's writings must remain no more than a possibility. It is not a certainty nor even a probability. Moreover, most of the Pauline texts that Luke is supposed to have used predate our latest dates for Luke-Acts. Given the uncertainty regarding Luke's use of Pauline texts that would lead us to significantly alter our preferred dates for Luke-Acts, such possible use has little to no bearing upon our chronological judgments in this book. Yet neither can it be shown with reasonable confidence that Luke did not know or use one or more letters from the Pauline corpus. If that could be shown, however, such nonuse would not entail a lower, middle, or higher date for Acts. So many factors go into an author's decision regarding which materials to use, how to present the characters, and so on, that I would be wary to draw any chronological conclusions from Acts's relationship to the Pauline corpus. Ultimately, the relationship of the Pauline corpus to Acts is best considered nonprobative for establishing the compositional date of Acts.

The Enigmatic Ending

Famously, Harnack twice revised his estimate for the date of Acts, each time downward.[70] Starting from a date ca. 93, he eventually concluded that the book must predate 70. Notably, Harnack identified the ending as a primary matter driving his revisions. That ending reads as follows: "[Paul] lived [in Rome] two whole years at his own expense and welcomed all who came to him, proclaiming the kingdom of God and teaching about the Lord Jesus Christ with all boldness and without hindrance" (Acts 28:30–31). Robinson

---

68. Cf. the discussion in chap. 6.

69. All the parallels that Pervo identifies between Luke-Acts and Ephesians are in fact between Acts and Ephesians, and all his parallels between Luke-Acts and Colossians are in fact between Acts and Colossians.

70. Cf. his final discussion of the matter in Harnack, *Date of the Acts*, 90–135. Cf. also his earlier discussions: Harnack, *Acts of the Apostles*, 290–97; Harnack, *Chronologie*, 246–50.

was greatly impressed by Harnack's thought on the matter, so much so that he begins his discussion of the ending with an extended quote from Harnack's *The Date of the Acts and the Synoptic Gospels*.[71] Here I find it valuable to follow suit and even quote more fully from Harnack than did Robinson himself.

> Only quite a short time could have elapsed since the expiration of the διετίαν ὅλην [two whole years]. If a longer time had elapsed the chronicler would have been obliged to relate either the place to which the Apostle [Paul] had now turned his steps or the nature of the greater restrictions to which he was now subjected. . . . Throughout eight whole chapters St. Luke keeps his readers intensely interested in the progress of the trial of St. Paul, simply that in the end he might disappoint them—they learn nothing of the final result of the trial! Such a procedure is scarcely less indefensible than that of one who might relate the history of our Lord and close the narrative with His delivery to Pilate, because Jesus had now been brought up to Jerusalem and had made His appearance before the chief magistrate in the capital city. One may object that the end of the Apostle was universally known, or one may also say that when the author had brought St. Paul to Rome he had attained the goal that he sets before himself in his book. For many years I was content to soothe my intellectual conscience with such expedients; but in truth they altogether transgress against inward probability and all the psychological laws of historical composition. The more clearly we see that the trial of St. Paul, and above all his appeal to Caesar, is the chief subject of the last quarter of Acts, the more hopeless does it appear that we can explain why the narrative breaks off as it does, otherwise than by assuming that the trial had actually not yet reached its close. It is no use to struggle against this conclusion. If St. Luke, in the year 80, 90, or 100, wrote thus he was not simply a blundering but an absolutely incomprehensible historian![72]

An initial observation needs to be made: Harnack's argument is not from silence. Rather, it is an argument from presence, indeed, the presence of an extended (eight chapters!) discussion of Paul's legal challenges and an ending that leaves said challenges unresolved. And Harnack makes a strong case. It is frankly difficult to either disagree with or improve upon his argument. Either Acts was completed ca. 62, when the Acts narrative ends with Paul in Rome, or Luke's aims in these last chapters remain opaque.

71. Robinson, *Redating*, 89–90. The quotation is from Harnack, *Date of the Acts*, 95–96. Cf. the fuller discussion of the ending of Acts in Robinson, *Redating*, 89–92; also the more recent treatment in Armstrong, *Dating Acts*, 97–123.

72. Harnack, *Date of the Acts*, 95–97.

Nevertheless, a range of theories aim to explain why Acts might have been written significantly later than ca. 62 and yet also end how it does. Karl Armstrong has helpfully organized these under four headings: fabrication, foreshadowing and silence, theological and political explanations, and linkage.[73] Of these, linkage is entirely taken up with the work of one scholar: Troy Troftgruben.[74] It seems best for our purposes here to include this in the discussion of theological and political explanations. In addition to these there is also what one might call the argument from missing material—that is, hypotheses according to which either Luke was unable to bring his work to completion or, alternatively, that parts of his work were lost. As such, in what follows, we will address arguments from missing material, arguments from fabrication, arguments from foreshadowing and silence, and arguments from theological and political explanations.

Beginning with arguments from missing material, one might argue that Luke intended to write a third volume, in which he would narrate Paul's death, but failed to do so; that Luke did write such a volume, but it has been lost; that Luke intended to write more but ran out of writing materials; or that Luke was interrupted before he could finish Acts. Harnack considered such arguments to be sufficiently weak that he relegated them merely to a footnote.[75] Armstrong does not consider these strong enough to merit their own category of explanation.[76] Such arguments are ad hoc, in the worst possible sense. For our purposes they can be dismissed as little more than speculation.

Armstrong's "fabrication" category includes "explanation[s] that Luke was aware of Paul's death but intentionally left that out and therefore fabricated (or falsified) his ending. . . . Essentially, scholars here explain Luke's silence on Paul's death because it would otherwise (1) be considered unedifying; (2) imply Paul's guilt; (3) implicate Christians who abandoned Paul; (4) blame the Roman Empire for Paul's death; (5) parallel the death of Jesus too closely."[77] Armstrong rightly notes that such explanations are argued against the more parsimonious one—namely, that Paul was yet alive when Luke was writing.[78] To this we might add that such explanations do not adequately explain the last quarter of Acts. On such explanations, Luke wants to elide the very thing to which the last quarter

73. Armstrong, *Dating Acts*, 110–23.
74. Troftgruben, *Conclusion Unhindered*.
75. Harnack, *Date of the Acts*, 96n2.
76. Cf. his discussion of such arguments in Armstrong, *Dating Acts*, 109–10.
77. Armstrong, *Dating Acts*, 111.
78. Armstrong, *Dating Acts*, 111.

of Acts draws attention. Surely Luke could have anticipated that at least some readers would know about Paul's fate and of the negative experiences of Christians during the last few years of Nero's reign.[79] Yet arguments from fabrication would have us believe that despite focusing upon the series of legal troubles that result in Paul being under house arrest in Rome, Luke does not want the reader to be concerned with Paul's ultimate fate in that city nor with conflicts between Christians and the Roman authorities. Arguments from fabrication render Luke's intentions in the last quarter of Acts almost entirely opaque.

Explanation from foreshadowing and silence proceeds "from the 'fabrication' view discussed above but emphasizes how Acts somehow provides 'hints' in the text that Paul had long been processed by Caesar (Nero) and that everyone was aware of the outcome."[80] Here the most relevant data are in Acts 20:22–25, 36–38a; and 21:13.

> "And now, as a captive to the Spirit, I am on my way to Jerusalem, not knowing what will happen to me there, except that the Holy Spirit testifies to me in every city that imprisonment and persecutions are waiting for me. But I do not count my life of any value to myself, if only I may finish my course and the ministry that I received from the Lord Jesus, to testify to the good news of God's grace. And now I know that none of you, among whom I have gone about proclaiming the kingdom, will ever see my face again." . . . When he had finished speaking, he knelt down with them all and prayed. There was much weeping among them all; they embraced Paul and kissed him, grieving especially because of what he had said, that they would not see him again. (Acts 20:22–25, 36–38a)

> Then Paul answered, "What are you doing, weeping and breaking my heart? For I am ready not only to be bound but even to die in Jerusalem for the name of the Lord Jesus." (Acts 21:13)

Admittedly, it is possible that the Lukan Paul intimates his death in Acts 20:22–25, 36–38a. Notably, however, Paul does not here state that he expects to die; moreover, he states explicitly that he does not know what fate awaits him.[81] Explicit denial of knowing his own fate does not sit easily with the hypothesis that he is predicting said fate. Further, Paul's statement that he expected never to be seen again by the Miletan and Ephesian Christians need

---

79. Cf. the discussion of the Neronian persecution in the introduction above.
80. Armstrong, *Dating Acts*, 113.
81. Cf. Acts 20:22.

not indicate that he expected to die. Rather, it is entirely consistent with his known intention at that time to travel from Jerusalem to Rome and then on to Spain.[82] If Paul had not expected to again minister in the eastern Mediterranean, it would have been entirely reasonable for him to anticipate that he would never again see the Christians of Ephesus and Miletus. Likewise, it would be difficult to argue that Acts 21:13 anticipates Paul's death in Rome when it speaks of the possibility that he might die in Jerusalem. But even if we grant that Acts 20–21 might well betray Luke's knowledge of Paul's death, we still want to ask why the author was prepared to obliquely imply but not explicitly narrate Paul's fate, especially after spending so much time focusing upon the travails that brought him to Rome. Foreshadowing something that never happens in the text is poor foreshadowing indeed.

Theological and political explanations argue that the ending of Acts "provides a sufficient literary or spiritual/theological explanation."[83] We should perhaps expand this category then to read "theological, political, or literary" explanations. One of the stronger variants of theological or political explanations is that with Paul's arrival in Rome, Luke has completed his aim of showing that the gospel was preached "to the ends of the earth."[84] Not only does this fail to account for Luke's emphasis upon Paul's legal troubles, but one might also ask why—if the climax of Acts is Paul bringing Christianity to Rome—Luke shows us that some believers were already in Rome before his arrival.[85] Also to be considered is Troftgruben's work, noted above, which Armstrong puts in its own category but which I place within his theological or political explanation.[86] Troftgruben argues that the ending to Acts is wholly intelligible on narrative grounds.[87] Armstrong contends that in building his argument, Troftgruben relies too heavily upon false analogies, such as between Acts and Homer's *Iliad*. More pressing for me, however, is that theological, political, and literary explanations do not in general define Luke's aim adequately. Surely any definition of Luke's aims at the end of Acts must account for why Luke devotes so much attention to Paul's legal troubles. Why devote so much time to something that one does not think needs to be resolved within one's narrative, whether for theological or political or literary reasons?

82. Cf. Rom. 15:28.
83. Armstrong, *Dating Acts*, 117.
84. Acts 1:8.
85. Cf. Acts 28:14–15.
86. Cf. Armstrong, *Dating Acts*, 118–23.
87. Troftgruben, *Conclusion Unhindered*.

All the above enumerated difficulties disappear entirely if Acts was completed ca. 62. Suddenly the failure to mention Paul's fate is wholly intelligible: Luke did not write of Paul's fate because Paul had yet to meet it. He devotes, I suggest, considerable attention to the events of 57 through 62 simply because he was frequently with Paul throughout that period.[88] A date ca. 62 is otherwise viable; on the basis of such significantly greater intelligibility, we should be inclined to suppose that Acts dates to around that time, thus also Luke's Gospel, and in turn Matthew's and Mark's most probably earlier. That is the position argued in this study.

Conclusion to Synchronization

Insofar as it is the case that

- external attestation should leave us wary of dating Matthew's Gospel or Mark's much later than 120, Luke's later than 150, and Acts later than 170;
- the best solutions to the Synoptic problem favor hypotheses in which Luke's Gospel postdates Matthew's, and Matthew's postdates Mark's;
- the tearing of the temple curtain (Matt. 27:51; Mark 15:38; Luke 23:45) is as equally intelligible before 70 as after 70;
- the Matthean addition to the parable of the wedding banquet in 22:7 is as equally intelligible before 70 as after;
- Jesus's prophecy that not one stone of the temple would remain in place (Matt. 24:1–2; Mark 13:1–2; Luke 21:5–6) is as equally intelligible before 70 as after;
- the (possibly false) report that Jesus predicted he would raise the temple in three days (Matt. 26:59–61; 27:39–40; Mark 14:57–58) is as equally intelligible before 70 as after;
- the Matthean and Markan "texts of desolation" (Matt. 24:15–31; Mark 13:14–27) are more fully intelligible before 70 than they are after;
- the Synoptic supposition that some of Jesus's contemporaries would live to see the eschaton (Matt. 24:34; Mark 13:30; Luke 21:32) favors lower or middle dates over higher ones;

88. As indicated by the Lukan we-passages. Cf. the discussion in chap. 2.

- the Synoptic supposition that some of Jesus's contemporaries would live to see the Son of Man come in his kingdom (Matt. 16:28) or the kingdom of God come (Mark 9:1; Luke 9:27) favors lower or middle dates over higher ones;
- Jesus's prediction of Jerusalem's destruction in Luke's Gospel (19:41–44; 21:20–28) is equally intelligible before 70 as after;
- the relationship of Luke's Gospel to Acts favors hypotheses in which the latter postdates the former;
- Luke and Josephus are mutually independent, and thus the date of one has no bearing upon the date of the other;
- Marcion most likely had access to a core text recognizable as Luke's Gospel, which he then proceeded to modify;
- the relationship between the Pauline corpus and Acts is sufficiently opaque as to have no bearing on the compositional date of Acts; and
- the ending of Acts favors hypotheses in which Acts was written ca. 62,

we conclude that Acts was written ca. 62 and the Synoptic Gospels prior to that date, with Matthew's Gospel likely written prior to Luke's, and Mark's Gospel prior to Matthew's.

2

Contextualization and Authorial Biography

Through the work of synchronization, chapter 1 concluded that Acts was written ca. 62 and the Synoptic Gospels prior to that date, with Matthew's Gospel likely written before Luke's, and Mark's Gospel prior to Matthew's. The aim of this chapter is to establish the most probable dates for the Synoptic tradition more precisely, via the work of contextualization and authorial biography.[1] This chapter argues that Mark's Gospel was written no earlier than 42 and no later than 45; Matthew's, no earlier than 45 and no later than 59; Luke's, ca. 59; and the Act of the Apostles, ca. 62.

Contextualization

In this section, we consider (1) the linguistic background of especially Mark's Gospel and (2) the closely related matters of mission and law. Building upon the work of synchronization, this work of contextualization will lead us to

---

1. In developing this chapter, I found the following particularly useful: Bauckham, *Jesus and the Eyewitnesses*; Bovon, *Luke*; Conzelmann, *Acts*; Crossley, *Date of Mark's Gospel*; Davies and Allison, *Matthew*; Donahue and Harrington, *Mark*; Evans, *Mark 8:27–16:20*; Fitzmyer, *Acts*; Fitzmyer, *Luke*; Guelich, *Mark 1–8:26*; Gundry, *Mark*; Gundry, *Matthew*; Hagner, *Matthew*; D. Harrington, *Matthew*; Hemer, *Book of Acts*; Hengel, *Four Gospels*; Hengel, *Gospel of Mark*; Hooker, *Mark*; Johnson, *Luke*; Keener, *Acts*; Luz, *Matthew*; Marcus, *Mark 1–8*; Marcus, *Mark 8–16*; Nolland, *Luke*; Wenham, *Redating Matthew, Mark and Luke*; Yarbro Collins, *Mark*.

the conclusion that Mark's Gospel likely predates 45; Matthew's Gospel and Luke's likely postdate 45 but predate 62; and that Acts dates ca. 62.

The Linguistic Background

Maurice Casey argues that careful linguistic study of Mark's Gospel supports a date ca. 40 for its composition.[2] Casey's contention that Mark's Gospel contains literal translations of Aramaic sources has been reasonably well received, although not without quibbles regarding details.[3] However, the presence of such literal translations can hardly suffice to establish that Mark's Gospel likely was written ca. 40, and this for at least two reasons: (1) Aramaic sources could have been produced later than 40, and (2) even if they were produced that early, Mark's Gospel could have incorporated translations of such sources decades later. Although the presence of such Aramaic material is certainly consistent with a lower date for Mark's Gospel, it should probably be considered nonprobative for establishing when the book was composed.

Mission and Law

James Crossley argues that the later one dates Mark's Gospel after 40, the more one should anticipate that the text will give a fuller account of the gentile mission.[4] On its own, such an argumentation would rise to little more than an argument from silence. The question, however, is not simply why Mark's Gospel takes so little notice of the gentile mission but rather why Matthew's and Luke's Gospels give the gentile mission so much more attention.[5] Once we have dispensed with the need to date any of the Synoptic Gospels later than 70 (and established that Mark's and Matthew's likely predate Luke), it becomes attractive in terms of both explanatory scope and parsimony to suggest that Matthew's and Luke's Gospels address the gentile mission more fully because they date from a time after that mission had become a significant factor in early Christianity. Mark's Gospel does not address the gentile mission because it dates from a time before that mission

---

2. Cf. esp. Casey, *Aramaic Sources*.
3. Cf., for instance, the discussions in Charlesworth, "Recover Aramaic Sources?"; Chilton, "Casey's *Aramaic Sources*."
4. Crossley, *Date of Mark's Gospel*.
5. A question emphasized by Crossley, *Date of Mark's Gospel*.

became significant. Such attractiveness only increases when we notice how Mark takes for granted that Jesus was Torah observant, whereas Matthew and Luke give a more explicit account.[6] The relative emphasis placed upon the question of Torah observance by Matthew's and Luke's Gospels is quite readily explained if Mark's Gospel was written before the full flourishing of the gentile mission provoked sustained reflection upon the extent to which non-Jewish converts must adhere to the Mosaic law. Such reflection seems to have emerged most fully in the mid to late 40s, reaching a climactic turning point with the Jerusalem Council (ca. 48). Insofar as the Matthean and Lukan Gospels demonstrate a greater awareness of such reflection than does the Markan Gospel, we can proceed on the hypothesis that Mark's Gospel is most fully intelligible if it dates earlier than the mid-40s and Matthew's and Luke's Gospels if they date later than the mid-40s. It should be stressed, however, that this hypothesis is sufficiently tentative that it should be supported by additional argumentation, which is what we seek to develop in the section on authorial biography below.

Conclusion to Contextualization

Insofar as it is the case that

- on the basis of synchronization we can reasonably conclude that Acts was written ca. 62 and the Synoptic Gospels prior to that date, with Matthew's Gospel likely written prior to Luke's, and Mark's Gospel prior to Matthew's;
- Markan use of Aramaic is nonprobative for establishing the date of Mark's Gospel; and
- Mark's Gospel is most fully intelligible if it dates earlier than the mid-40s and Matthew's and Luke's if they date later than the mid-40s,

we conclude that Mark's Gospel was most likely composed no later than 45; Matthew's and Luke's Gospels most likely no earlier than 45 and prior to 62, with Matthew's likely before Luke's; and Acts of the Apostles ca. 62.

6. As argued by Crossley, *Date of Mark's Gospel*, 82–124.

Authorial Biography

In this section, we consider the data of authorial biography for (1) Mark's Gospel, (2) Luke's Gospel and Acts, and (3) Matthew's Gospel. Given the data of authorial biography, it is argued that Mark's Gospel was most likely written no earlier than 42 and no later than 45; Matthew's, no earlier than 45 and no later than 59; Luke's, ca. 59; Acts, ca. 62.

Mark in Rome

With regard to authorial biography and Mark's Gospel, we consider several issues: (1) with whom Mark the Evangelist should be identified, (2) the relationship (if any) between Mark the Evangelist and Peter, (3) the tradition that identifies Rome as the origin of Mark's Gospel, and (4) whether Mark's Gospel should be dated after either Peter's departure from Rome or his death.[7]

Which Mark?

There is no evidence that the Second Gospel was ever known apart from its traditional attribution to someone named "Mark."[8] But who was this Mark? Apart from Mark the Evangelist, the putative author of Mark's Gospel, there are up to four Marks in the New Testament: the John Mark of Acts (cf. chaps. 12–13 and 15); the Mark of Colossians 4:10; the Mark of 2 Timothy 4:11; and the Mark of 1 Peter 5:13. Early Christian interpreters tended to treat these four figures as the same man, but early Christians also tended to conflate persons with identical or similar names. Thus we cannot exclude the possibility that these New Testament passages refer to up to four different men. For our initial purposes, it is sufficient to note that none, any, or all of these men could be identical with Mark the Evangelist.

Moving beyond the New Testament texts, we know relatively little about Mark the Evangelist, regardless of whether he is to be identified with John Mark, the Colossian Mark, the Pastoral Mark, the Petrine Mark, or none or all of these. Eusebius reports that Mark the Evangelist was the first missionary to Alexandria.[9] He dates this activity to ca. 43, according to

7. Cf. my earlier treatment of Markan origins in Bernier, *Quest*, 126–42.
8. Cf. the classic discussion of this matter in Hengel, *Four Gospels*, 48–57.
9. Eusebius, *Hist. eccl.* 2.16.1.

Jerome's Latin translation of Eusebius's *Chronicon*.[10] This is consistent with his statement that Philo (d. ca. 50) encountered Egyptian Christian communities that Mark had founded.[11] It is also clear, however, that Eusebius had read Philo's *On the Contemplative Life* and wrongly concluded that the Therapeutae—a Jewish ascetic sect similar to those who likely produced the Dead Sea Scrolls—whom Philo describes in that text were in fact early Egyptian Christians. Perhaps more useful for our purposes is Eusebius's report that Annianus succeeded Mark the Evangelist as bishop of Alexandria in the eighth year of Nero (i.e., 62/63).[12] This might indicate that Mark died at this time, but one should not insist upon this. Moreover, we cannot rule out the possibility that Eusebius has conflated another Mark with Mark the Evangelist.

For our purposes, there is little value in seeking to identify which New Testament Marks are the Evangelist. Any of the first-generation Christians known to us as Mark were plausibly operative in the 40s through the 60s. Thus a date for Mark's Gospel in the early 40s through to 70 is consistent with the traditional authorship.

Mark and Peter

A more promising line of inquiry lies in Mark the Evangelist's putative relationship with Peter. The main extracanonical evidence for this relationship is the famous statement of Papias of Hierapolis, writing most likely during the reign of Trajan (98–117) and preserved for us in Eusebius's *Ecclesiastical History* 3.39.15.

> And the Elder used to say this: "Mark, having become Peter's interpreter, wrote down accurately everything he remembered, though not in order, of the things either said or done by Christ. For he neither heard the Lord nor followed him, but afterward, as I said, followed Peter, who adapted his teachings as needed but had no intention of giving an ordered account of the Lord's sayings. Consequently Mark did nothing wrong in writing down some things as he remembered them, for he made it his one concern not to omit anything which he heard or to make any false statement in them."[13]

10. Jerome, *Chron.* 179, trans. Helm, *Die Chronik*, 525.
11. Eusebius, *Hist. eccl.* 2.17.3–24.
12. Eusebius, *Hist. eccl.* 2.24.1.
13. Eusebius, *Hist. eccl.* 3.39.15, trans. Holmes, *Apostolic Fathers*, 739–41.

John Robinson employs this passage in the work of developing a theory of Synoptic origins.[14] The passage can be licitly used as such.[15] Nonetheless, as intimated in the discussion of the Synoptic problem above, Robinson ties his arguments for the dates of the Matthean, Markan, and Lukan Gospels too much to his own somewhat idiosyncratic account of their source-critical relationships. My own approach is more pragmatic and leads me to focus upon two questions of relevance specific to authorial biography. The first question: Given what we know about Peter, is it plausible that he would have transmitted the materials attributed to him in Mark's Gospel? Admittedly, there is little positive evidence beyond Papias himself indicating that Peter was a primary source for Mark's Gospel.[16] Nevertheless, I have yet to see any argument that convincingly excludes this possibility. One might argue that Peter would never have transmitted material that presents himself at times in such a negative light. I am far from convinced by such argumentation. People can and do tell stories that put themselves in a negative light, for all sorts of rhetorical and psychological reasons. For our purposes, the possibility that Peter was a source for Mark is sufficient for us to consider whether a pre-45 date for Mark's Gospel is consistent with the external data.

On the basis of contextualization, we have already suggested that Mark's Gospel was written before 45. This leads to a second and, for our purposes, more relevant question: Can we establish contact between Peter and Mark as early as 45? If Mark the Evangelist is not to be identified with any of the New Testament Marks, then we would know almost nothing about his life during this period, and thus there would be no reason to exclude contact with Peter. It would be much the same if Mark the Evangelist is to be identified only with the Marks of the Pauline or Petrine corpora; in those cases we would again lack grounds to exclude early Markan-Petrine contact. If Mark the Evangelist is to be identified with the Mark of 1 Peter 5:13, then we would have positive evidence that this Mark was associated with Peter at least traditionally, if not in life. Without having yet offered a date for 1 Peter, we would still lack positive evidence that such association existed ca. 40, however. Yet neither could we exclude it. If Mark the Evangelist is to be identified with the John Mark of Acts, then Acts 12:12 would place Peter in the Jerusalem home of Mark's

---

14. Robinson, *Redating*, 95–96.

15. Cf. my earlier use of Eusebius's *Hist. eccl.* 3.39.15 to elucidate Synoptic origins in Bernier, *Quest*, 133–42.

16. Cf. the discussions in Bauckham, *Jesus and the Eyewitnesses*, 202–39; Hengel, *Gospel of Mark*, 47–53.

mother in 41 or 42. Peter was thus almost certainly familiar with John Mark by no later than this date. Cumulatively, the probability of Markan-Petrine contact as early as 40 ranges from plausible to virtually certain, depending upon which Mark is identified with the Evangelist.

Mark and Peter in Rome

The above discussion has demonstrated that Peter could have transmitted materials found in Mark's Gospel, and that Mark and Peter could have been in contact as early as 40. We should also consider the traditional view, which has Mark writing his Gospel in Rome after Peter taught in that community.[17] If this view is affirmed, can we also affirm Markan authorship in the early 40s? The answer appears to be yes. It is typically supposed that if Mark and Peter worked together in Rome, it could only have been in the 60s. Yet there is evidence that Peter journeyed to Rome in the early 40s.[18] Eusebius reports that Peter came to Rome during the reign of Claudius, where he disputed with Simon Magus. Eusebius and Jerome more specifically report that Peter arrived in Rome during the second year of Claudius (i.e., 42).[19] Nothing excludes the possibility that Mark journeyed with him at this time.[20] This evidence comes from relatively late sources; thus we should be wary about building too much on its foundation.[21] Nonetheless, given the evidence from Eusebius and the fact that we cannot exclude the possibility that Mark traveled with Peter in the early 40s, we can conclude that thus far the data of authorial biography is consistent with findings generated on the basis of synchronization and contextualization.

Peter's Departure

The broader patristic data does present two potential barriers to dating Mark's Gospel to the early 40s. First, some references in patristic literature

17. Cf. Eusebius, *Hist. eccl.* 2.15.1–2; 6.14.6–7. Cf. the discussion of this tradition in Robinson, *Redating*, 106–14. Robinson, in turn, leans heavily upon Edmundson, *Church in Rome*, 47–56.

18. As argued at length by Edmundson, *Church in Rome*, 47–56. Cf. the engagement with this tradition in Crossley, *Date of Mark's Gospel*, 11–12; Wenham, *Redating Matthew, Mark and Luke*, 146–72.

19. Cf. Eusebius, *Hist. eccl.* 2.14.6; Jerome, *Chron.* 179, trans. Helm, *Die Chronik*, 525; Jerome, *Vir. ill.* 1.

20. Robinson is also "prepared to take seriously" that Mark did indeed travel with Peter to Rome ca. 42 and that this led to the composition of his Gospel in that city (*Redating*, 114).

21. As rightly emphasized by Crossley, *Date of Mark's Gospel*, 11–12.

have been interpreted to indicate that Mark wrote his Gospel after the deaths
of Peter and Paul. The Anti-Marcionite Prologues claim that Mark wrote
his Gospel after Peter's departure (*post excessionem*). For his part, Irenaeus
reports that Mark handed on his Gospel after Peter's and Paul's departure
(*exodos*).[22] This language of "departure" could be—and has been—taken
to metaphorically reference Peter's (and Paul's) death.[23] If these prologues
refer to Peter's death and Irenaeus means Peter's and Paul's deaths, then
either the prologues and Irenaeus are mistaken or Mark's Gospel cannot
date to the 40s. However, it is unclear whether the prologue or Irenaeus are
reporting that either Peter or Paul departed from life before Mark's Gospel
was handed on. Indeed, immediately before the reference to their departure,
Irenaeus states that Peter and Paul were preaching in Rome.[24] Hence, it is at
least as possible to interpret this passage as referring to Peter's departure
from Rome rather than from this world. Similarly, Clement of Alexandria
reports Peter's response to Mark's Gospel.[25] The data converge to suggest
that Mark wrote his Gospel after Peter departed from Rome and was still
alive.

More challenging is the second difficulty posed by Irenaeus's aforemen-
tioned report that Mark handed on (*paradidonai*) his Gospel after Paul's
departure. If accepted as accurate, this report speaks against dating Mark's
Gospel any earlier than 62, which is the earliest time that we can plausibly
envision Paul having departed Rome. Yet we have already shown that Acts
and thus Mark's Gospel likely date no later than 62. Robinson too quickly
moves past this difficulty.[26] One might argue that by using the word *paradidōmi*
Irenaeus indicates not when Mark's Gospel was written but rather when it
was transmitted.[27] If this is granted, then one can envision a scenario in which
Mark composed his Gospel, Peter approved it, Peter and Paul departed (either
from Rome or life), and then Mark passed on his Gospel. This is not impossible. It would allow one to affirm Irenaeus's testimony in its entirety yet also

22. Irenaeus, *Haer*. 3.1.1.
23. Cf. such usage in Wis. 3:2; 7:6; Luke 9:31; 2 Pet. 1:15.
24. Irenaeus, *Haer*. 3.1.1.
25. According to Eusebius, *Hist. eccl*. 6.14.7.
26. Cf. the discussions in Crossley, *Date of Mark's Gospel*, 6–11; Ellis, *Making of the New Testament*, 360–64; Robinson, *Redating*, 110–11; Wenham, *Redating Matthew, Mark and Luke*, 138–42.
27. As argued by Ellis, *Making of the New Testament*, 361–63. Cf. the critique in Crossley, *Date of Mark's Gospel*, 6–9.

date Mark's Gospel to Peter's life.[28] It is difficult to imagine that Irenaeus had such detailed information regarding the transmission of Mark's Gospel. Irenaeus likely is mistaken regarding Paul's "depature."

The relevant data most fully indicate that Peter was present in Rome ca. 42. Meanwhile, the work of synchronization and contextualization suggest that Mark's Gospel dates earlier than the mid to late 40s. Given such data, we can reasonably conclude that Mark's Gospel was written sometime in the years running from 42 through 45.

Luke in Caesarea and Rome

For reasons that will become evident as we proceed, we will treat Luke's Gospel before Matthew's. With regard to authorial biography and Luke's Gospel, we consider (1) with whom Luke should be identified, (2) the so-called we-passages, and (3) Paul's imprisonment in Caesarea and Luke's activities during this time. As noted at the outset of this chapter, it is argued that Luke's Gospel was most likely written ca. 59.

Which Luke?

There is no evidence that Luke's Gospel was ever attributed to anyone other than the traditional Luke.[29] But who was this Luke? Just as there are multiple references to a person or persons named Mark in the New Testament, so there are multiple references to a person or persons named Luke (*Loukas*). These are all found in the Pauline corpus.[30] There are also two references to a person or persons named Lucius (*Loukios*), both of whom have some connection with Paul.[31] Insofar as *Loukas* represents an abbreviated form of *Loukios*, we should include these in our list of New Testament Lukes. For our purposes, whether these passages refer to one, two, three, four, or five persons named Luke, the evidence suffices for us to conclude that there was at least one person by that name in or near the Pauline orbit. Whether none, some, or all of these are to be identified with Luke the Evangelist is another question, and one largely immune to empirical resolution.

28. As does Ellis, *Making of the New Testament.*
29. Cf. again the discussion in Hengel, *Four Gospels*, 48–57.
30. Col. 4:14; 2 Tim. 4:11; Philem. 24.
31. Cf. Acts 13:1 (here identified as Lucius of Cyrene); Rom. 16:21.

The We-Passages

Of greater interest, however, is the evidence of the we-passages in Acts.[32] The narrator in these passages opted to write in the first-person plural; elsewhere he typically wrote in the third person. We might identify three broad categories of hypotheses by which to account for the we-passages: (1) literary artifact, (2) authorial access to an eyewitness source, and (3) author as eyewitness.[33] According to the first category of hypotheses, we should infer from these we-passages that the author employed a literary device, such as a style characteristic of ancient accounts of sea voyages, or alternatively that the author aimed at achieving nothing more than to present the narrator as someone whose proximity to the events in question guarantees his credibility to address the matter at hand.[34] This first category of hypotheses can be excluded with a high degree of confidence. Proponents of the sea-voyage hypothesis have been unable to demonstrate that the first-person plural was characteristic of sea voyages; indeed, its critics have shown positively that it was not.[35] Likewise, the narrative-credibility hypothesis supposes that the author wanted readers to think that he was present for the events of the we-passages. Such a hypothesis already concedes the foundations of the author-as-eyewitness hypothesis, to be discussed below, and one would want some warrant as to why the author wanted us to think he was present when in fact he was not, as well as why such an attempt at credibility is limited to just a few passages of the Acts. In this first category, the hypothesis to explain the we-passages seems to introduce more problems than it solves and thus should be affirmed only when other, simpler alternatives can be reasonably excluded.

The second and third categories can be initially evaluated as a unit. The second category of hypotheses argues that the author had access to a source of some sort, written in the first person and usually understood to be a travelogue belonging to one of Paul's companions.[36] According to the third

---

32. Acts 16:10–17; 20:5–15; 21:1–18; 27:1–28:16.

33. These three categories are developed from Hemer, *Book of Acts*, 312–13. Hemer identifies four categories, but two of these—authorial presence as eyewitness and a reproduction of the author's own diary or notes—are similar enough to justify conflating them into a single category for our purposes.

34. On the "sea-voyage" hypothesis: cf. Robbins, "By Land and by Sea"; Robbins, "We-Passages in Acts." On the "narrative credibility" hypothesis, cf. W. Campbell, "The Narrator"; W. Campbell, *The "We" Passages*. Cf. the response to W. Campbell in Keener, *Acts*, 3:2363–74.

35. Hemer, *Book of Acts*, 317–19.

36. For an accessible treatment of permutations of the travelogue hypothesis, see Dupont, *Sources of the Acts*, 75–165.

category, we should infer from these passages that the author was himself a companion of Paul, perhaps one or more of the Lukes known from the New Testament corpus. Here the evidence is more promising. In reading the we-passages more closely, we find that the first-person plural ends with Paul and his companions in Philippi, from whence Paul soon departs.[37] The first-person plural picks up again the next time Paul or any of his companions are associated with that same city.[38] The first category of hypotheses struggles to explain this data. By contrast, the second and third categories of hypotheses can readily explain this detail by suggesting that either the author of the putative travelogue or the author of Acts himself remained in Philippi when Paul and Silas moved on from that city. This is strengthened by recent work that suggests that Luke-Acts evinces greater geographical knowledge of the Aegean area than it does of Palestine.[39] Such research further shows that Luke-Acts evinces greatest geographical knowledge of the northeast Aegean. Such data are particularly interesting in that Philippi lies on the northern coast of the Aegean, and the we-passages describe an eastward journey along the coast from there. Such a patterning of the data makes sense if the author spent more time in the Aegean than in Palestine.

Cumulatively, the second and third categories of hypotheses are more consistent with the data than the first. Of these categories, parsimony should incline us to identify the author of the we-passages with the author of Acts.

Caesarea and Rome

Insofar as the we-passages are best understood as indicating that the author was present for the events under discussion, we can establish with reasonable precision that the author's movements were during the late 50s through the early 60s. In spring of 57, the author accompanied Paul on what turned out to be his final journey to Jerusalem.[40] Paul spent the next two years (ca. 57–59) imprisoned in Caesarea.[41] We do not know exactly how or where Luke spent the two years, but we do know that he was with Paul when he went to Rome.[42] Cumulatively, the above allows us to advance a hypothesis: that Luke spent

37. Cf. Acts 16:12.
38. Acts 20:6.
39. Kloppenborg, "Luke's Geography."
40. Acts 21:1–16.
41. Acts 24:27.
42. Acts 27:1.

the two years that Paul was in Caesarea undertaking the research for and perhaps also writing his Gospel. He made several trips back and forth from Caesarea to Jerusalem but spent little if any time in Galilee, thus giving him greater firsthand knowledge of the coastal regions. This is consistent with the evidence that the author of Luke-Acts was more familiar with the Palestinian coast than the interior.[43] It is not unreasonable to conclude that during this time he sought out eyewitnesses to Jesus's life.[44] Such knowledge incidentally entailed a largely secondhand familiarity with the interior. It is not unreasonable to think that during this time he also inquired into the history of the Jerusalem and Judean churches in preparation for writing Acts. Thus, Luke's Gospel might have been written ca. 59, at the end of this two-year period. If Luke was in Rome from 60 to 62, and given that Acts was likely finished not much later than this, then we do best to suggest that he wrote his second volume during those years.

Matthew in the Middle

Authorial biography is of limited utility in establishing the date of Matthew's Gospel. On the one hand, this is because Matthew's Gospel is the Synoptic Gospel most likely to be pseudonymous, and on the other hand, we have less potentially relevant information regarding the Matthean author than we do regarding the Markan or Lukan author. For this reason, we treat Matthew last with regard to authorial biography. We will consider several issues: (1) with whom Matthew should be identified, (2) the relationship between Matthew and the "Levi" of Matthew 9:9, and (3) patristic data regarding Matthew's life. It will be argued that Matthew's Gospel was most likely written no earlier than 45 and no later than 59, although it could have been written as late as 70.

There is no evidence that Matthew's Gospel was ever known apart from its traditional attribution to someone named Matthew.[45] Almost certainly, this traditional attribution has in mind Matthew, a member of the Twelve.[46] The Matthean Gospel almost certainly wants us to identify this figure with the tax collector whom Jesus called to be a disciple.[47] Whether this Matthew

---

43. Cf. Kloppenborg, "Luke's Geography."
44. Cf. Luke 1:1–4. Cf. the similar suggestion in Ellis, *Making of the New Testament*, 401–3.
45. Cf. again the discussion in Hengel, *Four Gospels*, 48–57.
46. Matt. 10:3; Mark 3:18; Luke 6:15.
47. Matt. 9:9; cf. 10:3, which refers to Matthew, a member of the Twelve, as a tax collector.

actually wrote the Matthean Gospel is another matter. Here the data are more complicated than those regarding either Mark's or Luke's Gospel.

We begin with the internal data. Where Matthew 9:9 narrates the call of a tax collector named Matthew, Mark's and Luke's Gospels narrate the call of a tax collector named Levi.[48] It is almost certain that "Matthew" and "Levi" here are not intended to be alternative names for the same person. It was quite common for a person to have both a Semitic name and a Greek or Roman one (Saul/Paul comes to mind). It would be exceptionally rare for a person to have two common Semitic names, such as Matthew and Levi.[49] These textual details have led to the argument that Matthew cannot be the author of the Matthean Gospel, as he would not have needed to repurpose the story of Levi's calling in order to narrate his own. Although we do not know enough about why (on the supposition of Markan priority) Matthew made this change for us to reject Matthean authorship with certainty, the biblical data are sufficiently ambiguous as to raise legitimate critical doubts.

The extracanonical data offer little more assistance. There seems to be general agreement that Matthew ministered for some years in Judea and that his Gospel dates from that period.[50] This offers us virtually nothing by which to narrow the range of probable compositional dates. Moreover, this general agreement might well be an inference from Papias's statement: "Matthew composed the oracles in the Hebrew language and each person interpreted them as best he could."[51] Again, Robinson utilizes this passage in developing a theory of Synoptic development.[52] Again, this is quite licit.[53] And again, such theorizing is far less helpful for purposes of establishing the date of composition than Robinson believes it to be. Moreover, this statement is no-toriously opaque and almost without use for our purposes. Two major schools of thought have developed from reading this passage. Most scholars hold that Papias understands there to have been an early Aramaic or Hebrew version of Matthew's Gospel, of which our Greek Gospel of Matthew is a translation. Others hold that Papias understands our Greek Gospel of Matthew to have

---

48. Cf. Matt. 9:9 with Mark 2:14 and Luke 5:27–28.
49. Cf. the discussion in Bauckham, *Jesus and the Eyewitnesses*, 108–12.
50. Cf. Eusebius, *Hist. eccl.* 3.24.6–7; Irenaeus, *Haer.* 3.1.1.
51. According to Eusebius, *Hist. eccl.* 3.39.16, trans. Holmes, *Apostolic Fathers*, 741.
52. Cf. Robinson, *Redating*, 95–96.
53. Cf. my own earlier efforts in using Eusebius, *Hist. eccl.* 3.39.16, to elucidate Synoptic origins in Bernier, *Quest*, 142–48.

been written in a Hebraic "style."[54] For our purposes, it is sufficient to note that virtually any resolution of this problem could accommodate virtually any proposed date of composition for our Matthean Gospel. As interesting as Papias is in his own right, he is of little relevance for establishing the compositional date of Matthew's Gospel.

Cumulatively, we can neither confirm nor refute Matthean authorship. Neither can it aid us in the task of narrowing down the most probable date of composition. Given what we have determined thus far, Matthew's Gospel likely postdates the composition of Mark's Gospel (ca. 42 to 45), and more specifically, the full flourishing of the gentile mission in the mid to late 40s.

Conclusion to Authorial Biography

Insofar as it is the case that

- on the cumulative basis of synchronization and contextualization Mark's Gospel was written no later than 45, Matthew's and Luke's after 45 but before 62, with Matthew's likely written prior to Luke's, and Acts ca. 62;
- Mark the Evangelist could be identified with any combination (or none) of the following: John Mark of Acts, the Mark of Colossians 4:10, the Mark of 2 Timothy 4:11, or the Mark of 1 Peter 5:13;
- the probability of Markan-Petrine contact as early as 40 ranges from plausible to virtually certain;
- we can plausibly place both Peter and Mark in Rome in the early 40s;
- both the Anti-Marcionite Prologues, which report that Mark handed on his Gospel following the departure of Peter either from life or Rome, and Irenaeus, who reports that Mark handed on his Gospel following the departure of Peter and Paul, are problematic enough that they cannot be used with confidence to exclude a date of composition for the Markan Gospel prior to the mid to late 40s;
- Luke the Evangelist could be identified with any combination (or none) of the following: the Luke of Colossians 4:14, the Luke of 2 Timothy 4:11, the Luke of Philemon 24, the Lucius of Acts 13:1, and the Lucius of Romans 16:21;

54. A position most fully associated in contemporary scholarship with Kürzinger, *Papias von Hierapolis*.

- the we-passages most likely indicate that the author of Acts was a companion of Paul;
- the two years that Paul spent imprisoned in Caesarea (57–59) would have afforded Luke the opportunity to undertake the research that he reports in Luke 1:1–4; and
- virtually any resolution of the critical doubts regarding Matthew's identity could accommodate virtually any proposed date of composition for our Matthean Gospel, as could virtually any reading of the relevant patristic dating,

we conclude that Mark's Gospel was written no earlier than 42 and no later than 45; Matthew's, no earlier than 45 and no later than 59; Luke's ca. 59; and the Acts of the Apostles ca. 62.

Cumulative Conclusion to Part 1: The Synoptic Gospels and Acts

Insofar as it is the case that

- the best solutions to the Synoptic problem favor hypotheses in which Luke's Gospel postdates Matthew's, and Matthew's postdates Mark's;
- the Matthean and Markan "texts of desolation" (Matt. 24:15–31; Mark 13:14–27) are more fully intelligible before 70 than they are after 70;
- Jesus's prediction of Jerusalem's destruction in Luke's Gospel (Luke 19:41–44; 21:20–28) is equally intelligible before 70 as after 70;
- the relationship of Luke's Gospel to Acts favors hypotheses in which the latter postdates the former;
- the ending of Acts favors hypotheses in which Acts was written ca. 62;
- Mark's Gospel is most fully intelligible if it dates no later than the mid-40s and Matthew's and Luke's if they date no earlier;
- the probability of Markan-Petrine contact as early as 40 ranges from plausible to virtually certain;

- we can plausibly place both Peter and Mark in Rome in the early 40s;
- the we-passages most likely indicate that the author of Acts was a companion of Paul; and
- the two years that Paul spent imprisoned in Caesarea (57–59) would have afforded Luke the opportunity to undertake the research that he reports in Luke 1:1–4,

we conclude that Mark's Gospel was written no earlier than 42 and no later than 45; Matthew's, no earlier than 45 and no later than 59; Luke's ca. 59; and the Acts of the Apostles ca. 62. This can be summarized via the following table:

Text	Probable Compositional Date
Gospel of Mark	42–45
Gospel of Matthew	45–59
Gospel of Luke	59
Acts of the Apostles	62

The Johannine Tradition

3

The Gospel of John

Part 2 of this study addresses the compositional dates of the Johannine tradition, defined broadly to also include Revelation.[1] Part 1 addressed the three Synoptic Gospels and Acts concurrently; part 2 will treat the Gospel of John in one chapter, then the Johannine Letters and Revelation in another. This difference in organization between parts 1 and 2 has to do with the nature of the evidence. The sheer quantity of material common to the Synoptic Gospels as well as the fact that Acts is a companion volume to Luke's Gospel makes it virtually impossible to treat them other than as a unit. By comparison, the similarities between the Johannine texts consist primarily of style rather than content (in the case of the Gospel and the Letters) and historical connections through putative authorship (in the case of all five texts). Therefore, treating them as a unit would confuse rather than clarify. Whereas most scholars favor a date for John's Gospel at or around 90, this study concludes that John's Gospel was most likely written sometime between 60 and 70.

1. In developing this chapter, I found the following particularly useful: Barrett, *St. John*; Beasley-Murray, *John*; Brown, *Gospel of John*; Keener, *Gospel of John*; Lincoln, *Saint John*; Moloney, *Gospel of John*.

Synchronization

In this section, we consider (1) the external attestation of John's Gospel, (2) the relationship of John's Gospel to the Synoptics, (3) the death of Peter, (4) the death of the Beloved Disciple, (5) the expulsion passages and the Birkat Haminim, (6) Jesus's reference in John 2:19 to the destruction of the temple, (7) Jesus's reference in John 4:21 to worship ceasing in Jerusalem and on Mount Gerizim, and (8) the narrator's reference in John 5:2 to the pool of Bethesda.

External Attestation

When it comes to external attestation, for the better part of a century it was supposed that $\mathfrak{P}^{52}$, a fragment of John's Gospel originally dated to the early to mid-second century, established that the Gospel cannot date much later than 125.[2] More recent estimates have suggested that $\mathfrak{P}^{52}$ could date to the late second century or even into the third.[3] Similar tales could be told about other early witnesses to the text of John's Gospel, such as $\mathfrak{P}^{66}$ and $\mathfrak{P}^{75}$. Although dates as early as the second century have been proposed for both, more recent work has tended toward the third or even fourth century.[4] Given the vagaries of the data, $\mathfrak{P}^{52}$, $\mathfrak{P}^{66}$, and $\mathfrak{P}^{75}$ cannot be used to establish that John's Gospel existed in the first half of the second century.[5] Indeed, on the strength of the manuscript data alone, one could not, for instance, rule out J. V. M. Sturdy's argument that John's Gospel was completed ca. 160.[6]

The reception-critical data are less conducive to such a later date. Charles Hill argues that there is already clear evidence of John's Gospel in the letters of Ignatius and the Shepherd of Hermas.[7] Hill has maximalist tendencies when it comes to identifying knowledge of the Johannine Gospel, and other scholars have tended to be more reticent on the matter.[8] Nonetheless, Hill does successfully show that perhaps as early as Trajan's reign (98–117, the traditional

---

2. See the classic treatment in Roberts, "Unpublished Fragment."

3. Cf. Nongbri, "Use and Abuse of P[52]"; Orsini and Clarysse, "New Testament Manuscripts"; Schmidt, "Zwei Anmerkungen zu P.Ryl. III 457."

4. Cf. Nongbri, "Paleographic Dating"; Nongbri, "Papyrus Bodmer XIV–XV (P[75])"; Orsini and Clarysse, "New Testament Manuscripts."

5. Cf. Nongbri, "Use and Abuse of P[52]," 46.

6. Following Sturdy, *Redrawing the Boundaries*, 75–80.

7. C. Hill, *Johannine Corpus*, 360–446.

8. Cf. P. Foster, "Epistles of Ignatius," esp. 183–84; Osiek, *Shepherd of Hermas*, 26; Schoedel, *Ignatius of Antioch*, 9.

date of Ignatius's letters) there existed a significant body of material that could be of Johannine provenance. Certainly by the late second century the Fourth Gospel is known to writers such as Clement of Alexandria and Irenaeus.[9] Cumulatively, although a mid-second-century date for John's Gospel cannot be excluded via external attestation, a date later than 120 is more likely to encounter reception-critical challenges than an earlier one.

Relationship of John's Gospel to the Synoptics

Scholars commonly suppose that among the canonical Gospels, John's was the last one written.[10] Irenaeus is often thought to indicate this, but he is arguably guided more by an emerging canonical order than by any particular knowledge about the chronology of Gospel composition.[11] Clement of Alexandria, too, is thought to suppose that John's Gospel was the last written.[12] Whether Clement of Alexandria is discussing the order in which the canonical Gospels were composed has, however, been contested.[13] Questions about what exactly Irenaeus and Clement claim, combined with uncertainty regarding the sources of their information, have led contemporary scholars to place relatively little weight upon patristic data when considering the order of the Gospels. Typically, such scholars turn to source-critical methodology in support of Synoptic priority.[14] On this matter, John Robinson notes that while he was writing *Redating the New Testament*, there was a general movement from supposing that John's Gospel depended upon at least Mark's Gospel toward thinking the two were independent.[15] Unless I misread current "straws in the wind," there is currently a general movement toward once again supposing that John knew Mark's Gospel.[16] I have some sympathies with this movement. Nonetheless, given the current state of Gospel source criticism, the relationship of John's Gospel to the Synoptics

9. Cf. the discussion in C. Hill, *Johannine Corpus*, 95–128.

10. For a dissenting minority report, cf. Robinson, *Priority of John*. Cf. more recently Matson, *Dialogue with Another Gospel?*

11. Irenaeus, *Haer.* 3.1.1. For a qualified defense of Irenaeus's knowledge about the order in which the Gospels were written, cf. Hengel, *Four Gospels*, 38–39.

12. According to Eusebius, *Hist. eccl.* 6.14.5–7, esp. 7.

13. Cf. Carlson, "Clement of Alexandria."

14. Cf. the classic discussion in Smith, *John among the Gospels*.

15. Robinson, *Redating*, 262.

16. As exemplified by Becker, Bond, and Williams, *John's Transformation*; North, *What John Knew*. Cf. also Barker, *John's Use of Matthew*, for fuller consideration of Synoptic-Johannine contact beyond John's possible use of Mark's Gospel. The term "straws in the wind" is from Robinson, *Twelve New Testament Studies*, 94.

is sufficiently unsettled that it should not be used to either exclude or favor any possible relative ordering of the texts in question.

The Death of Peter (John 21:18-19)

John 21:18–19 is often taken as evidence that John's Gospel postdates Peter's death. Robinson follows this tendency.[17] This allows him to date the Gospel after 65 with a high degree of confidence. There are two possible objections to Robinson's argumentation here. First, there is the matter of when Peter died. David Eastman has recently made two signal contributions to this matter.[18] He notes that while the relevant ancient material generally agrees that Peter died during Nero's reign (r. 54–68), the same material provides us with dates for Peter's death as early as 55 and as late as 69.[19] Thus in principle Robinson could be correct in affirming that John 21:18–19 was written after Peter's death, and yet the Gospel could date as early as 55. Second, there is the matter of whether John 21:18–19 does indeed postdate Peter's death.

Before proceeding, we need to consider the possibility that John 21 is a secondary addition to the book.[20] Unfortunately, the evidence for the secondary character of John 21 is not as strong as often supposed. The primary evidence is that the last two verses of John 20 (vv. 30–31) read as an intelligible conclusion to the Gospel. Given John 20:30–31, chapter 21 certainly reads as an epilogue to the Gospel. An epilogue need not be secondary, however, but rather could have been written as part of the original text.[21] Yet given its nature as an epilogue, John 21 could conceivably have been one of the last parts of John's Gospel to be written, possibly the very last. As such, if John 21 was written before Peter's death, then there is strong reason to think that John 1–20 was also written before he died. If John 21 was written after Peter's death, then the balance of the Gospel could date before his passing; however, since we are concerned with identifying the time at which the Gospel of John was more or less complete, this would make little difference for our present task.

John 21:18–19 reads as follows:

17. Robinson, *Redating*, 279–80.
18. Eastman, *Ancient Martyrdom Accounts*; Eastman, *Deaths of Peter and Paul*.
19. Eastman, *Deaths of Peter and Paul*, 69–102.
20. Cf. the discussion in Bultmann, *Gospel of John*, 700–702.
21. An insight owed to Bauckham, *Testimony of the Beloved*, 78–79.

"Very truly, I tell you, when you were younger, you used to fasten your own belt and to go wherever you wished. But when you grow old, you will stretch out your hands, and someone else will fasten a belt around you and take you where you do not wish to go." ([Jesus] said this to indicate the kind of death by which [Peter] would glorify God.) After this he said to him, "Follow me."

Two immediate questions demand our attention, one exegetical and the other historiographical. The exegetical question is whether, in John 21:18–19, John's Jesus anticipates that Peter will suffer a violent death. The historiographical question is whether Peter indeed suffered such a death. Our answers to these questions will establish the possible compositional dates of John 21:18–19 relative to the date of Peter's death. Let us consider the possibilities and their chronological implications, beginning with a helpful diagram.

	John's Jesus anticipates that Peter would suffer a violent death.	John's Jesus does not anticipate that Peter would suffer a violent death.
Peter suffered a violent death.	John 21:18–19 either predates or postdates Peter's death.	John 21:18–19 predates Peter's death.
Peter did not suffer a violent death.	John 21:18–19 predates Peter's death.	John 21:18–19 either predates or postdates Peter's death.

It takes little work to establish that someone writing after Peter's death could have used knowledge of his passing to present Jesus as a successful prophet. It is also altogether plausible that someone writing prior to Peter's death would correctly anticipate that such a prominent Christian figure would suffer much the same fate as other early leaders of the emerging movement, such as John the Baptist, Jesus of Nazareth, James son of Zebedee, and—depending upon exactly when John 21:18–19 was written—James the Just. It seems equally plausible that someone writing prior to Peter's death spontaneously (and correctly) supposed that he would live into old age and infirmity. It is also plausible that someone writing prior to Peter's death incorrectly anticipated that it would be violent in manner, or that someone writing prior to Peter's death incorrectly anticipated that it would be peaceful. It is markedly less plausible that a Christian author writing after Peter's death would have Jesus anticipate a peaceful passing if it had in fact been violent, or a violent passing if it had in fact been peaceful. Summarized succinctly, if the Johannine Jesus correctly anticipates the manner by which Peter died, then John 21:18–19 either predates or postdates his death; conversely, if the Johannine Jesus fails to correctly anticipate the manner in which Peter died, then John 21:18–19 most likely predates his death.

We must recognize that the relative probabilities of the four combinations enumerated in the diagram above are not equal. Exegetically, the passage does seem to anticipate a violent death. Historiographically, it seems more likely that Peter did in fact die a violent death, as—while discussing various persecutions suffered by the church—the probably first-century text 1 Clement 5.4 reports that Peter went to glory.[22] Thus the chronologist must reckon with the reality that the most likely exegetical and historical scenario regarding John 21:18–19 can quite plausibly either predate or postdate Peter's passing. Insofar as it is generally easier to know how someone died after they pass than before, there is some reason to think that John 21 was written after Peter's death. Nonetheless, the possibility that the author(s) of John 21 could have correctly anticipated that Peter would suffer a violent death is sufficiently greater than zero that we should be wary of using Peter's death to establish the date of John's Gospel.

The Death of the Beloved Disciple (John 21:22-23)

Throughout the Gospel of John are references to an enigmatic character known as the "Beloved Disciple."[23] In John 21:22–23, Jesus discusses the Beloved Disciple's fate in conversation with Peter.

> Jesus said to him, "If it is my will that he remain until I come, what is that to you? Follow me!" So the rumor spread in the community that this disciple would not die. Yet Jesus did not say to him that he would not die, but, "If it is my will that he remain until I come, what is that to you?"

From this statement, one could infer that the Beloved Disciple was already dead when John 21 was written. Alternatively, one could infer that it was written at a time when the Beloved Disciple was yet alive.[24] Both inferences are equally plausible. As such, we cannot reach any judgment regarding

---

22. On the likely compositional date of 1 Clement, cf. chap. 9 below. For an argument against a violent death, cf. Goulder, "Did Peter Ever Go to Rome?," esp. 378–83, arguing that Peter died peacefully in Jerusalem in the mid-50s.

23. Mentioned in John 13:23; 19:26–27; 20:2–8; 21:20–24; possibly also in 1:35–40; 18:15–16.

24. Robinson's preferred solution (cf. *Redating*, 280–82).

the date of John's Gospel on the basis of this passage. Moreover, even if it were granted that John 21 was written either prior or subsequent to the Beloved Disciple's death, we cannot with confidence identify who the Beloved Disciple might have been, much less when he might have died. At most we would be able to establish a relative date (either before or after the Beloved Disciple's death), but we would be unable to convert this into an absolute one. As such, we must consider John 21:22–23 to be nonprobative for purposes of establishing the date of the Fourth Gospel.

The Expulsion Passages (John 9:22; 12:42; 16:2)

The work of J. Louis Martyn inaugurated a tradition within Johannine scholarship wherein it was taken as given that the Johannine expulsion passages (9:22; 12:42; 16:2) refer allegorically to the implementation of the rabbinic prayer known as the Birkat Haminim ca. 85.[25] Unfortunately for this tradition, Martyn's empirical arguments are demonstrably false. These difficulties are crucial for our purposes because it is precisely the putative reference to the Birkat Haminim that allows Martyn to argue for dating the expulsion passages to the last decade or so of the first century.

In seeking to understand these empirical difficulties, it is useful to present the relevant texts here, beginning with those from John's Gospel:

> The Jews did not believe that he had been blind and had received his sight until they called the parents of the man who had received his sight and asked them, "Is this your son, who you say was born blind? How then does he now see?" His parents answered, "We know that this is our son, and that he was born blind; but we do not know how it is that now he sees, nor do we know who opened his eyes. Ask him; he is of age. He will speak for himself." His parents said this because they were afraid of the Jews; for the Jews had already agreed that anyone who confessed Jesus to be the Messiah would be put out of the synagogue [*aposynagōgos*]. Therefore his parents said, "He is of age; ask him." (John 9:18–23)

> Nevertheless many, even of the authorities, believed in him. But because of the Pharisees they did not confess it, for fear that they would be put out of the synagogue [*aposynagōgos*]. (John 12:42)

25. Martyn, *History and Theology*. On the development of this tradition, cf. Bernier, *Aposynagōgos and the Historical Jesus*, 1–18. Cf. also discussions in Instone-Brewer, "Eighteen Benedictions"; Langer, *Cursing the Christians?*; Marcus, "*Birkat ha-Minim* Revisited."

They will put you out of the synagogues [*aposynagōgos*]. Indeed, an hour is coming when those who kill you will think that by doing so they are offering worship to God. (John 16:2)

Each of these passages contains the word *aposynagōgos*, which means something like "out of the synagogue." Interpretation of these passages is complicated by the fact that *aposynagōgos* appears to be a Johannine neologism. At the very least, we have no evidence that anyone used the term prior to John. Normally, we could compare his usage to that found in other authors, but here we cannot. One should be slow to ground an entire theory of Johannine origins upon such relatively opaque passages. That, however, is essentially what Martyn did, doing so by appeal to a putative parallel in the form of the rabbinic prayer known as the Birkat Haminim, the "Benediction against Heretics."

In considering this text, Martyn follows the variant of the Birkat Haminim found in the Cairo Genizah in 1898.[26] Of particular interest for Martyn is the fact that this variant of the Birkat Haminim contains a previously unattested reference to נֹצְרִים (*notserim*), meaning "Nazarenes" or "Christians." For present purposes, it is best to follow the text as presented by Martyn:

1. For the apostates, let there be no hope
2. And let the arrogant government
3. be speedily uprooted in our days.
4. Let the Nazarenes [Christians] and the Minim [heretics] be destroyed in a moment
5. And let them be blotted out of the Book of Life and not be inscribed together with the righteous.
6. Blessed art thou, O Lord, who humblest the proud.[27]

The text of the Birkat Haminim itself contains little that would lead us to connect it with the Johannine expulsion passages, not least because it nowhere mentions expulsion from the synagogue. To connect the expulsion passages

---

26. Cf. Schechter and Abrahams, "Genizah Specimens," esp. 657.
27. Martyn, *History and Theology*, 62–63 (brackets original). Cf. the more recent treatments of the Genizah material in Instone-Brewer, "Eighteen Benedictions"; Langer, *Cursing the Christians?*, 187–95.

with the Birkat Haminim, Martyn relies upon a report from the Babylonian Talmud (b. Ber. 28b–29a) that this prayer was among the eighteen benedictions formulated by the seminal rabbinic academy, which is said to have gathered at Yavneh in the last quarter of the first century.[28] Again quoting from this text as followed by Martyn, it reads,

> Rabban Gamaliel said to the Sages: "Is there one among you who can word a benediction related to the Minim [heretics]?" Samuel the Small arose and composed it. The next year he [Samuel] forgot it and tried for two or three hours to recall, and they did not remove him [from his post as Delegate of the Congregation]. Why did they not remove him, seeing that Rab Judah has said in the name of Rab: If a reader made a mistake in any of the other benedictions, they do not remove him, but if in the benediction of the Minim, he is removed, because we suspect him of being a Min?—Samuel the Lesser is different, because he composed it. But is there not a fear that he might have recanted? Abaye said: We have a tradition that a good man does not become bad.[29]

A quick reading of this passage suffices to demonstrate that the supposed parallels between the Johannine expulsion passages and the Birkat Haminim simply do not exist.[30] With the expulsion passages (esp. 9:22; 12:42), declaring or even just being suspected of believing that Jesus is the Messiah leads to expulsion from the synagogue. By contrast, b. Ber. 28b–29a suggests that if one errs in reading the Birkat Haminim, then one is removed from the position of leading prayer on the suspicion of heresy. In one case, there is expulsion without prayer. In the other case, there is prayer without expulsion. The absence of parallels is injurious if not fatal to a hypothesis predicated upon such parallels. In addition, the Birkat Haminim plausibly postdates the Gospel of John. Dating to perhaps the last quarter of the second century, b. Ber. 28b–29a represents the earliest unambiguous reference to the Birkat Haminim.[31] More recent proponents of the Martynian approach often cite with approbation Joel Marcus, who argues that the Birkat Haminim not only existed in the late first century but also had antecedents in the Second

---

28. Martyn, *History and Theology*, 58–61.

29. b. Ber. 28b–29a, trans. Martyn, *History and Theology*, 59 (brackets original).

30. For the present argument, cf. Bernier, Aposynagōgos *and the Historical Jesus*, 41–46.

31. Cf. the earlier discussion in Bernier, Aposynagōgos *and the Historical Jesus*, 31–41. Cf. also Instone-Brewer, "Eighteen Benedictions"; Langer, *Cursing the Christians*, 16–39; Marcus, "*Birkat ha-Minim* Revisited."

Temple period.[32] For present purposes, however, Marcus opens the possibility that while the expulsion passages do indeed betray knowledge of the Birkat Haminim or an antecedent thereto, this in principle could have already existed as early as Jesus's lifetime.[33] Thus, even if the author of John's Gospel could have known the Birkat Haminim or its antecedents, we could not exclude a date for the Gospel as early as even 30.

Given the above considerations and even despite its widespread popularity in late twentieth-century Johannine scholarship, the supposed connection between the Birkat Haminim and the expulsion passages must be considered nonprobative when it comes to establishing when the Gospel of John was written.[34]

Raising the Temple in Three Days (John 2:19–22)

In discussing the destruction of the temple in relation to the date of John's Gospel, Robinson unfortunately indulges in his tendency to lapse into arguments from silence.[35] This tendency is evident in his treatment of John 2:19–22, which reads as follows:

> Jesus answered them, "Destroy this temple, and in three days I will raise it up." The Jews then said, "This temple has been under construction for forty-six years, and will you raise it up in three days?" But he was speaking of the temple of his body. After he was raised from the dead, his disciples remembered that he had said this; and they believed the scripture and the word that Jesus had spoken.

Robinson argues that if John's Gospel is indeed a post-70 composition, then we should expect a reference to the destruction of the temple here.[36] This is far from compelling. It is altogether plausible that Christians believed Jesus had predicted the destruction and reconstruction of the temple, and then when the destruction but not reconstruction later came to pass, they reinterpreted the prophecy as a reference to the resurrection. At the same time, these words are also plausible before 70. It is possible that Jesus did indeed prophesy or was believed to have prophesied the destruction of the temple, and that at some

---

32. Marcus, "*Birkat ha-Minim* Revisited."
33. Cf. also the arguments in Bernier, Aposynagōgos *and the Historical Jesus.*
34. Cf. the fuller discussion of this matter in Bernier, Aposynagōgos *and the Historical Jesus.* Cf. also the discussion in Robinson, *Redating,* 272–74.
35. Robinson, *Redating,* 276–77.
36. Robinson, *Redating,* 277.

time prior to 70 early Christians came to believe that he was referring to the events of the first Easter. Therefore, the reinterpretation of the prophecies of destruction as a reference to the resurrection seems equally intelligible both before and after 70. As a result, John 2:19–22 should be reckoned as nonprobative for purposes of establishing the date of John's Gospel.

The Temple and the Mountain (John 4:21)

Robinson addresses John 4:21 only in passing, noting that it does not unquestionably reflect the events of 70.[37] This is true, but nonetheless the passage merits closer attention. In John 4:21, Jesus says to the Samaritan woman at the well, "Woman, believe me, the hour is coming when you will worship the Father neither on this mountain [Gerizim] nor in Jerusalem." It could be argued that this prediction evinces an awareness of the events of the Jewish War, specifically the cessation of the Jerusalem cult. The difficulty with such a reading is that it risks making 4:21 into a failed prophecy after the fact. In principle, the passage could indeed be referring after the fact to the cessation of cultic worship with the destruction of Jerusalem in 70. It cannot, however, be referring after the fact to the cessation of cultic worship due to destruction at Mount Gerizim in 70, because Mount Gerizim did not suffer such destruction then nor did cultic worship cease there in 70. Hence it is probably best to consider 4:21 to be nonprobative for purposes of establishing the date of John's Gospel.

The Pool of Bethesda (John 5:2)

Robinson addresses this passage but does not give it the full weight that it deserves.[38] John 5:2 informs the reader that "in Jerusalem by the Sheep Gate there *is* a pool, called in Hebrew Beth-zatha [Bethesda], which *has* five porticoes" (emphasis mine). The present tense is not simply an artifact of translation into English but is native to the Greek text. The relevant verbs are *estin*, the third-person present active indicative of the verb *eimi* (to be); and *echousa*, a present active participle of *echō* (to have). The most natural reading of the present tense in this passage is that this pool existed when the author was writing.[39] Since the pool likely was destroyed in 70, we should prefer pre-70 composition for 5:2.

37. Robinson, *Redating*, 276.
38. Cf. Robinson, *Redating*, 277.
39. Cf. the discussion of tense and aspect below.

Although Robinson recognizes that this passage is most fully intelligible prior to 70, he does not fully appreciate the extent to which this is true.[40] In fairness to Robinson, he did not have access to Daniel Wallace's now-classic study on the matter, which appeared more than a decade after *Redating the New Testament*.[41] Wallace identifies and considers five possible categories of hypothesis by which one might defend a post-70 date for 5:2, which I will present and evaluate here from the weakest to the strongest: (1) the "error" view, which argues that the passage did in fact originate post-70 but that "the author made a mistake when he wrote that the pool was still intact";[42] (2) the "redactional" view, which argues that "the author(s) composed the Gospel at different stages, with some material being written before 70 (including 5,2)";[43] (3) the "anomalous present" view, which argues "that John uses the present tense in some unusual way";[44] (4) the "historical present" view, which supposes that the "author uses the present tense to refer to a place which is now just a memory"[45]; and (5) the "intact" view, "which argues that the pool survived the Jewish War intact."[46] Let us consider each in turn.

Wallace concludes that the error view is "irrational on its face: it is virtually impossible for any Jew or Christian of the late first century—regardless of his domicile—not to know the results of the war between Jerusalem and Rome."[47] Perhaps the only cavil that one might have with Wallace here is that an author might well have known that Jerusalem was destroyed without knowing the fate of the pool of Bethesda. Nonetheless, one would still need to consider how it is that someone who knew about Jerusalem's fate would erroneously suppose that the pool and its porticoes remained untouched. Given such a consideration, Wallace is correct in judging the error view to be less than compelling.

Wallace defines the redactional view as supposing that "much of the material in this [i.e., John's] gospel goes back to a tradition before the fall of Jerusalem" and that "the gospel has been worked over by at least two different hands."[48] Both suppositions can be granted in principle. For our purposes,

40. Cf. Robinson, *Redating*, 277–78.
41. Wallace, "John 5,2."
42. Wallace, "John 5,2," 183–84, quote from 183.
43. Wallace, "John 5,2," 193–97, quote from 193.
44. Wallace, "John 5,2," 184–85, quote from 184.
45. Wallace, "John 5,2," 197–205, quote from 197.
46. Wallace, "John 5,2," 185–93, quote from 185.
47. Wallace, "John 5,2," 183.
48. Wallace, "John 5,2," 193–94.

however, the first of these suppositions concedes the argument that John 5:2 is of pre-70 provenance, while the second allows but does not itself necessitate a post-70 date for the Gospel itself. Once that concession and allowance have been made, then absent compelling evidence that other material within the Gospel most likely postdates 70, we should, on the grounds of parsimony, be inclined to consider John's Gospel a pre-70 composition in toto.

What Wallace calls the "anomalous present" view might be more precisely termed the "comparison to Hebrews" view.[49] Writes Wallace of this view: "The argument is as follows: the epistle to the Hebrews was written after 70, yet it uses the present tense to refer to the Jewish sacrificial system which had already ceased. Thus, ἔστιν [estin] in John 5,2 might also belong to this category, therefore indicating nothing about the time of writing."[50] In critiquing such an argument, Wallace rightly notes that a post-70 provenance for Hebrews is far from certain.[51]

Turning to the historical present view, we must attend first to the verbal-aspect debate that has emerged since Wallace's article appeared in 1990. That debate was initiated within New Testament studies by Stanley Porter's *Verbal Aspect in the Greek of the New Testament*. Porter argues that Greek tense-forms—such as the present, aorist, future, and so on—are aspectual rather than temporal. Nonetheless, Porter also acknowledges that one of the major uses of the present tense-form is to be "present-referring."[52] As Porter further observes, the "past-referring" present tense-form is known as the "historic present."[53] Thus we are led back to the question posed by Wallace—namely, whether in John 5:2 *eimi* constitutes a historic present, such as we find when Josephus refers to the temple while using the present tense decades after the temple's destruction.[54] Wallace argues, however, that linguistically speaking, the historical present typically is associated with action verbs, not with verbs of being. But that is essentially the opposite of what we find in John 5:1–8. In this passage, John uses the aorist to report that Jesus arrived in Jerusalem (5:1); switches to the present to tell us about the pool called Bethesda, using the verb *eimi* (to be); then uses the aorist and imperfect tense-forms as he discusses what Jesus did at the pool (5:3–8). Moreover, Wallace observes that he could not find a single instance of *eimi* being used as a historical present

49. Wallace, "John 5,2," 184–85.
50. Wallace, "John 5,2," 184.
51. Wallace, "John 5,2," 183–84.
52. Porter, *Verbal Aspect*, 225.
53. Porter, *Verbal Aspect*, 189–90.
54. Cf. Josephus, *Ant.* 4.6.1–8 §§102–50; 4.7.1–7 §§151–87; 4.9.1–7 §§224–57.

within the New Testament.[55] In response to Wallace, Craig Blomberg writes, "It is difficult to know how much significance to attach to this observation. After all, most historical presents occur in narrative where a specific verb of speech or action is highlighted."[56] Blomberg's observation, however, seems to strengthen rather than weaken Wallace's argument that historical presents are not typical of verbs of being but rather of verbs of action. Considering the above, a historical present is unlikely. As such, it is probable that John 5:2 means to reference conditions as they stood at the time of composition.

Wallace rightly identifies the intact view as the strongest argument in favor of a post-70 provenance for John 5:2.[57] Here we must consider first the archaeological evidence. Contemporary scholars typically identify the pool of Bethesda with two pools located near St. Anne's Church in the Muslim Quarter. The present excavator of this area, Shimon Gibson, has argued that the southern of the two pools was a mikvah, that this was the pool mentioned in 5:2, and that the stirring of the water mentioned in 5:7 is the result of a sluice being opened between the two pools.[58] Responding to Gibson, Jodi Magness accepts that the southern pool was a mikvah but argues that "there is no indication in any of our sources—literary or archaeological—that Jews immersed in *miqva'ot* [mikvahs] for purposes other than purification, such as seeking miraculous healing."[59] Considering Gibson's argument to be speculative, Magness advances a speculation of her own: since we know that at some point after 70 this area would come to serve as an Asclepeion, Magness argues that John 5:6–7 might be alluding not to pre-70 practices associated with the God of Israel but rather to post-70 practices associated with the god Asclepius.[60] There are significant problems with this argument, however. For instance, it is not clear when the Asclepius cult began to operate at the site. Both André Duprez and Nicole Belayche discuss this cult within the context of pagan religious life in Aelia Capitolina, which from 135 was the official name for the city once known as Jerusalem. Although Duprez allows that this cult could have been in service as early as 70, he also states that the only certainty is that it was in service during the time of Aelia Capitolina.[61]

55. Wallace, "John 5,2," 203–4.
56. Blomberg, *Reliability of John's Gospel*, 43.
57. Wallace, "John 5,2," 185.
58. Gibson, "Pool of Bethesda."
59. Magness, "Sweet Memory," 327. On this Asclepeion, cf. Belayche, *Iudaea-Palestina*, 160–67; Duprez, *Jésus et les dieux guérisseurs*, 43–54.
60. Magness, "Sweet Memory," 328.
61. Duprez, *Jésus et les dieux guérisseurs*, 54.

We have seen already that reception-critical data make a date for John's Gospel much later than 120 unlikely. If indeed the Asclepeion was not in service until after 135, then on chronological grounds Magness's theory of anachronism is not impossible but certainly dubious.

More crucially, the practices described in John 5:6–7 do not strongly resemble those that Magness or her authorities on the matter—Belayche and Duprez—ascribe to the Asclepeion.[62] In Magness's own summary, "Ancient sources describe Asclepius and Serapis as healing patients through a combination of bathing in water and dreaming during incubation."[63] The absence of either dreaming or incubation vitiates, although does not entirely obviate, Magness's argument from parallel. Such vitiation is particularly problematic, as Magness's only grounds for concluding that John 5:6–7 does not suppose pre-70 conditions is the absence of parallel cases in which mikvahs were associated with healing. Moreover, Magness herself grants that given the archaeological data, John 5 might well constitute evidence that in at least one instance Second Temple Jewish persons did indeed use a mikvah for healing purposes.[64] This seems to be a more preferable solution than a poorly fitting parallel with an Asclepeion that might have come into existence only after John's Gospel.

Wallace further identifies a "fundamental problem" with "intact" arguments such as Magness's—namely, that they "attempt to divorce the porticoes from the pool."[65] Wallace notes rightly that John speaks about not only the pool of Bethesda as existing in the present but also the five porticoes that surround it. He thus correctly concludes that any iteration of the intact view should demonstrate that both pool and porticoes existed at the time that John 5:2 was written. As such, even if Magness could demonstrate that the pool was functioning as an Asclepeion as early as 70, she would still need to demonstrate that the porticoes remained intact. Unfortunately, precise knowledge about the state of the pool(s) and the porticoes after 70 eludes us. Given the extent of the destruction to Jerusalem, however, we can reasonably anticipate that the porticoes were indeed destroyed. This would be most consistent with the evidence provided to us by Josephus.[66]

62. Magness, "Sweet Memory," 328n16, cites Belayche, *Iudaea-Palestina*; Duprez, *Jésus et les dieux guérisseurs*.
63. Magness, "Sweet Memory," 328.
64. Magness, "Sweet Memory," 327.
65. Wallace, "John 5,2," 186.
66. Cf. Josephus, *J.W.* 7.1.1 §§1–3.

Considering the above, and absent evidence that suggests otherwise, it is probable that 5:2 was written prior to the destruction of 70, and with it the balance of the Gospel.

Conclusion to John's Gospel: Synchronization

Insofar as it is the case that

- the data of attestation should incline us to date John's Gospel no later than 120;
- the relationship of the Synoptic Gospels to John's Gospel resists confident resolution;
- the matter of Peter's death (cf. John 21:18–19) is likely nonprobative for establishing the date of John's Gospel, although if probative it would tend to support a date while Peter was yet alive (and thus no later than 69);
- John 21:22–23 does not necessitate that the Beloved was already dead when the Gospel was written, and in any case we cannot establish when he might have died;
- the expulsion passages (John 9:22; 12:42; 16:2) have no bearing on establishing the date of John's Gospel;
- Jesus's reference to the temple in John 2:19–22 is at least as intelligible before 70 as after;
- Jesus's reference to the temple in John 4:21 is at least as intelligible before 70 as after; and
- the narrator's description of the pool of Bethesda as a present reality in John 5:2 is more fully intelligible before 70 than after,

we conclude that John's Gospel was most likely written no later than 70.

Contextualization

In this section, we consider (1) the extent to which John's Gospel reflects conditions present in Palestine before 70, (2) the development of Johannine tradition, (3) the possibility of Gnostic influence on John's Gospel, and (4) the development of Johannine Christology. On the cumulative grounds of synchronization and contextualization, we can reasonably conclude that John's Gospel was written no later than 70.

Johannine Knowledge of Pre-70 Palestine

Robinson makes much of the extent to which John's Gospel reflects conditions present in Palestine before 70.[67] If anything, we now have stronger grounds to recognize that John's Gospel has reasonably accurate knowledge of pre-70 Palestine.[68] Nonetheless, while this does suggest that John's Gospel contains material that predates 70 and is thus consistent with a lower date, it is equally consistent with a middle or higher one. It should be considered nonprobative with regard to the date of John's Gospel.

The Development of Johannine Tradition

There is a long-standing scholarly tendency to understand John's Gospel as the product of an extended development of Johannine tradition. Such development did likely occur. As Robinson has emphasized, however, such development does not intrinsically require taking until the 90s or later to reach completion.[69] Robinson focuses upon the hypothesis elaborated in Raymond Brown's commentary on John's Gospel.[70] Regarding Brown, what matters for our purposes is that apart from the life and death of Jesus, the only absolute date that Brown offers for his sequence is the excommunication of Johannine Christians from the synagogue. For this, he relies upon the expulsion passages (John 9:22; 12:42; 16:2).[71] We, however, have already seen why they are nonprobative for purposes of dating John's Gospel.

Brown's work leads us to a conclusion that we would draw if we were to survey other comparable developmental sequences in depth: there is nothing intrinsic to theories of Johannine development that establishes an absolute date before, at, or after which the Gospel was written. For instance, Paul Anderson dates his "Middle Period" of Johannine Christianity to 70 through

---

67. Robinson, *Redating*, 264–72.

68. Cf. the summaries in von Wahlde, "Archaeology and John's Gospel"; and the more recent but briefer von Wahlde, "John and Archaeology."

69. Cf. Robinson, *Redating*, 269–72.

70. Following Brown, *Gospel of John*, 1:xxxiv–xli. Cf. later articulations of his developmental scheme in Brown, *Community of the Beloved Disciple*; Brown, *Introduction to the Gospel of John*, 64–69, 78–85.

71. Cf. esp. the discussion in Brown, *Community of the Beloved Disciple*, 22.

85, in part because he sees evidence of the Birkat Haminim in the expulsion passages but also in part because he sees John 20:28 as reflecting increased pressure to worship the emperor during Domitian's reign.[72] The introduction to this volume has already considered the extent to which Domitianic policies have received too much emphasis in New Testament studies. The reality is that, shorn of such tenuous connections with absolute dates, we can affirm virtually any given theory for the development of Johannine tradition and yet find that it will fit equally with a lower, middle, or higher chronology. One needs simply to shrink or expand the years assigned to each theorized stage. This stands apart from any consideration of whether such developmental theories in fact are warranted, given the relevant data. As such, we should consider hypotheses regarding the development of Johannine tradition to be nonprobative for purposes of establishing the date of John's Gospel.

Possible Gnostic Influences on John's Gospel

Scholars have sometimes argued for Gnostic influences upon the Gospel of John. This was most fully the case in the first half of the twentieth century, being epitomized in the work of Rudolf Bultmann.[73] Bultmann relied heavily upon the theory that Gnosticism predated Christianity and is evidenced in John's Gospel.[74] The theory of a pre-Christian Gnosticism was always on shaky empirical ground. Bultmann had to rely upon sources that postdate the Gospel of John by several centuries in some cases and posit that these nonetheless represent pre-Christian religion. For our purposes however, the most important point is that if these sources predate Christianity, then John's use of them is equally compatible with a lower, middle, or higher date. Moreover, Bultmann wrote on the relationship between Gnosticism and the Gospel of John prior to the discoveries at Qumran and Nag Hammadi. He emphasized dualism as an aspect of Gnostic thought. As a result of the discoveries at Qumran, however, we now know that there was a strong tradition of dualistic imagery within non-Gnostic Jewish literature. Accordingly, John's imagery of light and dark are intelligible within a thoroughly Jewish, non-Gnostic

72. Cf. the discussion in Anderson, *Fourth Gospel and the Quest*, 197–98.

73. Cf. the overview of Bultmann's thought on the matter in Schmithals, introduction to Bultmann, *Gospel of John*, esp. 7–9.

74. For his theory of a pre-Christian Gnosticism, Bultmann relied heavily upon the work of Reitzenstein, *Das iranische Erlösungsmysterium*.

context. From Nag Hammadi, we now know more fully the extent to which "Gnostic" writers were themselves dependent upon the Gospel of John.[75]

Contemporary scholarship tends to see Christian Gnosticism—whatever it is—as a largely second-century development.[76] Given the current state of our knowledge, there is little ground for thinking that John's Gospel betrays knowledge of the largely second-century developments typically grouped under the rubric of Gnosticism.

The Development of John's Divine Christology

John's Gospel explicitly affirms Jesus's divinity more fully than most New Testament texts. The prologue to the Gospel (1:1–18) is of particular significance in this regard. John 1:1 affirms that the Word was God. John 1:14 explicitly declares that the Word became flesh. John 1:15 and 17 leave little doubt that Jesus was this enfleshed—incarnate—Word. "The Word was God," proclaims John, and "the Word became flesh" in Jesus Christ. The idea that Jesus is God incarnate is often described as a "high Christology." The question before us is the earliest time at which a high Christology such as we find in John's Gospel could have emerged.

The last thirty years have seen significant advances in the study of early Christology.[77] For our purposes, we can divide current and historical views into two broad categories, which we might define as "early high Christology" and "late high Christology." "Early high Christology" is held by scholars who argue, to use Richard Bauckham's memorable words, that the "earliest Christology was already the highest Christology."[78] In addition to Bauckham himself, proponents of such a view include Martin Hengel and Larry Hurtado.[79] Such scholars hold that divine Christology was an almost immediate response to the ministry of Jesus and the experience of the first Easter. The primary argument for such "early high Christology" is that Paul takes for granted that Jesus is to be accorded many of the honors and titles normally reserved for the God of Israel. Three passages in particular have become the focus of attention in these discussions:

75. Cf. the classic discussion in Pagels, *Johannine Gospel in Gnostic Exegesis.*
76. Cf. the overview of the current consensus in King, "'Gnostic Myth.'"
77. Cf. the recent typology that seeks to organize these theories, in Loke, *Origins of Divine Christology*, 3–6.
78. Bauckham, *Jesus and the God of Israel*, x.
79. Cf. Bauckham, *Jesus and the God of Israel*; Hengel, *Son of God*; Hurtado, *Lord Jesus Christ.*

Yet for us there is one God, the Father, from whom are all things and for whom we exist, and one Lord, Jesus Christ, through whom are all things and through whom we exist. (1 Cor. 8:6)

For you know the generous act of our Lord Jesus Christ, that though he was rich, yet for your sakes he became poor, so that by his poverty you might become rich. (2 Cor. 8:9)

Let the same mind be in you that was in Christ Jesus, who, though he was in the form of God, did not regard equality with God as something to be exploited, but emptied himself, taking the form of a slave, being born in human likeness. And being found in human form, he humbled himself and became obedient to the point of death—even death on a cross. Therefore God also highly exalted him and gave him the name that is above every name, so that at the name of Jesus every knee should bend, in heaven and on earth and under the earth, and every tongue should confess that Jesus Christ is Lord, to the glory of God the Father. (Phil. 2:5–11)

Hurtado describes these as the "Pauline pre-existence passages" and argues that they "reflect two key christological convictions: (1) Jesus's origins and meaning lie in God, above and beyond human history, making his appearance an event of transcendent significance (e.g., Phil. 2:6–8; 2 Cor. 8:9); and (2) Jesus's agency in creation corresponds to his central role in redemption (1 Cor. 8:6), expressing his unique significance and the unity of divine purpose in creation and redemption."[80] In addition to these, we might add 1 Corinthians 1:24 and 30, which describe Jesus as God's wisdom. Wisdom is often presented as a personified being—divine Wisdom, rather than just "wisdom"—in the Hebrew Bible / Old Testament and the Deuterocanon/Apocrypha.[81] Although a proponent of what we might call a relatively "late high Christology" (cf. below), James D. G. Dunn in particular has emphasized that in 1 Corinthians 1:24 and 30 Paul understands Jesus to be the embodiment of divine Wisdom.[82] As argued in chapter 6 (below), 1–2 Corinthians and Philippians likely date to the late 50s, although Philippians could plausibly date to the early 60s. For our purposes, if in the 50s Paul could identify Jesus not only as divine in origin but also as an agent in creation and redemption—and perhaps also

---

80. Hurtado, *Lord Jesus Christ*, 126.
81. Cf. esp. Prov. 8:22–31; Sir. 24; Wis. 6:12–11:1.
82. Cf. Dunn, *Christology in the Making*, 163–212; Dunn, *Theology of Paul*, 267–81.

as divine Wisdom—then we must wonder why John's Gospel could not, by roughly the same time, have likewise identified Jesus as having divine origin, as an agent in creation and redemption, and as the divine Word.

Scholars who advocate late high Christology take up this question. Against the idea that the earliest Christology was already high, such scholars argue that there is a general movement from low to high Christology throughout the first and second Christian generations. Prominent proponents of late high Christology include Wilhelm Bousset, Maurice Casey, and James D. G. Dunn.[83] These theorists differ with respect to details, but all agree that John's Gospel represents the highest development of Christology present in the New Testament.[84] The significance can best be explicated by Dunn's statement: "As the first century of the Christian era drew to a close we find a concept of Christ's real pre-existence beginning to emerge, but only with the Fourth Gospel can we speak of a full-blown conception of Christ's personal pre-existence and a clear doctrine of incarnation."[85] Dunn argues that Paul did not think Christ to have been personally preexistent as Wisdom but rather that Wisdom was embodied in Christ; by contrast, John's Gospel declares that Christ was personally preexistent as the Word. Thus the doctrine of the incarnation proper did not develop until John's Gospel. I am more inclined than Dunn to consider Jesus as the embodiment of divine Wisdom to be conceptually closer to Jesus as the incarnation of the divine Word. More important for our purposes is that Dunn dates the doctrine of the incarnation to the end of the first century because he dates the Gospel of John to the end of the first century. If John's Gospel is indeed the earliest extant document to contain the doctrine of the incarnation, and if John's Gospel dates prior to 70, then the doctrine of the incarnation emerged earlier than 70. For his part, Casey similarly argues that while the doctrine of Jesus's preexistence was already present in Paul's Letters, it is with John's Gospel that Jesus is recognized not only as preexistent but also as fully divine.[86] Much as with Dunn, if we grant Casey's argument, then the doctrine of Jesus's full divinity emerged no later than the Gospel of John; this, however, does not tell us when the Gospel of John itself was written.

---

83. Cf. Bousset, *Kyrios Christos*; Casey, *From Jewish Prophet to Gentile God*; Dunn, *Christology in the Making*.

84. Cf. Casey, *From Jewish Prophet to Gentile God*, 141–61; Dunn, *Christology in the Making*, 213–50.

85. Dunn, *Christology in the Making*, 258 (emphasis omitted).

86. Cf. Casey, *From Jewish Prophet to Gentile God*, 124, 159.

Given the above considerations, christological development cannot rule out a pre-70 date for John's Gospel. Nonetheless, we should be wary of dating John's Gospel much earlier than the letters containing Paul's "preexistence passages": 1–2 Corinthians and Philippians. As such, John's Gospel likely does not predate 60.

Conclusion to John's Gospel: Contextualization

Insofar as it is the case that

- on the grounds of synchronization we can reasonably conclude that John's Gospel was written no later than 70;
- Johannine knowledge of conditions within pre-70 Palestine is equally consistent with pre-70 and post-70 dates;
- virtually any scheme for Johannine development can plausibly accommodate any proposed date for John's Gospel;
- John's Gospel does not betray knowledge of the largely second-century developments typically grouped under the rubric of Gnosticism; and
- the Christology of John's Gospel is approximately as high as that articulated by Paul,

we conclude that John's Gospel was likely written no earlier than 60 and no later than 70.

Authorial Biography

Through the work of synchronization and contextualization, the previous two sections led to the judgment that John's Gospel was likely written no earlier than 60 and no later than 70. Greater precision eluded us. The section that follows considers the identity of the putative author and whether that can aid us in establishing when John's Gospel was written. It concludes that, unfortunately, the data of authorial biography do not aid in narrowing down the likely date of composition of John's Gospel.

As we saw with regard to the Synoptic Gospels, there is no evidence that John's Gospel was ever known apart from its traditional attribution to someone named John.[87] Apart from John the Evangelist, the putative author of our Gospel, up to seven different men by that name appear in the New Testament: John the Baptist; John son of Zebedee; John Mark; the John who appears in Galatians 2:9; the putative author of 1 John; the putative author of 2 John; the putative author of 3 John; and John, the author of Revelation.[88] There is, in addition, "John the Elder" (alternatively, "the Elder John"), an apparent follower of the historical Jesus mentioned by Papias.[89] Given that the Baptist dies within the Fourth Gospel, we can definitively exclude him as author. John son of Zebedee is almost certainly to be identified with the John of Galatians 2:9; he is also the figure most frequently identified as the author of the Fourth Gospel. Although few today seriously consider John Mark to be the author of the Fourth Gospel or the Johannine Letters, he cannot in principle be excluded.[90] We can be virtually certain, however, that John son of Zebedee is not to be identified with John Mark since they appear as distinct characters in Acts.[91] Likewise, Papias seems to distinguish John son of Zebedee from John the Elder. We cannot exclude the possibility that John Mark and John the Elder are the same person, but there is also little reason to think that they are.

The above discussion is intended primarily to give readers some sense of the messiness surrounding any biographical engagement with the various first-century Christians named John. This messiness no doubt stems from the reality that "John" was one of the most common male Jewish names in Roman Palestine.[92] Fortunately for our purposes, it is sufficient to note that if the author of the Fourth Gospel is to be identified with an otherwise known, named individual, then John son of Zebedee, John the Elder, and to a lesser extent John Mark are the most likely candidates. Chronologically, all three appear to have been active by 40 at the latest. John son of Zebedee and John the Elder are both remembered as followers of Jesus, and John Mark labored alongside both Peter and Paul in the 40s. Regarding the son of Zebedee and the Elder, there are

---

87. Cf. the classic discussion of this matter in Hengel, *Four Gospels*, 48–57.

88. Both John the Baptist and John son of Zebedee appear throughout the gospel tradition. John son of Zebedee also appears throughout the early chapters of Acts. John Mark appears in Acts 12–13 and 15. Cf. the discussion of John Mark in chap. 2 above. Revelation identifies its author as "John" in Rev. 1:1, 4, 9; 22:8.

89. According to Eusebius, *Hist. eccl.* 3.39.4.

90. Cf. the argument by Parker, "John and John Mark."

91. Cf. Acts 1:13; 3:1–4, 11; 4:1, 13, 19; 8:14, 17, 25; 12:2, all of which likely refer to John son of Zebedee; and Acts 12:12, 25; 13:13; 15:37, 39, which refer to John Mark.

92. Cf. the discussion in Bauckham, *Jesus and the Eyewitnesses*, 67–92.

indications that one or both lived until the reign of Trajan.[93] As we noted in the previous chapter, Eusebius reports that Annianus succeeded Mark the Evangelist as bishop of Alexandria in the eighth year of Nero (i.e., 62/63).[94] If Mark the Evangelist and John Mark are different persons, and if Eusebius has conflated them, and if John Mark in fact wrote John's Gospel, and if this reported succession indicates that John Mark died at this time, then this might indicate that John the Evangelist died at this point. One would hardly want to insist upon this as anything more than a possibility, and a fairly improbable one at that.

Cumulatively, what we know about these men can do little to narrow down the compositional date of the Fourth Gospel, and that is apart from considerations of pseudepigraphy. We simply do not know enough about the author's identity for external data regarding his identity to be of relevance.

Conclusion to John's Gospel: Authorial Biography

Insofar as it is the case that

- on the cumulative basis of synchronization and contextualization we can reasonably conclude that John's Gospel was written no later than 70; and
- we cannot identify the putative author with confidence because potential candidates could have been alive as late as Trajan's reign,

we conclude that John's Gospel was written no later than 70.

Cumulative Conclusion to Chapter 3: John's Gospel

Insofar as it is the case that

- Jesus's reference to the temple in John 4:21 is at least as intelligible before 70 as after;
- the narrator's description of the pool of Bethesda as a present reality in John 5:2 is more fully intelligible before 70 than after; and

93. Cf. Irenaeus, *Haer.* 2.22.5; 3.4.4.
94. Eusebius, *Hist. eccl.* 2.24.1.

· the Christology of John's Gospel is approximately as high as that articulated by Paul,

we conclude that John's Gospel was likely written no earlier than 60 and no later than 70.

This conclusion is based primarily upon three judgments. First, we have argued that John 5:2 supposes that the pool of Bethesda still stands. Since this pool was probably destroyed in 70, it is likely that John 5:2 was written before this time. The second judgment is that there is no material in the Gospel of John that is more intelligible after 70 than before. Thus we favor a date prior to 70. The third is that insofar as John's Gospel more explicitly acknowledges Jesus's divinity, we should be wary of dating it earlier than Paul's Letters.

Obviously, greater and stronger evidence would be preferable, but we must work with what we have. Therefore, of the four canonical Gospels, John's is the most likely to postdate 70. Nonetheless, the data more fully warrant a pre-70 date than a post-70 date, and that is the judgment reflected here.

We can thus summarize the likely compositional dates of the texts considered thus far in this study via the following table:

Text	Likely Date of Composition
Gospel of Mark	42–45
Gospel of Matthew	45–59
Gospel of Luke	59
Acts of the Apostles	62
Gospel of John	**60–70**

4

The Epistles of John and Revelation

Chapter 4 considers the compositional dates of the Epistles of John and Revelation.[1] It argues that 1, 2, and 3 John were likely written ca. 60–100, and Revelation ca. 68–70.

The Epistles of John

The Epistles of John offer little joy to the chronologist. There are virtually no chronological indicators in these three letters. In this section we need to settle for the general conclusion that 1, 2, and 3 John were written ca. 60–100. This position is close to when most scholars date the Johannine Epistles, although they might prefer a slightly higher range.

Synchronization

In this section, we will consider (1) external attestation and (2) the relationship of John's Letters to John's Gospel. We will conclude on the basis of synchronization that 1 John was written no later than 150, 2 John no later than 175, and 3 John no later than 225.

---

1. In developing this chapter, I found the following especially useful: Aune, *Revelation 1–5*; Aune, *Revelation 6–16*; Aune, *Revelation 17–22*; Boxall, *Revelation*; Brown, *Epistles of John*; W. Harrington, *Revelation*; Koester, *Revelation*; Moloney, *Apocalypse of John*; Painter, *1, 2, and 3 John*; Smalley, *1, 2, 3 John*; Strecker, *Johannine Letters*.

External Attestation

It is likely that Polycarp of Smyrna refers to 1 John and possibly also 2 John.[2] Since in his *Letter to the Philippians* (13.2), Polycarp asks for information about Ignatius's fate, and since Ignatius is usually thought to have died during Trajan's reign, Polycarp's *Letter to the Philippians* is typically dated sometime prior to 120. That being said, while 13.2 in this work most likely dates from around the time of Trajan, it has been argued that 1–12, the section of the letter wherein we find potential references to 1 and 2 John, was originally separate and dates to ca. 135–137.[3] Further, recent work has opened the possibility that Ignatius died later than Trajan's reign.[4] Nonetheless, given that Polycarp himself likely died sometime around 155, we should be wary of dating 1 John later than 150.

Irenaeus, writing in the last quarter of the second century, certainly knows 1 and 2 John.[5] This suggests that 2 John likely existed by ca. 175. For 3 John, we need to look to the third century for attestation. Eusebius tells us that Origen knew of two "further" epistles attributed to John (other than what is likely 1 John) and that they were extremely short.[6] This is almost certainly a reference to 2 and 3 John. As such, external attestation allows us to conclude that 1 John was written no later than 150, 2 John no later than 175, and 3 John no later than 225.

Relationship to the Gospel

The style and content of the Johannine Letters are sufficiently close to the Johannine Gospel that they are most likely related in some way. However, what is the nature of that relationship? The majority of scholars probably presume common authorship or at least a common "community." I admit that I have strong sympathies in this direction, although I would stridently argue that one cannot reconstruct the history of this community from the Gospel. Nonetheless, the existence of such a community is far from certain.[7] Moreover, whether the relationship between the Johannine Letters and the

2. Cf. Pol. *Phil.* 7.1 to 1 John 2:18, 22; 4:2–3; 2 John 7. Cf. the discussion in Holmes, "Polycarp's *Letter to the Philippians*," esp. 223–26.
3. Harrison, *Polycarp's Two Epistles*.
4. Cf. the overview of this work in Lookadoo, "Date and Authenticity."
5. Cf. Irenaeus, *Haer.* 1.16.3, citing 2 John 11. *Haer.* 3.16.5, citing 1 John 2:18–19, 21–22. *Haer.* 3.16.8, citing 2 John 7–8; 1 John 4:1–2; 5:1.
6. Eusebius, *Hist. eccl.* 6.25.10.
7. Cf. the classic critiques of gospel communities in Bauckham, *Gospels for All Christians*; the engagement with these critiques in Klink, *Audience of the Gospels*; and more recently, Méndez, "Did the Johannine Community Exist?"

Johannine Gospel results from common authorship, common community, or source relations, the exact chronological order of the respective texts remains opaque. There is a tendency to suppose that John's Gospel was written before 1, 2, and 3 John.[8] John Robinson's position is more complicated, arguing that the letters were written after a "first edition" of John's Gospel but before the final edition.[9] John Painter concludes that the letters were written either just before or just after the Gospel.[10] This perhaps best accounts for the similarities between the Gospel and the letters, as in this case they would all represent the state of Johannine tradition around the same time. Nonetheless, the relationship between the Gospel and letters is such that we should be wary of using it to establish dates of composition.

Conclusion to the Epistles of John: Synchronization

Insofar as it is the case that

- 1 John was written no later than 150, 2 John no later than 175, and 3 John no later than 225; and
- the relationship of the Johannine Letters to the Johannine Gospel resists confident resolution,

we conclude that 1 John was written no later than 150, 2 John no later than 175, and 3 John no later than 225.

Contextualization

In this section we will address (1) the ecclesiology supposed by 2 and 3 John and (2) the Christology of 1 and 2 John. We argue that the work of contextualization should incline us to date 1 and 2 John later than 60.

Ecclesiology

The Letters of 2 and 3 John are attributed to someone called the "Elder" who was engaged in a struggle with a person named Diotrephes.[11] It is tempting to

---

8. Brown, *Epistles of John*, 69–115; Bultmann, *Johannine Epistles*, 1; Smalley, *1, 2, 3 John*, xxxi.
9. Robinson, *Redating*, 307. Cf. the similar position in Anderson, *Fourth Gospel and the Quest*, 126.
10. Painter, *1, 2, and 3 John*, 74.
11. Cf. 2 John 1; 3 John 1, 9.

imagine that the Elder of 2 and 3 John (and perhaps also Diotrephes) occupied a position comparable to the monarchical bishop known from the Ignatian corpus.[12] It is tempting further to argue that 2 or 3 John originated roughly coeval with Ignatius. Yet there are several problems with such argumentation. First, there is a very concrete difference in the terminology used. Ignatius envisions a singular bishop (*episkopos*) and a collective group known as the "presbytery" (*presbyterion*).[13] By contrast, 2 and 3 John envision a single "presbyter" or "elder" (*presbyteros*), with neither bishop nor presbytery mentioned. It is possible that "the bishop" of the Ignatian *Letters* is equivalent to the Elder of 2 and 3 John; equally, it is possible that it is not. Further, it is not self-evident that "Elder" is even meant to reference an ecclesial role. It could, for instance, be a nickname indicating that the Elder is quite aged. Turning to the chronological implications, even if we could show that the Elder of 2 and 3 John is the functional equivalent to a bishop as known to Ignatius, we remain unclear regarding when such bishops first emerged. As a result, we should consider the ecclesiology of 2 and 3 John to be nonprobative for purposes of establishing an absolute date for these letters.

Christology

First and 2 John are greatly concerned with matters of Christology. Unfortunately, it is not clear when we should best situate these concerns. As with the Gospel of John, the Letters of John contain a Christology approximately as "high" as that of Paul's undisputed letters. And again, as with the Gospel of John, we should be wary of dating the letters much earlier than Paul's Letters. However, insofar as both 1 and 2 John on the one hand and Ignatius on the other are concerned with persons who in some fashion deny Jesus Christ's fleshly existence, it is not unreasonable to suspect that they are addressing the same doctrines.[14] Unfortunately, neither is this certain or even probable.[15] Indeed, Larry Hurtado presents two bodies of doctrines that with equal plausibility account for the data that we find in 1 and 2 John and yet are mutually exclusive.[16] Moreover, even if we could say that 1 and 2 John and

12. Ign. *Eph.* 1.3; 2.2; 4.1; Ign. *Magn.* 2.1; 15.1; Ign. *Trall.* 1.1.
13. Cf. Ign. *Eph.* 2.2.
14. Cf. 1 John 4:2–3a and 2 John 7 with Ign. *Smyrn.* 1.1–3.3 and Ign. *Trall.* 9.1–10.1.
15. Cf. the discussions in Brown, *Epistles of John*, 58–59; Hurtado, *Lord Jesus Christ*, 417; Schoedel, *Ignatius of Antioch*, 155.
16. Hurtado, *Lord Jesus Christ*, 419–23.

Ignatius are addressing the same body of doctrines, it is not self-evident that they would have to be doing so around the same time. Given that we should be wary of dating the Christology of 1 and 2 John prior to Paul's Letters, we should consider it probable that these letters date later than 60.

Conclusion to the Epistles of John: Contextualization

Insofar as it is the case that

- on the grounds of synchronization 1 John was written no later than 150, 2 John no later than 175, and 3 John no later than 225;
- the ecclesiology of 2 and 3 John does not permit us to narrow down possible dates; and
- the Christologies of 1 and 2 John are not likely earlier than Paul's Letters,

we conclude that 1 John was written ca. 60–150, 2 John ca. 60–175, and 3 John perhaps as late as 225.

Authorial Biography

As with the canonical Gospels, the Letters of John do not identify their author by name, yet there is no evidence that they ever circulated independent of their traditional attribution to someone named John. We have already surveyed authorial biography regarding the Gospel of John. Insofar as 2 and 3 John are attributed to the "Elder," John the Elder stands out as a preferable option for at least these letters. Most important for our present purposes is that the two most likely authors—John son of Zebedee and John the Elder—each permit a date prior to 70 and as late as Trajan's reign. Further, insofar as John son of Zebedee and John the Elder were apparently both followers of the earthly Jesus, it seems unlikely that they were active much past 100. As such, I find myself inclined to date these letters no later than 100.

This conclusion of course supposes that on the basis of traditional attribution we can reasonably conclude that either John son of Zebedee or John the Elder is the probable author. If this supposition is rejected, then 1 John was plausibly written as late as 150, 2 John as late as 175, and 3 John as late as 225.

Conclusion to the Epistles of John: Authorial Biography

Insofar as it is the case that

- on the cumulative grounds of synchronization and contextualization, 1 John was written no later than 150, 2 John no later than 175, and 3 John no later than 225; and
- the most probable candidates for authorship of 1, 2, and 3 John—John son of Zebedee and John the Elder—are unlikely to have been active much past 100,

we conclude that 1 and 2 John date ca. 60–100 and 3 John no later than 100.

Cumulative Conclusion to the Epistles of John

Insofar as it is the case that

- the data of attestation date 1 John as late as 135, 2 John as late as 175, and 3 John as late as 225;
- the relationship of the Johannine Letters to the Johannine Gospel resists confident resolution;
- the Christologies of 1 and 2 John are not likely earlier than Paul's Letters; and
- the most probable candidates for authorship of 1, 2, and 3 John are unlikely to have been active much past 100,

we conclude that 1 and 2 John date ca. 60–100, and 3 John no later than 100.

Revelation

The aim of this section is to establish the most probable dates for the book of Revelation. Although most scholars favor a date for Revelation in the 90s, this study concludes that Revelation was most likely written ca. 68–70.

Synchronization

In this section, we consider (1) external attestation, (2) the "king count" of Revelation 17:9–11, (3) the relationship of the text to Nero's reign, and

(4) the matter of 70. We conclude that, on the grounds of synchronization, Revelation was likely written no earlier than 68 and no later than 70.

External Attestation

Justin Martyr almost certainly knew of Revelation, as he writes in *Dialogue with Trypho* that a man "named John, one of Christ's Apostles, received a revelation and foretold that the followers of Christ would dwell in Jerusalem for a thousand years, and that afterwards the universal and, in short, everlasting resurrection and judgment would take place."[17] Here Justin names the author as John and identifies him as an apostle; describes the "revelation" using the word ἀποκάλυψις (*apokalypsis*), which is the Greek title for Revelation; and offers what reads as a précis of Revelation 20:4–6. Reference to Revelation is virtually certain. *Dialogue* itself was likely written sometime between 154 and 167.[18] Thus the data from *Dialogue* would in principle allow for Revelation to have been written perhaps as late as 160.

Andrew of Caesarea reports that Papias knew Revelation.[19] Eusebius fails to mention Papias's knowledge of Revelation and attributes this chiliasm not to Revelation but rather to material that we would be inclined to call apocrypha and agrapha.[20] Nonetheless, Eusebius's description of Papias's chiliasm would be consistent with a more literal interpretation of Revelation 20:4–6.[21] It cumulatively seems likely that Papias knew Revelation, and as such we should be wary of dating Revelation later than 120. Insofar as Papias's knowledge of Revelation is not certain, however, we cannot exclude a date as late as 160 on the basis of external attestation.

Counting Kings (Rev. 17:9–11)

In Revelation 17:9–11 we read the following.

The seven heads are seven mountains on which the woman is seated; also, they are seven kings, of whom five have fallen, one is living, and the other has not

17. Cf. Justin Martyr, *Dial.* 81.4, trans. Falls, *Saint Justin Martyr*, 278.
18. Cf. the discussion in Allert, *Revelation, Truth, Canon*, 32–34.
19. Andrew of Caesarea, *Commentary on Revelation*, prologue and 12.34 (enumerated as T27 and T28 in Carlson, *Papias of Hierapolis*).
20. Eusebius, *Eccl. Hist.* 3.39.10–11. Cf. the discussion of Andrew of Caesarea and Eusebius in Stevens, "Did Eusebius Read Papias?," esp. 168–69.
21. Eusebius, *Eccl. Hist.* 3.39.12.

yet come; and when he comes, he must remain only a little while. As for the beast that was and is not, it is an eighth but it belongs to the seven, and it goes to destruction.

The seven mountains here almost certainly refer to Rome.[22] This inclines us to expect that the seven kings are Roman emperors. Arguments for a pre-70 date for Revelation often insist that we should begin the count with Augustus and simply count forward. In that case, the sixth and living king was Galba, who reigned following Nero's death in June of 68 until his own death on January 15 in 69. Robinson strongly argues for this position.[23] Yet the "king count" is more complicated than this might suggest.[24] It is questionable, for instance, whether we should leave Julius out of the count because no less a figure than Suetonius treated him in his *Lives of the Caesars*. If we start with Julius, then Nero would be the sixth and current king. Objections have also been raised regarding the inclusion of Vitellius, Galba, and Otho, given their short reigns (although Suetonius includes them in *Lives*). If indeed the kings are meant to be Roman emperors, then probably the most we can say is that 17:9–11 was written sometime following the accession of the fifth "Caesar" (i.e., Nero) in 54.

The Neronian Non-error (Rev. 13)

The introduction to this volume addressed what we called the Domitianic error on the one hand and the Neronian on the other. By way of reminder, the Domitianic error tends to suppose that any unspecified reference to persecution should be situated toward the end of Domitian's reign, while the Neronian error—endemic to Robinson's *Redating the New Testament*—tends to suppose that any unspecified reference to persecution should be situated toward the end of Nero's reign. It is the position of this study that absent specific data that strongly incline us to prefer a situation either in Domitian's reign or in Nero's reign (or any other time), we should suppose that any unspecified reference to persecution can be situated anytime otherwise permissible for the book in question. In the case of Revelation, however, Robinson probably is right in seeing a connection with Nero.[25] In order to see why this is the case, we begin with Revelation 13:18.

22. For recent qualification (but not rejection) of this probability, cf. Moloney, *Apocalypse of John*, 263–70.
23. Robinson, *Redating*, 242–49.
24. For an especially helpful tabulation of the possible "counts," cf. Koester, *Revelation*, 72–73.
25. Cf. Robinson, *Redating*, 234–36.

This calls for wisdom: let anyone with understanding calculate the number of the beast, for it is the number of a person. Its number is six hundred sixty-six.

There is a general consensus that the "number of the beast" is a coded reference to Nero.[26] Not only would 666 constitute the sum of the letters in "Neron Caesar" when written in Hebrew, but also the variant "616," found in certain early manuscripts, constitutes the sum of the letters of the same name when written in Latin.[27] This renders tenuous any other identification. Hence we should probably consider it likely that Revelation was written after Nero's accession in 54.

Revelation 13 earlier suggests that the beast had been wounded but not really killed.[28] If indeed the beast is allegorically Nero, then this seems to make better sense after Nero's demise than before. Indeed, these verses should probably be read as a Christian articulation of the widespread rumors following Nero's death—namely, that he either was not dead or would be raised back to life.[29] This rumor continued for some time. Although Tacitus records that Achaia and Asia were specifically afflicted by rumors of Nero's return in 69, such rumors continued for at least another twenty years. Cumulatively, Revelation 13:1–18 was most likely composed sometime after the death of Nero in June of 68, but it could be consistent with dates into at least the late 80s and potentially into the 90s.

The Events of 70 (Rev. 11:1-13)

Once again, we confront the matter of 70. Revelation 11:1–13 contains the material most relevant for thinking about the matter. Here I reproduce the sections most relevant for our purposes.

Then I was given a measuring rod like a staff, and I was told, "Come and measure the temple of God and the altar and those who worship there, but do not measure the court outside the temple; leave that out, for it is given over to the nations, and they will trample over the holy city for forty-two months." (Rev. 11:1–2)

26. For a recent dissenting opinion, cf. Moloney, *Apocalypse of John*, 207–8.
27. Cf. the detailed discussion of the gematria involved in Bauckham, *Climax of Prophecy*, 387–94.
28. Rev. 13:3, 12.
29. Cf. Dio Cassius, *Hist. rom.* 66.19.3; Dio Chrysostom, *Pulchr.* 21.10; Suetonius, *Nero* 57; Tacitus, *Hist.* 2.8–9. Cf. once again the extensive discussion in Bauckham, *Climax of Prophecy*, 407–31.

At that moment there was a great earthquake, and a tenth of the city fell; seven thousand people were killed in the earthquake, and the rest were terrified and gave glory to the God of heaven. (Rev. 11:13)

Revelation 11:1–2 typically receives the greatest emphasis when discussing the question of compositional date. Given these verses by themselves, it is possible that the author is to measure the physical temple still standing at the time of composition. It is also possible that he is to measure some sort of heavenly or symbolic temple, a possibility that Robinson perhaps moves past too quickly.[30] The physical temple does, however, seem more likely, given the reference to an outer court that will be trampled by the gentiles. Nonetheless, the possibility that the temple is something symbolic or heavenly is sufficiently strong that we should be wary of relying too heavily on 11:1–2.

The matter is different when we turn to Revelation 11:13. There can be little doubt that the city of 11:13 is meant to be the earthly Jerusalem, since verse 8 identifies it as the city in which the Lord of the two witnesses was crucified. If 11:13 is meant to be a prophecy after the fact of 70, then the destruction of but a tenth of the city dramatically understates the actual fall of Jerusalem. Whereas Josephus (*J.W.* 7.1.1 §§1–4) tells us that the whole city was razed, only a tenth of the city fell according to Revelation 11:13. Further, the text is not accurate in attributing the destruction to an earthquake rather than to Roman soldiers. In part cognizant of these difficulties, the history of interpretation often seeks to interpret not only the city but also the temple and the two witnesses of Revelation 11 in more allegorical terms.[31] There is probably much truth to such interpretations. Nevertheless, such arguments are largely irrelevant for our current interest in establishing the most likely compositional date of Revelation. It is difficult to imagine that an author writing after 70 would employ the fall of Jerusalem for symbolic effect and yet grossly misrepresent the nature of that fall and, more to the point, underestimate its extent. As such, unless we can demonstrate the presence elsewhere in Revelation of material that likely derives from a post-70 context, the balance of probabilities should incline us toward a pre-70 date for the book.

30. Robinson, *Redating*, 239–40.
31. For recent such efforts, cf. Mangina, *Revelation*, 139–40; Moloney, *Apocalypse of John*, 154–61.

Conclusion to Revelation: Synchronization

Insofar as it is the case that

- external attestation permits a date for Revelation as late as 160, although we should be wary of dating it later than 120;
- the succession of kings in Revelation 17:9–11 is ambiguous for establishing when the text might have been written;
- Revelation 13:1–18 is more intelligible after the death of Nero than before; and
- Revelation 11:1–2 and to a greater extent 11:13 are significantly more intelligible before than after 70,

we conclude that Revelation was written no earlier than July of 68 and no later than 70.

Contextualization

In this section, we consider (1) Revelation's concern with food sacrificed to idols, (2) whether references to Rome as "Babylon" necessitate a post-70 composition, (3) Revelation's Christology, and (4) Revelation's ecclesiology. The primary contribution of contextualization is to demonstrate that the results in these four areas are consistent with, but do not necessitate, a date for Revelation ca. 68–70.

Food Sacrificed to Idols (Rev. 2:14, 20)

In Revelation 2:14, 20, the risen Christ has the following to say to the churches in Pergamum and Sardis, respectively:

> But I have a few things against you: you have some there who hold to the teaching of Balaam, who taught Balak to put a stumbling block before the people of Israel, so that they would eat food sacrificed to idols and practice fornication. (Rev. 2:14)

> But I have this against you: you tolerate that woman Jezebel, who calls herself a prophet and is teaching and beguiling my servants to practice fornication and to eat food sacrificed to idols. (Rev. 2:20)

Robinson addresses Revelation 2:14 and 2:20 concerning matters of immoral-
ity, but without explicit reference to food sacrificed to idols.[32] This nonetheless
requires some attention. On independent grounds, we have good reason to think
that it was primarily during the 40s through 60s that the Christian movement
was preoccupied with the extent to which believers, either gentile or Jewish,
should avoid eating food sacrificed to idols.[33] We cannot exclude the possibility
that such debates continued beyond the 60s. Nonetheless, the later one wants to
date Revelation after 100, the more 2:14 and 2:20 will look out of place. Admittedly, apocalyptic literature frequently sets its visions in a period much earlier
than the time of composition, and thus the concern about food sacrificed to
idols could stem from a later time. But insofar as concern with food sacrificed
to idols is quite consistent with what we know about the Christian movement
during the 40s through 60s, 2:14 and 2:20 tend to be more consistent with a date
toward the middle of the first century than one in the 90s or later.

Babylon (Rev. 14:6; 16:19; 17:4; 18:2, 10, 21)

Revelation refers several times to "Babylon."[34] Most commentators take it
as given that this is a metaphorical reference to Rome. It is generally recognized
that such usage is attested from the post-70 era.[35] Comparable attestation is
lacking for the pre-70 period. In and of itself, this could constitute an argument for a post-70 date. Such an argument, however, is from silence. As such,
the absence of independent evidence that "Babylon" could be used to refer to
Rome prior to 70 should be given less weight than the positive evidence that
Revelation was written before the destruction of Jerusalem. Revelation's use of
"Babylon" in reference to Rome should thus be considered an instance of such
usage prior to 70 rather than a reason to exclude a pre-70 date for the book.

Christology

Revelation has one of the "highest" Christologies within the New Testament.[36] Few texts as fully identify Jesus Christ with the God of Israel.

32. Cf. Robinson, *Redating*, 175n157, 227.
33. Cf. Acts 15:20, 29, which is set ca. 48; 1 Cor. 8:4–13.
34. Rev. 14:8; 16:19; 17:5; 18:2, 10, 21.
35. Among texts often cited as examples are 4 Ezra 3:1–2, 28–31; 2 Bar. 10:1–3; 11:1; 67:7;
Eusebius, *Hist. eccl.* 2.15.2, quoting Clement of Alexandria's lost *Hypotyposes*; Sib. Or. 5.143, 159.
36. Cf. the discussions in Bauckham, *Climax of Prophecy*, 118–49; Bauckham, *Jesus and the God of Israel*, 127–51, esp. 141–42; Hurtado, *Lord Jesus Christ*, 590–94.

Just as God is the Alpha and Omega, the beginning and the end, so too is Christic.[37] But even more incredible is Revelation 5:8–14, where the Lamb is worshiped in heaven. Hurtado describes such heavenly worship of Jesus as "completely unparalleled" and states, "In the religious values of the author, it would be difficult to imagine a more direct and forceful way to express Jesus' divine status."[38] Hurtado describes the early Christian decision not only to frame Jesus in such a fashion but also to worship him as a "mutation" in their Jewish heritage.[39] There is no reason, however, to think that the worship dimension of this "mutation" could not have already been operative as early as the "high" Christology that we find in Paul.[40] Moreover, there seems to be a certain "primitivity" to Revelation's Christology. Perhaps most notably, Christ is clearly cast as the Danielic Son of Man.[41] Such imagery brings us extremely close to the Synoptic presentation of Jesus, and arguably even to Jesus's own language for describing himself. Yet we must acknowledge that such "primitive" Christology in no way guarantees an earlier date for the text. Given what we know about the development of Jesus-belief, Revelation's Christology is conceivable from the 30s through to the second century. As such, the matter of Christology should be considered nonprobative for purposes of establishing the compositional date of Revelation.

Ecclesiology

Revelation contains a series of profound reflections upon the church life of its time, especially in the seven letters.[42] My primary interest here is in the ecclesiastical roles evident in the book. Revelation evinces clear awareness of only two roles within the early church: apostle and prophet.[43] The Seer seems to understand himself to be numbered among the prophets.[44] Twenty-four "elders" appear throughout the book. It is not clear, however, whether these

---

37. Cf. Rev. 1:8 and 21:6, where God claims such titles, to Rev. 1:17 and 22:13, where Christ claims the same. Cf. the discussion of these comparisons in Bauckham, *Jesus and the God of Israel*, 38–39.

38. Hurtado, *Lord Jesus Christ*, 592–93.

39. Hurtado, *One God, One Lord*, 97–130.

40. Cf. the discussion of the Christology of John's Gospel above.

41. Cf. esp. Rev. 1:12–16 and 14:14 with Dan. 7:13–14.

42. Cf. Rev. 2–3.

43. For apostles, cf. Rev. 2:2; 18:20; 21:14 (the last of these referring specifically to the Twelve). For prophets, cf. 2:20; 11:18; 16:6; 18:20.

44. Cf. Rev. 1:3; 10:11; 22:7, 9, 10, 18, 19.

elders correspond to any specific role within the earthly churches as known to the Seer. There is no hint of a monarchical bishop in the Christian communities, unless one understands the seven angels of the seven churches to represent such persons. This is of particular interest, given that the letters of Ignatius attest to the presence of bishops at Ephesus, Philadelphia, and Smyrna—to whom John the Seer also writes—in the early second century. Overall, Revelation supposes an ecclesiology closer to that depicted in Acts than what we see emerging in the second century. While this is certainly friendly to a lower date for Revelation, we should not suppose that ecclesiastical roles developed uniformly everywhere across the early Christian movement. Given this reality, the data of ecclesiology cannot be used to exclude a high or a middle date for Revelation.

Conclusion to Revelation: Contextualization

Insofar as it is the case that

- on the grounds of synchronization, we judge it likely that Revelation was written no earlier than 68 and no later than 70;
- Revelation's concern with food sacrificed to idols is consistent with what we know about the Christian movement during the 40s through 60s;
- references to Rome as "Babylon" are consistent with a post-70 date for Revelation but cannot exclude a pre-70 one;
- Revelation's Christology is intelligible as early as the 50s or 60s; and
- Revelation supposes an ecclesiology more consistent with the first century but not inconsistent with the second,

we conclude that Revelation was written no earlier than 68 and no later than 70.

Authorial Biography

We have already considered the difficulties endemic to identifying any of the Johannine authors with any particular first-generation Christians known by the name "John." John son of Zebedee and John the Elder are probably the best candidates for identification with John of Patmos, although John Mark cannot be excluded. Adjudicating between them, however, is difficult. Moreover, we cannot rule out the possibility that John of Patmos is in fact another, otherwise unknown person by the name of John, nor the possibility that the text is pseudonymous. Thus we can do little with his biography. We do, however, need to consider Irenaeus's famous testimony, which seeks to situate Revelation within Domitian's reign.

A mid-90s date for Revelation rests heavily upon a statement uttered by Irenaeus that tells us that the vision regarding the number of the beast (which he identifies explicitly as "666") came "recently," at the end of Domitian's reign.[45] George Edmundson, whose arguments Robinson elsewhere follows quite closely, argues that Irenaeus actually means to say that *John* was seen at the end of Domitian's reign, not the vision.[46] Robinson rightly rejects this reading, concluding that Irenaeus understood the visions of Revelation were seen near the end of Domitian's reign.[47]

It is wonderful when all relevant data converge without significant difficulty. One cannot always expect to be full of wonder, however, and indeed the internal and external data regarding Revelation present a less-than-wonderful case. All things being equal, it is reasonable to prefer those hypotheses better warranted by the internal data over those better warranted by the external data. The internal data relevant to the date of the Revelation are such that a date no earlier than 68 and no later than 70 is probable. Irenaeus's statement, however, rules out any date earlier than 81 (the beginning of Domitian's reign). In weighing the balance of probabilities, it seems most judicious to favor the internal data and thus a date earlier than 70.

45. Irenaeus, *Haer.* 5.30.3.
46. Edmundson, *Church in Rome*, 164–65.
47. Robinson, *Redating*, 221.

Conclusion to Revelation: Authorial Biography

Insofar as it is the case that

- on the cumulative grounds of synchronization and contextualization, we judge it likely that Revelation was written no earlier than 68 and no later than 70; and
- Irenaeus's late-second-century report that Revelation dates from the end of Domitian's reign does not suffice to overturn the internal data,

we should date Revelation no earlier than July of 68 and no later than 70.

Cumulative Conclusion to Revelation

Insofar as it is the case that

- Revelation 13:1–18 is more intelligible after the death of Nero than before;
- Revelation 11:1–2 and 11:13 are significantly more intelligible before than after 70;
- Revelation's concern with food sacrificed to idols is consistent with what we know about the Christian movement during the 40s through 60s; and
- Irenaeus's late-second-century report that Revelation dates from the end of Domitian's reign does not suffice to overturn the internal data,

we conclude that Revelation was written no earlier than July of 68 and no later than 70.

Cumulative Conclusion to Chapter 4:
The Epistles of John and Revelation

This chapter has concluded that 1 and 2 John were likely written between 60 and 100; 3 John prior to 100; and Revelation between 68 and 70. We can thus summarize the likely compositional dates of the texts considered thus far in this study via the following table:

Text	Likely Date of Composition
Gospel of Mark	42–45
Gospel of Matthew	45–59
Gospel of Luke	59
Gospel of John	60–70
1 and 2 John	**60–100**
Acts of the Apostles	62
Revelation	**68–70**
3 John	**before 100**

PART 3

The Pauline Corpus

5

Critical Matters in Dating the Pauline Corpus

Part 3 aims to ascertain the most probable dates of the thirteen letters that, among the New Testament Letters, are attributed to Paul.[1] The structure of part 3 differs significantly from that of parts 1 and 2. Chapter 5 considers several critical matters related to establishing the compositional dates of the Pauline corpus; chapter 6 undertakes the work of determining when this corpus was written. To be considered in the present chapter, then, are (1) the question of authenticity, (2) the broader question of method, and (3) the "indispensability of Acts" for purposes of Pauline chronology.

The Matter of Authenticity

Of the thirteen canonical Pauline Letters, scholars agree that Paul certainly contributed to Romans, 1 and 2 Corinthians, Galatians, Philippians, 1 Thessalonians, and Philemon. New Testament scholars are probably more or less evenly divided between those who affirm that Paul contributed to Ephesians, Colossians, and 2 Thessalonians. Probably only a minority affirm that he contributed to one or more of the so-called Pastoral Epistles (1 and 2 Timothy and

---

1. In developing this chapter, I found the following particularly useful: D. Campbell, *Framing Paul*; D. Campbell, "Anchor for Pauline Chronology"; D. Campbell, "Inscriptional Attestation"; Hemer, *Book of Acts*; Jewett, *Chronology of Paul's Life*; Knox, *Life of Paul*; Lüdemann, *Paul, Apostle*; Reicke, *Re-examining Paul's Letters*; Riesner, *Paul's Early Period*.

Titus). I do not engage in the work of demonstrating or refuting the authenticity of the canonical Pauline Letters. This study is already long enough without replicating such earlier work. Instead, I refer readers to relatively recent studies arguing in favor of the authenticity of various disputed works within the Pauline corpus.[2] I accept that Paul contributed to Ephesians, Colossians, and 2 Thessalonians, as I find the arguments against their authenticity to be particularly weak. I offer two possible dates or date ranges for the Pastoral Epistles: that which follows if they are authentic, and that which follows if they are not. This is done out of recognition that due to our inability to convincingly situate the Pastoral Epistles within Paul's career as can be reconstructed from Acts, these are the least likely to represent authentic Pauline writings.

The Matter of Method

Within the Pauline Letters is a general absence of data relevant for the work of synchronization. Since the data regarding attestation would, in the case of each letter, establish a date later than that of Paul's death, we will not in most cases consider matters of attestation. Although there are perennial questions regarding the relationship of the Pauline corpus to non-Pauline texts, I have found it best to restrict discussion of these relationships to the non-Pauline texts in question. So, for instance, although in this study I consider the relationship between the Pauline Letters and the Epistle of James, that discussion is in chapter 7 below, which deals with the date of James. Likewise, I have found it most expedient throughout this study to treat the Pauline Epistles as constituting our primary contextual data for the state of Christian development in the 50s and 60s, emphasizing the undisputed epistles over the disputed ones whenever I am discussing relevant contextual matters. Treating the Pauline Epistles as the fixed variable in discussions of textual relationships and Christian development allows me to minimize the number of moving parts that I need to coordinate at any given moment. Consequent to these considerations, we will not have sections dedicated to either synchronization or contextualization in our investigation of the respective Pauline Letters.

2. Asiedu, *Paul and His Letters*, 231–72; Bray, *Pastoral Epistles*, 7–15; D. Campbell, *Framing Paul*, 204–16, 247–53, 282–304, 309–34. D. Campbell accepts the authenticity of Ephesians (which he considers to be the letter to the Laodiceans mentioned in Col. 4:16), Colossians, and 2 Thessalonians, but not 1 and 2 Timothy or Titus.

Virtually everything that follows in this chapter, then, can be grouped under the broad rubric of "authorial biography." Paul is the only putative New Testament author to receive an extended biographical treatment within the New Testament itself. That treatment is found in the Acts of the Apostles. When approaching any given Pauline Letter, our first question will be to ask whether it can be situated within Paul's career as known from Acts, and if so, where. If it can be, and if there is no compelling reason to date the letter elsewhere in his career, we should favor the most probable date ascertainable from Acts. If it cannot be, then we must consider whether it can be situated within Paul's career as can be reconstructed apart from Acts.

The last time we hear of Paul in Acts, we learn that he spent two years under house arrest in Rome.[3] As we will see in chapter 6, these two years ran from early 60 through 62. As such, it is likely that Paul was still alive in mid-62. There is a venerable tradition that Paul was executed during Nero's reign.[4] Since Nero died in June 68, we can thus conclude that Paul likely died sometime from mid-62 through mid-68. Robert Jewett argues that Paul was executed sometime in spring 62 through August 64; Harry Tajra holds that he was executed ca. 63 or 64.[5] Regardless of our preferred judgment on the matter, the data are such that we should be wary of dating any letter written by Paul later than mid-68. Exactly what Paul was doing during those years is unclear. We will have occasion to treat his activities in greater depth when we come to the Pastoral Epistles.

In many ways the procedural decision to foreground Acts is out of step with current trends in Pauline chronology. Therefore, before considering any specific Pauline Epistle, an initial justification of what I call "the indispensability of Acts" is in order.

The Indispensability of Acts

Contemporary Pauline scholarship exhibits some tendency to relegate Acts to a secondary role in determining Pauline chronology. Among current scholars, this position is best represented by Douglas Campbell's recent effort to revive

3. Cf. Acts 28:30–31.
4. Most prominently reported by Eusebius in *Hist. eccl.* 2.25.5 and 3.1. Cf. the primary literature collected in Eastman, *Ancient Martyrdom Accounts*; also, the discussion of these texts in Eastman, *Deaths of Peter and Paul*; Tajra, *Martyrdom of St. Paul*.
5. Jewett, *Chronology of Paul's Life*, 45–46; Tajra, *Martyrdom of St. Paul*, 27–32.

and complete John Knox's project of developing a Pauline chronology from the epistles alone.[6] Knox most fully developed his project in his *Chapters in a Life of Paul*, which rightly has been described as one of the most important studies of Paul to appear in the twentieth century.[7] Campbell has most fully built upon Knox's work in his *Framing Paul*, which a hundred years from now will itself likely be recognized as one of the more important studies on Paul to appear in the twenty-first century.

Despite the undoubted significance of Campbell's work, in this section I contend that his effort to establish the dates of the Pauline Epistles without reference to Acts suffers insuperable conceptual and empirical difficulties.[8] Regarding the conceptual, Campbell writes, "The data concerning Paul in the book of Acts, the second principal reservoir for his life [after his letters], is something of an unknown quantity. We do not know who wrote Acts, when, where, or—perhaps most importantly—why. We do not know—and certainly not at first glance—what the relationship was between the author and Paul."[9] Granted. Absolutely, at first glance and before I engage in the actual work of knowing, I cannot know who wrote Acts where, when, or why. This is equally true of the Pauline Letters. At first glance, I do not know the relationship between the author(s) and Paul. This latter fact is especially dramatized by the distinction between Pauline and pseudo-Pauline letters. The reality that Paul did not write every letter attributed to him (think 3 Corinthians, apart from questions regarding the canonical letters) means that we must engage in considerable work beyond the first glance before we can use these texts to investigate Paul's life. Campbell seems to engage in some special pleading here: when he comes to the Lukan data, he makes much out of the uncertainty endemic to empirical investigation, but when he comes to the Pauline data, that same endemic uncertainty appears to trouble him little.

Of course, one must manage the uncertainty somehow, and Campbell is perfectly correct in seeking ways to do so. Indeed, the work of historiography could be defined precisely as the work of managing uncertainty about the past via the judicious construal of relevant data. With this reality in mind,

---

6. Cf. D. Campbell, *Framing Paul*, esp. 19–36; also D. Campbell, "Anchor for Pauline Chronology"; D. Campbell, "Inscriptional Attestation"; Knox, *Life of Paul*.

7. Hare, introduction to Knox, *Life of Paul*, ix–xxii.

8. Cf. my previous engagement with D. Campbell's chronological work in Bernier, "When Paul Met Sergius."

9. D. Campbell, *Framing Paul*, 20.

the great *Annales* historian Marc Bloch writes, "The narrative sources—to use a rather baroque but hallowed phrase—that is, the accounts which are consciously intended to inform their readers, still continue to provide valuable assistance to the scholar. Among their other advantages, they are ordinarily the only ones which furnish a chronological framework, however inconsistent. What would not the prehistorian or historian of India give to have a Herodotus at his disposal?"[10] Unable to escape this need for a narrative source, Campbell turns to Josephus, the Herodotus of the Second Temple era. Indeed, Josephan data are at least as foundational for Campbell's Pauline chronology as are Pauline data, for he anchors his chronology explicitly by way of inference from Pauline *and* Josephan data.[11] From this combination of data, for instance, he infers that Paul could have fled Damascus only in late 36 or early 37.[12] Campbell interprets Pauline data alongside data from non-Pauline sources, precisely what he refuses to do on programmatic grounds elsewhere. He is obligated to account for why it is licit to treat Josephan data as foundational within a chronology that aims to build exclusively upon the Pauline Letters, yet not licit to similarly introduce Lukan data. I have found no such account in his work.

This negative critique does not, however, build a positive argument for the indispensability of Acts in the work of Pauline chronology. To such an argument we must now turn.

The Lukan Prologue (Luke 1:1–4)

Luke-Acts helpfully informs us about the author's intention in writing. The relevant text is Luke 1:1–4:

> Since many have undertaken to set down an orderly account of the events that have been fulfilled among us, just as they were handed on to us by those who from the beginning were eyewitnesses and servants of the word, I too decided, after investigating everything carefully from the very first, to write an orderly account for you, most excellent Theophilus, so that you may know the truth concerning the things about which you have been instructed.

10. Bloch, *Historian's Craft*, 61.
11. Most specifically, 2 Cor. 11:32–33 and Josephus, *Ant.* 18.109–25.
12. D. Campbell, *Framing Paul*, 30, 182–89; D. Campbell, "Anchor for Pauline Chronology." Cf. the comparable arguments in Bowersock, *Roman Arabia*, 65–69; Jewett, *Chronology of Paul's Life*, 30–33. Cf. the responses to D. Campbell in Bernier, "When Paul Met Sergius"; and in Bunine, "Visite de Paul à Jérusalem."

Luke tells us that, like other writers (modern scholars tend to suppose at least those of Mark's Gospel and of either Q or Matthew), he has set out to write an account of the things that have been fulfilled among the Christians. The fulfillment of scriptural prophecy is a major theme throughout Luke-Acts. It is likely also in view here. Luke understands it to be the case that in the life of Jesus and the emergence of the early church, the God of Israel has been fulfilling promises once made. Thus one might advance the hypothesis that Luke's theology guided his historiography to such an extent that his conception of God and God's role in history displaced any interest in factuality. This is a perfectly legitimate hypothesis, but like any hypothesis, it must be checked against the data before it can be affirmed.

Unfortunately, such a hypothesis requires us to suppose that Luke operated exactly in opposition to how he claims to have operated. Such a supposition is not necessarily fatal to this hypothesis, but it is certainly less than friendly. Luke tells us that in his investigation he went back to the "the very first" (*anōthen*); has been distinctly thorough, investigating everything (*pasin*); and has proceeded with significant care (*akribōs*) in his investigation, in his compositional practice, or both. As such, he is able to write an orderly (*kathexēs*) account; Luke can thus offer Theophilus certainty (*asphaleian*) about that which Theophilus was taught (*katēchēthēs*). It has been shown that such claims are characteristic of specific genres.[13] Yet it does not follow from this that the claims are empty. Rhetoric is not identical with truth, but neither is it mutually exclusive thereof. Absent compelling evidence to the contrary, the words of the Lukan prologue provide initial support for the premise that Luke was interested in factuality.

The We-Passages

An initial but tentative confirmation that Luke was both concerned with historical factuality and sufficiently knowledgeable as to generally achieve it in the writing of Acts comes from the famous we-passages.[14] We have already considered these passages at length in chapter 2. As we argued there, it is likely that Luke had access to an eyewitness source for these passages, or more likely that he himself was present for the events therein described. Either case would

13. Cf. the discussions in Alexander, *Preface to Luke's Gospel*; Bauckham, *Jesus and the Eyewitnesses*, 116–24.
14. Acts 16:10–17; 20:5–15; 21:1–18; 27:1–28:16.

support the conclusion that Luke was plausibly knowledgeable regarding at least some of what he wrote about. More to the point for our present purposes, they strengthen the conclusion that Luke was most plausibly knowledgeable precisely when it comes to Pauline biography.

Narrative Sequence as Data

In this section, we consider the extent to which the relative order of the Acts narrative (the narrative sequence) corresponds to the relative order in which the narrated events are known on independent grounds to have occurred (the historical sequence).[15] Douglas Campbell argues that such a correspondence is a nonstarter. His Luke is altogether willing to place events out of temporal sequence.[16] As far as hypotheses go, this is one worth testing. Such testing must take place in two steps. First step: identify events that are narrated within the narrative sequence of Acts and that can also be dated independent of Lukan data. Second step: compare the order in which they appear in the narrative sequence of Acts to the order in which they appear in the historical sequence. To the extent that these sequences correlate, we are justified in stating that Luke evinces an interest in presenting events in their proper historical sequence.

There are four independently datable events that meet our criteria as specified in the first step above: the crucifixion (Acts 1:3), the death of Herod Agrippa (12:23), the governorship of Gallio in Corinth (18:12–17), and the succession from Felix to Festus as governor of Judea (24:27). As noted in the introduction, Jesus was crucified no earlier than 29 and no later than 34.[17] Any date within this range would place the crucifixion earlier than the next reported, datable event. Of this event, Josephus reports that Agrippa reigned three years as king under the emperor Claudius, and because Claudius began to reign in 41, Agrippa must have died in 44.[18] From the well-known Delphi Inscription, we can infer that Gallio was likely governor of Corinth from July 1, 51, through June 30, 52.[19] Although the exact date of the succession from Felix to Festus has been disputed, it

---

15. For an earlier discussion of this matter, cf. Bernier, "When Paul Met Sergius," 837–42.

16. Cf. D. Campbell, *Framing Paul*, 20–26; D. Campbell, "Inscriptional Attestation," 21.

17. Cf. Bond, "Dating the Death of Jesus"; Pitre, *Jesus and the Last Supper*, 251–73.

18. Cf. Josephus, *Ant.* 19.8.2 §351; Josephus, *J.W.* 2.11.6 §219.

19. Cf. the fuller discussion of the inscription and its significance for Pauline chronology in chap. 6 below.

certainly postdates Gallio's term as governor in Corinth; 59 is probably the strongest candidate.[20]

Before proceeding to the second step enumerated above, two notes are in order. First, in earlier published work I treated the tenures of Felix and Festus as two distinct events or situations.[21] This was wholly warranted, as Acts correctly identifies that Felix preceded Festus. I have here decided to treat their succession as a singular event. This has the potential effect of blunting the strength of my argument. I decided, however, that this is preferable to being accused of overemphasizing the significance of the Felix and Festus connection. The second caveat has to do with the expulsion of Jewish persons from Rome under Claudius, mentioned in Acts 18:2. From the extra-Lukan data, I am persuaded that this occurred in 49.[22] Given the admitted chronological uncertainties surrounding this event, however, I have omitted it from the list of confidently datable events.

We can now move to the second step, in which we compare the order that these events are reported in the narrative sequence (in Acts) with the order that they occurred in the historical sequence. This comparison is summarized in the following table:

Event	Location in Narrative Sequence (in Acts)	Location in Historical Sequence (Independent Date)
Crucifixion of Jesus	1:3	ca. 29–34
Death of Herod Agrippa	12:23–24	44
Gallio's tenure in Corinth	18:12–17	mid-51–mid-52
The succession from Felix to Festus	24:27	59

These comparisons demonstrate a clear correlation between the narrative sequence of Acts and the historical sequence as we can most confidentially recover it on independent grounds. They suffice to demonstrate that Luke in Acts betrays at least some interest in and success at ensuring that events within his narrative are properly situated in time.

20. Cf. the discussion in Jewett, *Chronology of Paul's Life*, 40–44; Riesner, *Paul's Early Period*, 219–24.

21. Bernier, "When Paul Met Sergius," 837–42.

22. On the date of the expulsion, with a specific focus on Pauline chronology, see Jewett, *Chronology of Paul's Life*, 36–38; Lüdemann, *Paul, Apostle*, 164–71; Riesner, *Paul's Early Period*, 157–204.

This is borne out further by Acts 11:19–20, which refers to events narrated in 8:1. Although Acts 11:19–20 is placed just prior to events occurring in the early 40s, it refers to events that likely occurred some years earlier. Yet we know this precisely because Acts explicitly tells us that he is resuming that earlier narrative. We know that here Acts is narrating events that took place up to a decade or so prior to the time upon which the narrative is currently focused, but we only know this because Luke references those earlier events. The very fact that Acts evinces a concern to let us know when the narrative sequence diverges from the historical sequence demonstrates again that Luke was interested in achieving a high degree of correspondence between the two sequences.

The only instance in which we have strong reason to at least suspect that Acts places independently and confidently datable events out of historical sequence and without signaling that this is the case is Acts 5:36–37. In that text, Gamaliel I dates Theudas's revolt before that of Judas, whereas Josephus tells us that Judas's revolt predated Theudas's by approximately forty years.[23] Since this report lies outside the book's narrative sequence proper, it does not speak to the relationship between narrative and historical sequence in Acts. This, however, represents more the triumph of definitions than the fruits of careful investigation. It is instructive rather to expand our view to consider the entirety of Luke-Acts. Doing so, we find that Luke 2:2 situates the Nativity during a census carried out when Quirinius was governing Syria. Since Luke 1:5 seems to indicate that Jesus was at least conceived if not born during Herod the Great's reign, on his data the census cannot reasonably be thought to date much later than Herod's death in 4 BCE. However, Josephus reports that Quirinius became governor of Syria only in 6 CE.[24] A pattern begins to emerge. When Luke is interested in narrating events that involve either the Jerusalem disciples and church (e.g., the crucifixion and the Agrippan persecution) or Paul (e.g., the meetings with Gallio, Felix, and Festus), he does not vary from the historical sequence as can be reconstructed on the basis of independent data. By contrast, when he is concerned to narrate events that either predate or do not directly involve such figures, there is greater reason to suspect chronological error. This is of great significance for the present study. For our purposes, Acts is most crucial precisely regarding

23. Josephus, *Ant.* 18.1.1 §§1–10; 20.5.1 §§97–99; Josephus, *J.W.* 2.8.1 §118; 2.17.8 §433; 7.8.1 §253.
24. Cf. Josephus, *Ant.* 18.2.1 §26.

the authorial biography of Paul, and the available data suggest that Luke is generally knowledgeable regarding the chronological sequence of Paul's life.

Narrative Episodes as Data

Given the focus of this study, questions about the relevance of chronological sequence are generally of greater significance for our investigation than questions about the relevance of individual narrative episodes. Nonetheless, insofar as these episodes describe Paul's activities and indeed the early Christian movement more generally, we cannot avoid questions about their relevance. Nonetheless, the relatively circumscribed nature of our investigation allows us to restrict the discussion of such questions about relevance to a manageable range.

All things being equal, we can expect that Luke is generally of greatest historiographical relevance on the matters in which he was a personal participant. Insofar as he was probably a personal participant in the we-passages, we can expect that these passages will be especially relevant for the work of historical reconstruction. This statement is made with full recognition of relatively recent discussions among New Testament scholars regarding the reliability of eyewitness testimony.[25] It goes without saying that eyewitness reports are not verbatim transcripts of what was said or done. No less than any other piece of writing, eyewitness reports are subject to the vicissitudes of memory, the demands of polemic, and the crafting of narrative. Nonetheless, given Luke's intention to include factuality, he is less likely to make egregious errors when reporting something in which he participated than when reporting something in which he had no part.

Of perhaps less but still significant historiographical relevance are those passages wherein Luke reports matters for which we can identify his informants. Again, insofar as Luke was a personal participant in the we-passages, we can identify Paul as a primary informant for the balance of the material regarding the latter's life and ministry. If the we-passages indicate that Luke was indeed a companion of Paul, then he demonstrably worked alongside a person who knew Peter, James, and John.[26] Luke would have also been in

---

25. Cf. the various discussions in Bauckham, *Jesus and the Eyewitnesses*, 319–57; Crook, "Collective Memory Distortion"; Le Donne, "Selectivity in Memory Research"; Redman, "How Accurate Are Eyewitnesses?"

26. Gal. 1:18; 2:9; cf. also Acts 15.

direct contact with James.[27] Moreover, given that the we-passages continue to the end of Acts, combined with the data that put Paul and Peter together in Rome at the end of their lives, we can consider the possibility (although no more than the possibility) that Luke and Peter met sometime during those final years. Nonetheless, it seems quite probable that Luke at least knew people who knew Peter.

Yet our knowledge about what happened in the past is limited. Our capacity to state that a given event occurred is restricted by the empirical data available to us. Such restriction tends to increase as we attempt to describe any given event in detail. Such is the reality of historiography, and perhaps especially ancient historiography. Nonetheless, there is reason to believe that Luke was concerned with and had access to the resources needed to achieve a significant degree of factuality; thus we are justified in concluding that the narrative episodes in Acts provide significant insight into the actual events of the first Christian decades. Such reason is particularly strong when it comes to Paul and to a lesser extent when it comes to James and Peter. This is stated with recognition that some degree of abstraction is typically necessary. For instance, it is probably impossible to verify whether Peter spoke to a slave girl named Rhoda after fleeing prison around Passover in 41, but we are justified in judging it probable, on the basis of Acts 12, that at that time Herod Agrippa was pursuing an anti-Christian policy that resulted in the death of one or more Christian leaders. For most of what we are doing in this monograph, such a degree of abstraction is generally adequate.

With that all having been said, let us turn to the work of establishing the dates of the Pauline correspondence.

27. Acts 21:18.

6

The Compositional Dates
of the Pauline Corpus

Chapter 6 aims to establish the compositional dates of the Pauline corpus.[1] This chapter concludes that Galatians was written sometime from 47 through 52; 1 and 2 Thessalonians sometime from 50 through 52; 1 Corinthians in early 56; 2 Corinthians in late 56; Romans in the winter of 56/57; Ephesians, Colossians, Philemon, and Philippians in 57 to 59; 1 Timothy in 63 or 64 if Pauline, no earlier than 60 and no later than 135 if pseudo-Pauline; Titus in 63 or 64 if Pauline, no earlier than 60 and no later than 175 if pseudo-Pauline; and 2 Timothy sometime in 64 through 68 if Pauline, no earlier than 60 and no later than 135 if pseudo-Pauline. These dates are close to the majority

1. In developing this chapter, I found the following particularly useful: Barrett, *First Epistle to the Corinthians*; Barrett, *Romans*; Barrett, *Second Epistle to the Corinthians*; Barth, *Ephesians*; Barth and Blanke, *Colossians*; Best, *Ephesians*; Best, *Epistles to the Thessalonians*; Betz, *Galatians*; Bockmuehl, *Philippians*; Bray, *Pastoral Epistles*; D. Campbell, *Framing Paul*; D. Campbell, "Anchor for Pauline Chronology"; D. Campbell, "Inscriptional Attestation"; Conzelmann, *1 Corinthians*; Cranfield, *Romans*; Dibelius and Conzelmann, *Pastoral Epistles*; Dunn, *Galatians*; Fitzmyer, *First Corinthians*; Fitzmyer, *Philemon*; Fitzmyer, *Romans*; P. Foster, *Colossians*; Furnish, *II Corinthians*; Hemer, *Book of Acts*; Jewett, *Chronology of Paul's Life*; Jewett, *Romans*; Johnson, *Letters to Timothy*; Keener, *Galatians*; Knox, *Life of Paul*; Lambrecht, *Second Corinthians*; Lohse, *Colossians and Philemon*; Lüdemann, *Paul, Apostle*; Malherbe, *Letters to the Thessalonians*; Marshall, *Pastoral Epistles*; Martin, *2 Corinthians*; Martyn, *Galatians*; Muddiman, *Letter to the Ephesians*; Reicke, *Re-examining Paul's Letters*; Reumann, *Philippians*; Riesner, *Paul's Early Period*; Thrall, *Second Epistle to the Corinthians*.

position with regard to the undisputed Pauline Epistles (Romans, 1 and 2 Corinthians, Galatians, Philippians, 1 Thessalonians, and Philemon) and close to the dates affirmed by about half of working New Testament scholars regarding Ephesians, Colossians, and 2 Thessalonians. While only a minority of scholars affirm that 1 and 2 Timothy and Titus are Pauline texts, a majority probably consider these to be earlier compositions than the latest allowed on a hypothesis of pseudo-Pauline authorship.

Regarding the treatment of secondary literature, John Robinson and I are in general agreement in regard to the compositional dates of Romans, 1 and 2 Corinthians, Ephesians, Philippians, Colossians, 1 and 2 Thessalonians, and Philemon. Thus I engage relatively little with his argumentation regarding these letters. We significantly disagree with regard to Galatians, 1 and 2 Timothy, and Titus. Therefore I will engage more heavily with Robinson's argumentation regarding these letters.

1 and 2 Thessalonians

In this section, we consider the compositional dates of 1 and 2 Thessalonians. There are two primary matters of concern: the correlation of 1 and 2 Thessalonians with Acts and the date of the Corinthian sojourn. On the basis of these considerations, we argue that 1 and 2 Thessalonians were most likely written no earlier than 50 and no later than 52.

Correlation with Acts

Although Paul wrote several letters with Timothy (2 Corinthians, Colossians, Philippians, and Philemon), 1 and 2 Thessalonians are the only letters attributed not only to Paul and Timothy but also to Silas. From this common attribution, we can reasonably infer at least two things: (1) prior to the composition of 1 and 2 Thessalonians, there was a preexisting relationship between the Thessalonian Christians on the one hand and Silas and Timothy on the other; (2) 1 and 2 Thessalonians were written at a time when Paul, Timothy, and Silas were working closely together. Both conditions are met in Acts 16–18. Paul, Silas, and Timothy set out together on a missionary journey (cf. 15:40–16:2); traveled together to Thessalonica (cf. 17:1); traveled together to Berea, about 70 km away (cf. 17:10); and separated in Berea (cf. 17:14), with Paul traveling to Athens (cf. 17:15). From there, Paul sent word for Timothy and Silas to join him (17:15). The three were reunited not in Athens, however, but rather in Corinth, with Silas and Timothy arriving from Macedonia (18:5; cf. 1 Thess. 3:6, wherein Paul tells the Thessalonians that Timothy has just rejoined him after visiting Thessalonica, a major Macedonian center).

The reference to a recent reunion situates 1 Thessalonians most probably within the so-called Corinthian sojourn, and one suspects earlier rather than later therein. The absence of a reference to such a reunion in 2 Thessalonians opens the possibility that they wrote this letter before separating in Berea. This, however, does not seem likely. In 2 Thessalonians 1:4 Paul writes, "Therefore we ourselves boast of you among the churches of God for your steadfastness and faith during all your persecutions and the afflictions that you are enduring." The plural "among the churches of God" (*en tais ekklēsiais tou theou*) indicates the authors have been boasting of the Thessalonians at multiple churches, suggesting they have traveled beyond just Berea. This shifts probability away from Berea and toward Corinth. It is thus best to situate 2 Thessalonians during the Corinthian sojourn, along with 1 Thessalonians.

Date of the Corinthian Sojourn

According to Acts 18:11, Paul was in Corinth for at least eighteen months. During this time, he appeared before the governor, Gallio.[2] Efforts to date the Corinthian sojourn thus typically and rightly begin with the Delphi Inscription, from which we infer that Gallio's governorship lasted from July 1, 51, to June 30, 52.[3] If the meeting with Gallio occurred within these eighteen months, the sojourn probably began between January 1, 50, and June 30, 52, and ended between July 1, 51, and December 31, 53. Acts 18:18, however, states that Paul stayed in Corinth for "a considerable time," which could refer either to the eighteen months or to time spent in the city after the end thereof. As such, we should allow for the possibility that Paul at this time remained in Corinth for upward of two years. Cumulatively, we should best conclude that within the period extending from mid-49 through mid-54, Paul spent a consecutive stretch of time in Corinth equaling eighteen months to two years.

2. Acts 18:12–17.
3. Cf. the discussions in Jewett, *Chronology of Paul's Life*, 38–40; Lüdemann, *Paul, Apostle*, 163–64; Riesner, *Paul's Early Period*, 202–8.

We can narrow down the likely time of Paul's sojourn, however. Acts 18:2 says Priscilla and Aquila arrived in Corinth not long before Paul, having come recently from Italy after being expelled by Claudius. Although not incontestable, there is good reason to think that this expulsion occurred in 49.[4] Thus we can infer that Priscilla and Aquila arrived in Corinth sometime in 49 or perhaps early 50. This provides warrant to conclude that the Corinthian sojourn began closer to mid-49 than to mid-54, although 49 is perhaps a bit too early given Paul's activities after the Jerusalem Council in 48.[5] I am inclined to date Paul's arrival in Corinth to 50 and his departure to 52. Therefore I date both 1 and 2 Thessalonians to 50 through 52.

But was 2 Thessalonians written before or after 1 Thessalonians? The hypothesis that 2 Thessalonians was written after 1 Thessalonians seems to make the best sense of the data. First Thessalonians makes much of the fact that Timothy has just come from Thessalonica. If 2 Thessalonians was written during the Corinthian sojourn but prior to 1 Thessalonians, then it seems strange that Paul would not have mentioned Timothy's recent visit in 2 Thessalonians. Although I will not alter the suggested date range for these letters on this basis, it still seems best to conclude that 2 Thessalonians was written after 1 Thessalonians.

Conclusion to 1 and 2 Thessalonians

Insofar as it is the case that

- 1 and 2 Thessalonians most likely were written during Paul's Corinthian sojourn; and
- the Corinthian sojourn most likely dates to 50 through to 52,

we conclude that 1 and 2 Thessalonians were written no earlier than 50 and no later than 52.

Including absolute dates relevant for our purposes as discussed and established in this chapter, our cumulative chronological framework can be summarized in the following table (with dates of composition shown in bold):

---

4. Once again, cf. the discussions in Jewett, *Chronology of Paul's Life*, 36–38; Lüdemann, *Paul, Apostle*, 164–71; Riesner, *Paul's Early Period*, 157–204.

5. Contra Robinson, who wants to date the beginning of the Corinthian sojourn to autumn of 49; cf. Robinson, *Redating*, 35. On Paul's activities following the council and before arriving in Corinth, i.e., in the so-called second missionary journey, cf. Acts 15:30–18:1.

Event	Date
Crucifixion of Jesus	ca. 29–34
Death of Herod Agrippa	44
Paul's Corinthian sojourn	50–52
1 Thessalonians	**50–52**
2 Thessalonians	**50–52**
Gallio's tenure in Corinth	mid-51–mid-52
The succession from Felix to Festus	59

1 Corinthians

In this section, we consider the compositional date of 1 Corinthians. We deal with two primary matters of concern: (1) the correlation of 1 Corinthians with Acts and (2) the date of the Ephesian sojourn. On the basis of these considerations, we argue that 1 Corinthians was written in early 56.

Correlation with Acts

First Corinthians 16:5–8 indicates that Paul wrote this letter from Ephesus and that he anticipated soon traveling to Macedonia. Almost certainly this corresponds with the Ephesian sojourn, after which he did indeed go to Macedonia.[6] Given that Paul anticipates soon traveling to Macedonia, it seems likely that he wrote this text closer to the end of the Ephesian sojourn than the beginning. As such, we should seek to establish the date of the Ephesian sojourn, which requires us to consider Paul's movements from the end of the Corinthian sojourn.

Date of the Ephesian Sojourn

After leaving Corinth, Paul traveled to Ephesus with Priscilla and Aquila, then on to Caesarea and (probably) Jerusalem.[7] If Paul indeed set out from Corinth in 52, as argued above, we might reasonably infer that these travels took up the balance of that year. He is then said to have spent some time in Antioch,[8]

6. Acts 19:1–20:1.
7. Acts 18:18–22a.
8. Acts 18:22b.

which we might reasonably identify with the winter of 52/53. After this he is said to have returned to Ephesus by way of Galatia, Phrygia, and the "interior regions" back to Ephesus.[9] These travels probably took up much of 53. It thus seems probable that the Ephesian sojourn began in late 53 or perhaps early 54. The Ephesian sojourn extended at least twenty-seven months, perhaps as long as three years.[10] Thus we can suggest that whether Paul arrived in late 53 or early 54, the sojourn most likely ended in 56. It could not have ended much later than this, given Paul's subsequent travels.[11] Thus I date 1 Corinthians to 56. Given that Paul indicates he intends to stay in Ephesus until Passover (1 Cor. 16:8), we can deduce that he was writing this letter in early 56.

Conclusion to 1 Corinthians

Insofar as it is the case that

- 1 Corinthians most likely was written near the end of Paul's Ephesian sojourn; and
- the Ephesian sojourn likely dates to 54 through 56, and 1 Corinthians 16:8 suggests that Paul was writing early in the year,

we conclude that 1 Corinthians was written in early 56.

Including absolute dates relevant for our purposes as discussed and established in this chapter, our cumulative chronological framework can be summarized in the following table (with dates of composition shown in bold):

Event	Date
Crucifixion of Jesus	ca. 29–34
Death of Herod Agrippa	44
Paul's Corinthian sojourn	50–52
1 Thessalonians	**50–52**
2 Thessalonians	**50–52**
Gallio's tenure in Corinth	mid-51–mid-52
Paul's probable visit to Jerusalem of Acts 18	late 52
Paul's Ephesian sojourn	54–56

9. Acts 18:23b; 19:1.
10. Acts 19:8, 10, 22; 20:31.
11. Cf. the relevant discussions below.

Event	Date
1 Corinthians	early 56
The succession from Felix to Festus	59

2 Corinthians

In this section, we consider the compositional date of 2 Corinthians. We deal with three matters of concern: (1) Paul's flight from Damascus, (2) the correlation of 2 Corinthians with Acts, and (3) the integrity of 2 Corinthians. On the basis of these considerations, we argue that 2 Corinthians most likely was written in late 56.

The Flight from Damascus (2 Cor. 11:32)

In 2 Corinthians 11:32 Paul tells us, "In Damascus, the governor under King Aretas guarded the city of Damascus in order to seize me." The Aretas in question is almost certainly Aretas IV of the Nabateans.[12] Since Aretas IV began to reign ca. 9/8 BCE, likely before Paul was born, this information does little to narrow the range of earliest possible dates for the letter. Conversely, the letter need not have been written after the end of Aretas's reign, ca. 39 or 40, since Paul could potentially be writing while the king yet ruled.[13] Overall, the flight from Damascus referenced in 2 Corinthians 11:32 is important for larger questions about Pauline biography but is nonprobative for establishing the compositional date of 2 Corinthians.

Correlation with Acts

Paul appears to have written 2 Corinthians either during or following a recent journey to Macedonia, at a time when he was contemplating a trip to Judea by way of Corinth (cf. 2 Cor. 1:16; 2:13). This correlates well with his movements as reported in Acts 20–21. Having departed Ephesus in most likely 56, he traveled to Macedonia.[14] He then came to Greece, from which

12. Cf. the classic discussion of Aretas IV in Bowersock, *Roman Arabia*, 51–69.
13. On the final year of Aretas IV's reign, cf. Riesner, *Paul's Early Period*, 76–77.
14. Cf. Acts 20:1–2a.

he departed for Syria and ultimately Palestine.[15] Since at the time of writing, Paul had apparently not yet visited Corinth nor continued on to Palestine, we should situate the provenance in the latter half of 56, either from Macedonia or from somewhere in Greece rather than Corinth.

The Integrity of 2 Corinthians

There is a strong tradition of seeing our 2 Corinthians as the conflation of several Pauline letters.[16] Scholars working within this tradition most frequently argue that 2 Corinthians 1–9 represents one letter, and 10–13 another.[17] Second Corinthians 12:18 is probably the strongest evidence for such a division, as it could easily be reflecting upon the visit by Titus, which Paul mentions as forthcoming in 8:16–23. Yet there are concrete differences between the visits, most notably that three delegates are mentioned in 8:16–23 (cf. vv. 18, 22) whereas only two are mentioned in 12:18.[18] Indeed, given that only Titus is mentioned by name in reference to both visits, we cannot be certain that either of the fellow delegates mentioned in 2 Corinthians 8:16–23 are to be identified with the delegate of 12:18. Moreover, Paul refers to another trip undertaken by Titus in 2 Corinthians 8:6. This trip might be the one mentioned in 2 Corinthians 12:18.[19] Alternatively, it could refer to an otherwise unattested trip undertaken by Titus. Thus it is not self-evident that Paul is referring to the same visit in these two passages.

Even if 2 Corinthians 12:18 refers to the same visit as 8:16–23, 2 Corinthians 1–9 and 10–13 were still written closely together. According to 12:20, Paul still intended to come to Corinth. We know of only one more Pauline visit to Corinth after late 56, the one in the winter of 56/57, during which he likely wrote Romans.[20] We have no evidence of even an intended visit later in his career. It is possible that while in prison in Caesarea he intended to visit Corinth on the way to Rome; indeed, I argue that he intended to visit Colossae on this westward journey. Likewise, it is possible that he intended

---

15. Cf. Acts 20:2b–21:17 and the discussion below.

16. Cf. D. Campbell's recent, comprehensive, and highly insightful treatment of the integrity of 2 Corinthians in relation specifically to Pauline chronology (*Framing Paul*, 98–121).

17. Cf. Barrett, *Second Epistle to the Corinthians*, 9–10; Furnish, *II Corinthians*, 36–41.

18. As noted in D. Campbell, *Framing Paul*, 119; Thrall, *Second Epistle to the Corinthians*, 2:854–55.

19. As argued by Martin, *2 Corinthians*, 643–44; Thrall, *Second Epistle to the Corinthians*, 2:854–55.

20. Cf. the discussion below.

to visit Corinth during his hypothetical post-Acts career. Nonetheless, if we judge 2 Corinthians 1–9 and 10–13 to constitute separate letters, it is more parsimonious to conclude that both were written in anticipation of his journey at the end of 56. As argued above, on the basis of 2 Corinthians 1:16 and 2:13, Paul likely wrote at least 2 Corinthians 1–9 from either Macedonia or Greece, both of which would have facilitated relatively rapid communications between Paul and the Corinthians. If 2 Corinthians 1–9 and 10–13 were indeed separate letters, then they were probably both written as part of an ongoing interaction with the Corinthian church in the latter part of 56.

Conclusion to 2 Corinthians

Insofar as it is the case that

- the flight from Damascus reported in 2 Corinthians 11:32 is nonprobative for establishing the compositional date of 2 Corinthians; and
- 2 Corinthians most likely was written just prior to Paul's final recorded journey to Greece, which took place in the latter part of 56,

we conclude that 2 Corinthians 1–9 and 10–13 either are both original to 2 Corinthians or were written during an ongoing interaction between Paul and the Corinthians in the latter part of 56 and that 2 Corinthians was thus written in late 56.

Including absolute dates relevant for our purposes that we have thus far discussed and established in this chapter, our cumulative chronological framework can be summarized in the following table (with dates of composition indicated in bold):

Event	Date
Crucifixion of Jesus	ca. 29–34
Death of Herod Agrippa	44
Paul's Corinthian sojourn	50–52
1 Thessalonians	**50–52**
2 Thessalonians	**50–52**
Gallio's tenure in Corinth	mid-51–mid-52
Paul's probable visit to Jerusalem of Acts 18	late 52

Event	Date
Paul's Ephesian sojourn	54–56
1 Corinthians	**early 56**
Paul leaves Ephesus for Macedonia and then on to Greece	56
2 Corinthians	**late 56**
The succession from Felix to Festus	59

Romans

In this section, we consider the compositional date of Romans. We deal with two primary matters of concern: (1) the correlation of Romans with Acts and (2) the integrity of Romans. On the basis of these considerations, we argue that Romans most likely was written in the winter of 56/57.

Correlation with Acts

Probably no biblical text can be dated as precisely as Romans. Romans 16:1–2 suggests that Paul was writing from Cenchreae, Corinth's port, while Romans 15:28 suggests that Paul was about to depart to deliver the collection, presumably to Jerusalem. This almost certainly situates the composition of our letter in the three months that Paul spent in Greece before his final recorded trip to Jerusalem.[21] These three months can moreover be situated with reasonable precision. If Paul set out from Ephesus to Macedonia in 56, then he reasonably can be expected to have arrived in Greece toward the end of that year. Acts 20:4–6 reports that Paul and certain companions again departed Greece for Macedonia by land, then sometime after Passover were followed by certain other companions. From this, we infer that Paul departed Greece early in 57. That the year of departure was 57 is further confirmed by the probable dates of the Caesarean captivity, which began not long after Paul's arrival in Jerusalem and ended two years later with Festus's succession in 59.[22] Cumulatively, we can conclude that the three months of Acts 20:2b–3a likely extended from the very end of 56 through late winter or early spring of

21. Cf. Acts 20:2b–3a.
22. Cf. discussion of the Prison Epistles below.

57. On the strength of the evidence from Romans 15 and 16, the letter likely dates to this narrow slice of time.

The Integrity of Romans

The previous section supposes the integrity of Romans. There are, however, legitimate questions regarding whether Romans 15 and especially Romans 16 are original to the letter. The textual tradition surrounding these chapters is messy.[23] Textual criticism has proposed both that Romans first appeared in a fourteen-chapter form, with chapters 15–16 added later, and that it first appeared in a fifteen-chapter form, with chapter 16 added later. Other proposals suggest that some but not all of chapters 15–16 is original to Romans. For our purposes, the crucial question is what would be the case if 15:28, 16:1–2, or both are secondary to the letter. If 15:28 with its reference to Paul's plan to visit Jerusalem with the collection (but not 16:1–2) is original to the letter, then we would probably still date Romans to shortly before the final recorded visit to Jerusalem. Since that visit dates to 57, we would date the letter to 56 or 57. If 16:1–2 (but not 15:28) is original, then we should date the letter to the periods when Paul was known to be in and around Corinth. The Corinthian sojourn (50–52; cf. above) and again the winter of 56/57 would thus be the most likely candidates. If neither is original to the letter, then we would know only that Paul was writing at a time during which he hoped to soon visit Rome, apparently for the first time (cf. 1:7, 10–15). Under such conditions, we would be justified in thinking that this time postdates the Greek mission of the early 50s, as Paul seems to have consistently turned his attention further west over the years before his arrival in Rome in early 60. Cumulatively then, the mid to late 50s are the best dates for Romans, with the possible combinations of material original to the text favoring the winter of 56/57. This, then, remains the most probable date.

Conclusion to Romans

Insofar as it is the case that

- Romans most likely was written from Corinth, just prior to Paul's final recorded journey to Jerusalem; and

23. Among major English-language commentators, Jewett, *Romans*, 4–18, offers a particularly thorough treatment of this messiness.

· the integrity of Romans is more probable than not,

we conclude that Romans was written in the winter of 56/57.

As such, including absolute dates relevant for our purposes as discussed and established thus far in this chapter, our cumulative chronological framework can be summarized in the following table (with dates of composition shown in bold):

Event	Date
Crucifixion of Jesus	ca. 29–34
Death of Herod Agrippa	44
Paul's Corinthian sojourn	50–52
1 Thessalonians	**50–52**
2 Thessalonians	**50–52**
Gallio's tenure in Corinth	mid-51–mid-52
Paul's probable visit to Jerusalem of Acts 18	late 52
Paul's Ephesian sojourn	54–56
1 Corinthians	**early 56**
Paul leaves Ephesus for Macedonia and then on to Greece	56
2 Corinthians	**late 56**
Romans	**winter of 56/57**
Paul's visit to Jerusalem of Acts 21	57
The succession from Felix to Festus	59

Galatians

At first glance, Galatians might appear among the easier New Testament texts to situate temporally. Indeed, no other epistle in the New Testament corpus provides such explicit relative dates as does Galatians.[24] The difficulty, however, is that there is significant ambiguity surrounding these relative dates, which only increases as we attempt to correlate them with absolute ones. In what follows, we need to consider the following issues: (1) the visit to Jerusalem reported in

24. Cf. Gal. 1:18; 2:1.

Galatians 1:18, (2) the implications of the North Galatian theory relative to the South Galatian theory, (3) the visit to Jerusalem reported in Galatians 2:1, and (4) Paul's visits to Jerusalem reported in Acts. Cumulatively, it is concluded that Galatians was most likely written no earlier than 47 and no later than 52.

The Jerusalem Visit of Galatians 1:18

According to Galatians 1:17–18, three years after his conversion to Christianity, Paul went to Arabia and Damascus, then on to Jerusalem for his first postconversion visit. "Three years" here might refer idiomatically to a length of time greater than two years but no greater than three. Regarding the date of the conversion, Acts reports that Paul engaged in activities against the church at some point after the Pentecost immediately following Jesus's death.[25] Here I must register significant differences of opinion with Robinson. First, Robinson is persuaded by the now-discredited position that the crucifixion could have only occurred in 30 or 33.[26] Second, Robinson supposes that a year's interval is too short a time to account for all the developments that occur in Acts 1–8.[27] Robinson dates Paul's conversion no earlier than 33 and the Jerusalem visit of Galatians 1:18 no earlier than 35. But I am not persuaded by Robinson's argumentation. First, we have already seen that the crucifixion could have occurred at or around Passover anytime from 29 through 34.[28] Second, relatively few developments occur in Acts 1–8, and none requires a great amount of time. Acts 1 suggests that the Twelve reconstituted themselves with a core of Jesus's followers numbering about 120.[29] Acts 2 indicates that this happened before the first Pentecost—which is to say, seven weeks after Jesus died.[30] The church is said to have experienced a rapid numerical expansion, beginning at that Pentecost.[31] Conflicts arose with the local authorities, culminating in Stephen's martyrdom and in persecution of the disciples by Paul.[32] Those scattered by the Pauline persecution fled throughout the Judean countryside and into Samaria.[33]

25. Cf. Acts 2:1–9:2.
26. Cf. Robinson, *Redating*, 37.
27. Cf. Robinson, *Redating*, 37.
28. Cf. the discussion above; Bond, "Dating the Death of Jesus"; Pitre, *Jesus and the Last Supper*, 251–373.
29. Acts 1:12–15.
30. Acts 2:1.
31. Cf. Acts 2:41, 47; 6:7.
32. Acts 3:1–8:3.
33. Acts 8:1b.

This is presented as the beginning of the Samaritan—and indeed the world—mission.[34] Throughout this period, the earliest Christian community is forced to create novel ways of addressing the material needs of those who join the movement.[35] Insofar as these developments are localized to Judea and indeed primarily to Jerusalem, we need not suppose that they took several years to occur. Indeed, there are some indications that these were quite rapid developments. For instance, the so-called community of goods was reliant upon the liquidation of capital for funding and seems to have lacked any formal means by which to police corruption in its midst.[36] This could plausibly indicate the lack of development that is characteristic of a community only just beginning to wrestle with the endemic problems associated with overdependence upon the liquidation of capital on the one hand and corruption on the other.

Consequent to the considerations above, the earliest year possible for the crucifixion—namely, 29—is also the earliest year possible for Paul's conversion. As such, the journey to Jerusalem reported in Galatians 1:18 cannot date any earlier than 31. Given only the data considered thus far then, 31 must be reckoned as the earliest date for the composition of Galatians.

North versus South Galatia

In Galatians 4:13, Paul writes, "You know that it was because of a physical infirmity that I first announced the gospel to you." "The first" (*to proteron*) could reference the first visit of two (or more), or it could simply reference a visit that took place prior to the writing of the letter. Given this passage, we conclude that Paul wrote Galatians after his first visit with the churches in Galatia, and possibly after a second visit.

Acts first reports that Paul ministered in a region explicitly designated as "Galatia" in 16:6, during the so-called second missionary journey. Older scholarship thus supposed that the Letter to the Galatians must postdate the apostolic council reported in Acts 15, which is typically dated to 48. By the end of the nineteenth century, however, it was known that the words "Galatia" and "Galatians" could be defined either ethnically or politically.[37] An ethnic definition entails reference to "North Galatia," the region peopled historically

---

34. Acts 8:2–40.
35. Acts 4:32–37; 6:1–7.
36. Cf. Acts 4:32–5:10.
37. Cf. the history of scholarship on this matter as well as overview of the relevant data in Hemer, *Book of Acts*, 277–307.

by Celtic-speaking groups, while a political definition would entail reference to a "South Galatia," the Roman province known as "Galatia." The cities of Iconium, Lystra, and Derbe lie within South Galatia, and Paul is reported to have ministered there shortly before the Acts 15 council, during the so-called first missionary journey.[38] Notably, Acts 14:21 reports that Paul and Barnabas returned to Lystra and Iconium on their way to Antioch, just before the events that led to the Acts 15 council. Thus it is possible that Paul wrote Galatians prior to the Acts 15 council, although almost certainly after the beginning of the first missionary journey.

There is considerable ambiguity regarding the absolute chronology of Paul's first missionary journey. Acts narrates the journey after the death of Agrippa I in 44.[39] However, it is plausible that the first missionary journey began during Agrippa's life. In Acts 11:29–30 Luke says that Barnabas and Paul traveled from Antioch to Jerusalem; immediately afterward he reports the events of the Agrippan persecution of 41 or 42. After describing Agrippa's death, Luke mentions that Paul and Barnabas returned to Antioch (cf. 12:20–25). Unless we suppose that Paul and Barnabas spent two or three full years in Jerusalem (from before the persecution to after Agrippa's death), we should judge that Luke is here employing what for him is a very typical technique: using journeys between locales to indicate narrative shifts. Given the Lukan data alone, we would probably be close to the mark if we suggested that the first missionary journey began sometime between 40 and 45. A year or so beyond this range in either direction would not be impossible but would probably strain credulity. Thus, given only this data and those considered in the previous section, the earliest reasonable date for Galatians is 40.

The Jerusalem Visit of Galatians 2:1

In Galatians 2:1, Paul reports that he went to Jerusalem again after fourteen years. This datum requires close attention. First, as with "three years," "fourteen years" in Pauline usage likely indicates a length of time greater than thirteen but no greater than fourteen. Second, these thirteen to fourteen years could be concurrent or consecutive with the two to three years of Galatians 1:18—that is, the fourteen years could be reckoned from the conversion and thus include the three years (concurrent), or from the first visit to Jerusalem

38. Cf. Acts 13:13–14:23.
39. Cf. Acts 12:20–25.

and thus in addition (consecutive). If concurrent, then the visit of Galatians 2:1 could date just over thirteen years after the conversion but no more than fourteen; if consecutive, then the visit of Galatians 2:1 could date between just over fifteen years after the conversion but no more than seventeen. Given that the conversion most likely dates no earlier than summer of 29, the visit of Galatians 2:1 should date no earlier than 42 on a concurrent chronology and no earlier than 44 on a consecutive one. For our immediate purposes, the earlier of these dates is the most important, as it effectively excludes any date for Galatians earlier than 42.

Paul's Visits to Jerusalem as Reported in Acts

Here we get most fully into the thorny matter of relating the Pauline data to the Lukan. Paul enumerates two visits to Jerusalem: those of Galatians 1:18 and 2:1. By comparison, Luke enumerates at least four and probably five visits: those of Acts 9:26; 11:29–30 and 12:25 (henceforth referred to more succinctly as the visit of Acts 12); 15:2b; possibly 18:22; and 21:17.[40] Most scholars identify the visit of Acts 9:26 with that of Galatians 1:18. Absent other considerations, parsimony should incline us to identify the visit of Galatians 2:1 with that of Acts 12. On this "Acts 12" hypothesis, then, the prophecy that according to Galatians 2:2 prompted Paul and Barnabas to go to Jerusalem is to be identified with the prophecy that led to the Antiochian church, sending them to Jerusalem according to Acts 11:28–30, and the conflict reported in Galatians 2:11–14 parallels that reported in Acts 15:1–2a. There would then be no parallel between Galatians and the balance of Acts 15, since the Letter to the Galatians was written before the events described in Acts 15.

Most scholars, however, identify the visit reported in Galatians 2:1 with that reported in Acts 15. This is for a number of reasons. Whereas Acts 11 and 12 mention no discussions between Paul and Barnabas on the one hand and leading apostolic figures on the other, this is precisely the focus of Acts 15; thus, it is argued, Acts 15 can more reasonably be thought to parallel Galatians 2:1–10. Such an argument, however, is limited in strength for at least four reasons: (1) Luke is always highly selective in what he presents; (2) as

40. English translations of Acts 18:22 typically state that Paul went up to Jerusalem. "Jerusalem," however, does not appear in the Greek text. Nonetheless, Luke reports that Paul went up from Caesarea to greet the church at an undisclosed location; almost certainly this is an idiomatic way of stating that Paul went to Jerusalem. As such, although we cannot say with absolute confidence that Acts 18:22 reports a journey to Jerusalem, it is highly probable.

recognized since at least Ferdinand Christian Baur in the nineteenth century, Luke tends to emphasize the irenic side of interapostolic relationships and is not necessarily inclined to report every single conflict that took place; (3) Acts 15 makes no mention of a prophecy, the very thing that according to Galatians 2:2 motivated Paul and Barnabas's journey to Jerusalem, and as such, the Acts 15 hypothesis is as vulnerable to arguments from silence as is the Acts 12 hypothesis; (4) if (as on the Acts 12 hypothesis) Galatians 2:1–10 reports the sort of discussions that led up to the later dispute that led to the council of Acts 15, then it should hardly surprise us if Luke decided to focus upon the later, more significant, and defining discussion reported in Acts 15 rather than the earlier discussion reported in Galatians 2:1–10.

More challenging for the Acts 12 hypothesis is the fact that whereas Acts 15:2a presents Paul and Barnabas as united against the people from Judea, Galatians 2:13 shows them divided. This is indeed a problem, but hardly an insuperable one. Acts 15:2a reports that Paul and Barnabas took the same side on the question of whether gentile believers need to be circumcised, whereas Galatians 2:13 reports that Barnabas refused to eat with gentiles. Barnabas's conduct in these two passages conflicts only if we suppose it impossible that he would object to circumcision as a requirement yet also withdraw from eating with gentile believers. Paul clearly thought that these two matters were of a piece: if one did not think it necessary for gentile believers to be circumcised, he reasoned, then surely one would have no problem eating with them. It is not self-evidently the case that Barnabas either shared this opinion or could bring himself to follow its dictates in practice. Moreover, again, insofar as Luke tends to emphasize the unity among early Christians, it is hardly inconceivable that he has elided conflict between Paul and Barnabas prior to the council.

Ultimately, whether one prefers the Acts 12 or the Acts 15 hypothesis will in large part come down to which parallels one chooses to emphasize. If, following the Acts 12 hypothesis, we affirm that the conflict of Galatians 2:11–14 parallels that of Acts 15:1–2a, then we should probably conclude that Galatians was written not long before the Acts 15 council. A date in late 47 or early 48 would then probably be preferred. Insofar as one dates the Epistle to the Galatians later than the probable visit of Acts 18:22 and the certain visit of 21:17, to that extent one must account for why Paul omitted or Luke added not only one but two or possibly even three visits.[41] Thus Galatians was most likely written

41. A problem faced by Robinson, who dates Galatians to 57 (*Redating*, 55–57).

before the visit of Acts 18:22 and almost certainly prior to the visit of Acts 21:17.[42] Because we have already suggested that the visit of Acts 18:22 should date to ca. 52 and the visit of 21:17 to 57, then on the Acts 15 hypothesis, the letter cannot predate 48, and we should be wary of dating the Epistle to the Galatians later than 52. Given the relative strengths and weaknesses of both the Acts 12 and Acts 15 hypotheses, I do not think that we can date Galatians more precisely than sometime from 47 through 52.

Conclusion to Galatians

Insofar as it is the case that

- the visit that Paul mentions in Galatians 1:18 can date no earlier than 31;
- the South Galatia theory permits a date for Galatians as early as 40;
- the visit that Paul mentions in Galatians 2:1 can date no earlier than 42; and
- correlation between Acts and Galatians favors either a date for Galatians of 47 or 48 (on the Acts 12 theory) or 48 through 52 (on the Acts 15 theory),

we conclude that Galatians was written no earlier than 47 and no later than 52.

Including absolute dates relevant for our purposes and dates we have thus far discussed and established in this chapter, our cumulative chronological framework can be summarized in the following table (with dates of composition shown in bold):

Event	Date
Crucifixion of Jesus	ca. 29–34
Conversion of Paul	no earlier than late 29
Paul's visit to Jerusalem of Acts 9 // Gal. 1:18	no earlier than late 31
Paul's first missionary journey	40–45

42. Contra those who would identify the visit of Gal. 2:1–10 with that of Acts 18:22. Cf. Jewett, *Chronology of Paul's Life*, 78–87; Knox, *Life of Paul*, 43–49; Lüdemann, *Paul, Apostle*, 141–46.

Event	Date
Paul's visit to Jerusalem of Gal. 2:1–10*	no earlier than 42
Death of Herod Agrippa	44
Paul's visit to Jerusalem of Acts 12	prior to 45
Galatians	**47–52**
Paul's visit to Jerusalem of Acts 15	48
Paul's Corinthian sojourn	50–52
1 Thessalonians	**50–52**
2 Thessalonians	**50–52**
Gallio's tenure in Corinth	mid-51–mid-52
Paul's probable visit to Jerusalem of Acts 18	late 52
Paul's Ephesian sojourn	54–56
1 Corinthians	**early 56**
Paul leaves Ephesus for Macedonia and then on to Greece	56
2 Corinthians	**late 56**
Romans	**winter of 56/57**
Paul's visit to Jerusalem of Acts 21	57
The succession from Felix to Festus	59

* As discussed in the body of this study, Paul's visit of Gal. 2 is likely synonymous with either his visit of Acts 12 or of Acts 15. But I have listed them as three separate events here so as not to take a position on something that need not be resolved for purposes of our current work.

The Prison Epistles

Ephesians, Philippians, Colossians, and Philemon are often referred to as the "Prison Epistles," as they all suppose that Paul is writing from prison (cf. Eph. 3:1; 4:1; 6:20; Phil. 1:7, 13–14; Col. 4:18; Philem. 1, 10). Crucial to determining the date of any given prison letter is establishing the location from which Paul was writing. There is a general disciplinary supposition that if indeed Ephesians and Colossians are authentic Pauline compositions, then they must have been written around the same time as Philemon. This is due in large part to the similarities and connections between the three letters. Thus, it is expedient to consider them as a unit and to consider Philippians separately.

Ephesians, Colossians, and Philemon

In this section we consider the probable dates for Ephesians, Colossians, and Philemon. As we do so, we consider (1) the relationship between Philemon and Colossians, (2) the earthquake that struck the Lycus Valley (where Colossae is located) in 60, (3) the relationship between Colossians and Ephesians, and finally (4) the location of composition. We argue that all three letters likely date from Paul's Caesarean imprisonment, thus no earlier than 57 and no later than 59.

Philemon and Colossians

It is generally held that the historical Philemon was located in Colossae. This supposition is based upon certain correlations between the Letters to the Colossians and to Philemon.[43] In Philemon 2, Paul greets Archippus, who is similarly greeted in Colossians 4:17; the Letter to Philemon is focused upon Onesimus's return to his master (cf. esp. v. 10), and Colossians 4:7–9 states that not only is Onesimus coming to Colossae but also that Onesimus is a Colossian Christian; in Philemon 23–24, Paul sends greetings from Epaphras, Mark, Aristarchus, Demas, and Luke, and these are among those who are said to send greetings in Colossians 4:10–14. There is thus a long-standing assumption that (granting Pauline authorship) Paul dispatched the Epistle to the Colossians and the Epistle to Philemon to the same locale and (more importantly for our purposes) at the same time.

The Earthquake of ca. 60

The city of Colossae was devastated by an earthquake ca. 60, as were neighboring Hierapolis and Laodicea. Scholarship has sometimes assumed that following this earthquake Colossae was sufficiently depopulated that there would have been no one to write to there. This would quite helpfully narrow down the possible date for the letter. There are two concerns to address here, however.[44] First, it is unclear exactly when the earthquake took place. Our earliest report of the earthquake comes from Tacitus, who dates it to 60.[45] Eusebius, however,

---

43. Cf. the argument against making such correlations in Balabanski, "Where is Philemon?" Balabanski's argument is predicated upon the supposition that Colossians is a pseudo-Pauline work. For those who reject that supposition, the argument loses much of its force.

44. On both, cf. the discussions in P. Foster, *Colossians*, 3–8; and Huttner, *Christianity in the Lycus Valley*, 101–3, 114–15.

45. Tacitus, *Ann.* 14.27.

dates the earthquake to 63 and Jerome to 64.[46] Ulrich Huttner suggests that the only certainty we can have is that an earthquake struck the Lycus Valley in the early 60s and caused great devastation, although he raises the possibility that there were two or more such earthquakes during the first half of that decade.[47]

Also of concern is the extent of the devastation, and more specifically whether the earthquake or earthquakes would have precluded Paul writing a letter to the Colossians. There is evidence of recovery efforts, most notably an inscription from Colossae dating to the late first or early second centuries that discusses the rebuilding of public baths and water channels.[48] Moreover, Laodicea was also affected by the earthquake and yet was among the churches addressed in Revelation. Admittedly, Tacitus mentions recovery efforts only in Laodicea. It would, however, be a dubious argument from silence to thus conclude that comparable efforts did not also take place in Colossae. Indeed, Tacitus does not mention recovery efforts in Hierapolis, yet they undoubtedly took place.[49] Given that we do not know the extent to which the earthquake(s) of the early 60s would have precluded a letter from Paul, this matter should be considered nonprobative for purposes of establishing the compositional date of Colossians and Philemon. If considered probative, it would at most exclude only the latest possible dates for the letters.

Colossians and Ephesians

Both Colossians and Ephesians expect that Tychicus will arrive alongside the letter (cf. Eph. 6:21; Col. 4:7). On the supposition that Ephesians is indeed a Pauline composition, the most likely inference is that Paul wrote this letter around the same time as Colossians, probably intending for Tychicus to deliver both these letters along with the one to Philemon. The three letters should thus be dated at the same time.

Location of Composition

Three cities are typically given for the location from which Paul wrote any given prison epistle: Ephesus, generally thought to be in connection with the

46. Cf. the discussion in Huttner, *Christianity in the Lycus Valley*, 101.
47. Huttner, *Christianity in the Lycus Valley*, 101–2.
48. Published in Cadwallader, "Repairer of the Baths at Colossae"; Cadwallader, "Repairer of the Baths: A New Inscription." Cf. also the discussion in Cadwallader, "Scholarship on Colossae."
49. Cf. the discussion in Huttner, *Christianity in the Lycus Valley*, 102.

riot described in Acts 19:23–41; Caesarea, as Paul was imprisoned there for two years (23:33–24:27); Rome, since he spent at least two years under house arrest there (28:30–31) and was probably there again at the end of his life. Given our previous discussion of Pauline chronology, if Paul was imprisoned following the riot in Ephesus, this was likely toward the end of the Ephesian sojourn (54–56). The Caesarean imprisonment ended with the succession from Felix to Festus in 59, and because it lasted two years, it must have begun in 57.[50] Paul was sent to Rome late in the shipping season, but due to shipwreck did not arrive until early in 60. The first Roman imprisonment began in 60, as Paul was sent to Rome for trial late in 59 but did not arrive until early 60 (cf. 27:1–28:11). This imprisonment lasted the next two years (cf. Acts 28:30), thus ending in 62. As discussed more fully below on the Pastoral Epistles, Paul's second Roman captivity likely began no earlier than 64 and ended no later than 68. Thus, a prison letter written from Ephesus likely dates to 55 or 56; from Caesarea, 57 through 59; from Rome, 60 through 62, or possibly during a hypothetical second imprisonment likely starting no earlier than 64 and ending no later than 68.

Joseph Fitzmyer suggests that Rome has most frequently been seen as the place of composition; he himself prefers Ephesus and notes that Caesarea is rarely argued today.[51] We thus consider them in this order, moving from the traditional Roman origin, through the Ephesian, and on to the Caesarean. The "Roman hypothesis" typically seeks to situate the origin of the Letter to Philemon during Paul's house arrest in Rome from 60 to 62. This is attractive in principle since Acts 28:30–31 indicates that Paul was able to operate without hindrance during those two years. A variant of the Roman hypothesis might also locate the composition of our letter during a hypothetical second Roman imprisonment. This is also attractive, as later in this chapter we argue that if 2 Timothy is a Pauline composition, then it dates to the second imprisonment. Further, 2 Timothy has certain personalia in common with Philemon, Colossians, and Ephesians.[52] Against the Roman hypothesis, it is often objected that Rome and Colossae are too far apart for Onesimus to have fled there to see Paul. This is somewhat unconvincing. Indeed, one could easily reverse the argument and suggest that a slave in trouble with his master might well prefer a more distant locale to a closer one. More problematic, though, is Paul's expectation

---

50. Cf. again the discussion in Jewett, *Chronology of Paul's Life*, 40–44; Riesner, *Paul's Early Period*, 219–24.

51. Fitzmyer, *Philemon*, 9–11. Cf. Lohse, *Colossians and Philemon*, 188, who argues likewise.

52. Cf. 2 Tim. 4:10–12 with Eph. 6:21; Col. 4:10, 14; and Philem. 24.

that he will visit Philemon in relatively short order.[53] Admittedly, Paul's request that Philemon prepare a guest room for him is quite conceivably an expression of hope for his own release rather than a concrete, logistical request. Nonetheless, the implication is that he expects to travel in the direction of Colossae upon his release. This, however, is the opposite of what we know about Paul's travel plans during the first Roman imprisonment. According to Romans 15:28, his plan had always been to travel west from Rome, not east. And one rather imagines that Paul's hopes for an imminent release were significantly lower during the second imprisonment than the first. That having been said, Rome cannot be ruled out definitively.

The Ephesian hypothesis seeks in large part to address the distance between Colossae and Paul's locale. As noted above, however, the question of distance is largely a nonissue, as it is unclear whether Onesimus would have preferred to run to a closer or a more distant locale. Having said that, an Ephesian origin does not stand as clearly at variance with Paul's known movements and aims at the relevant time as does a Roman origin. According to Acts 20:1, Paul leaves Ephesus and sets out for Macedonia, and never again in Acts does he travel through the regions in and around Colossae. Nonetheless, we know that Paul operated with a changing itinerary during this period.[54] Thus, it is far from impossible that during an Ephesian imprisonment Paul had anticipated traveling to Colossae, and then for whatever reason this did not happen. The single most significant challenge to the Ephesian hypothesis is that we have no account of Paul being in prison while in Ephesus. Of course, that does not mean that he was not; such an argument from silence would be wholly illicit. Nonetheless, operating on the principle of parsimony, I prefer known events to unknown ones whenever possible.[55]

Compared to both the Roman and the Ephesian hypotheses, the Caesarean hypothesis has notable advantages. We know from Romans 15:25–28 that prior to his final recorded journey to Palestine, Paul had intended to travel west toward Rome afterward. According to Acts 25:11, he did not appeal to Caesar until the end of the two years in Caesarea. Thus, it is conceivable that throughout most (if not all) of his Caesarean imprisonment he anticipated traveling to Rome by foot and stopping in Colossae along the way. Due to his appeal to Caesar, however, he ultimately was forced to sail. Unlike either the Roman or the Ephesian

53. Cf. Philem. 22.
54. Cf. 2 Cor. 1:16.
55. Thus I am also inclined to opt against, for instance, the recent argument that Paul was writing from Apamea, advanced by D. Campbell, *Framing Paul*, 274–76.

hypotheses, we can thus readily account both for Paul's expectation that he would travel through Colossae after his release and also for his change of plans.

None of the above considerations fully excludes the Roman or a hypothetical Ephesian captivity as the provenance for Ephesians, Colossians, and Philemon. Nonetheless, this study concludes that the Caesarean imprisonment makes the greatest sense of the balance of probabilities, thus dating Ephesians, Colossians, and Philemon to no earlier than 57 and no later than 59.

Conclusion to Ephesians, Colossians, and Philemon

Insofar as it is the case that

- the Letter to Philemon was most likely written to Colossae at the same time as Colossians;
- the earthquake that struck the Lycus Valley ca. 60 through 64 is nonprobative for purposes of establishing when the Letters to Philemon and Colossians were most likely written;
- Ephesians was most likely written at the same time as the Letter to the Colossians; and
- Ephesians, Colossians, and Philemon were most likely written during Paul's imprisonment in Caesarea ca. 57 through 59,

we conclude that Ephesians, Colossians, and the Letter to Philemon are to be dated no earlier than 57 and no later than 59.

Philippians

In this section, we consider the compositional date of Philippians. We treat two primary matters of concern: (1) the most likely location of composition and (2) the integrity of Philippians. On the basis of these considerations, we argue that Philippians, too, was most likely written during the Caesarean imprisonment, ca. 57 through 59.

Location of Composition

The most relevant datum for establishing where Philippians was written is found in Philippians 1:13: "It has become known throughout the whole imperial guard and to everyone else that my imprisonment is for Christ." Paul's reference here to an "imperial guard" has frequently led to the conclusion that he must be writing from Rome. The word translated here as "imperial guard" is *praitōrion*, and its use is not limited to Rome. Indeed, the only location in which Paul is explicitly said to be situated at a *praitōrion* is during the Caesarean imprisonment (cf. Acts 23:35). As such, on the basis of Philippians 1:12–13, Caesarea is at least as likely a candidate for the origin of Philippians as is Rome. Yet Ephesus cannot be ruled out, because a governor's residence was frequently referred to as a *praetorium* (from which *praitōrion* derives).[56] Indeed, in principle, neither can an unknown imprisonment in any other locale be excluded. Nonetheless, given that only in Caesarea is Paul associated with a *praitōrion* in our earliest account of his life, I am inclined toward a Caesarean origin for Philippians.

The Integrity of Philippians

Discussions of Philippians are complicated by scholarly doubts regarding its integrity. The currency of such doubts is evident if we consult two relatively recent commentators on Philippians in respected commentary series: in his Black's Commentary on Philippians, Markus Bockmuehl considers it most likely that Philippians represents a single letter; John Reumann, in his Anchor Commentary, considers it most likely that Philippians contains parts of three different letters, all written by Paul.[57] The present author is persuaded, however, that the various partition theories fail on the test of parsimony, introducing a greater number of questions than they resolve. Yet if one favors a partition theory, then any chronological judgment based upon Philippians 1:12–13 would apply only to the part of the letter that contains this passage.

Conclusion to Philippians

Insofar as it is the case that

- Philippians most likely was written from Caesarea, during Paul's imprisonment there and
- the integrity of Philippians is more probable than not,

we conclude that Philippians should be dated no earlier than 57 and no later than 59.

---

56. Cf. the discussion in Reumann, *Philippians*, 171–72.
57. Bockmuehl, *Philippians*, 20–25; Reumann, *Philippians*, 1–19, esp. 8–13.

Conclusion to the Prison Letters

Insofar as it is the case that

- the Letter to Philemon was most likely written to Colossae at the same time as Colossians;
- the earthquake that struck the Lycus Valley ca. 60 is nonprobative for purposes of establishing when the Letters to Philemon and Colossians were written;
- Ephesians was most likely written at the same time as the Letter to the Colossians;
- Ephesians, Colossians, and Philemon were most likely written during Paul's imprisonment in Caesarea ca. 57 through 59;
- Philippians most likely was written from Caesarea during Paul's imprisonment there; and
- the integrity of Philippians is more probable than not,

we conclude that Ephesians, Philippians, Colossians, and Philemon were written no earlier than 57 and no later than 59.

Including absolute dates relevant for our purposes as discussed and established thus far in this chapter, our cumulative chronological framework can be summarized in the following table (with dates of composition shown in bold):

Event	Date
Crucifixion of Jesus	ca. 29–34
Conversion of Paul	no earlier than late 29
Paul's visit to Jerusalem of Acts 9 // Gal. 1:18	no earlier than late 31
Paul's first missionary journey	40–45
Paul's visit to Jerusalem of Gal. 2:1–10	no earlier than 42
Death of Herod Agrippa	44
Paul's visit to Jerusalem of Acts 12	prior to 45
Galatians	**47–52**
Paul's visit to Jerusalem of Acts 15	48
Paul's Corinthian sojourn	50–52
1 Thessalonians	**50–52**

Event	Date
2 Thessalonians	50–52
Gallio's tenure in Corinth	mid-51–mid-52
Paul's probable visit to Jerusalem of Acts 18	late 52
Paul's Ephesian sojourn	54–56
Paul's possible imprisonment in Ephesus	55 or 56
1 Corinthians	early 56
Paul leaves Ephesus for Macedonia and then on to Greece	56
2 Corinthians	late 56
Romans	winter of 56/57
Paul's visit to Jerusalem of Acts 21	57
Paul's imprisonment in Caesarea	57–59
Ephesians, Colossians, Philemon, and Philippians	57–59
The succession from Felix to Festus	59
Paul's first imprisonment in Rome	60–62
One or more earthquakes strike the Lycus Valley	60–64

The Pastoral Epistles

In this section, we discuss the most vexed of Pauline literature for a chronologist's purpose. These Pastoral Epistles are vexed because few currently working New Testament scholars consider it probable that all three can be attributed to Paul. Reasonable grounds do exist for at least suspecting one or more of the Pastorals to be pseudo-Pauline. Most notable for purposes of this study, the Pastorals cannot be easily situated within Paul's career as reconstructed from Acts. This does not make them pseudo-Pauline, but it does mean that Pauline authorship requires one to posit a hypothetical post-Acts career. Such a necessity reduces the probability that they are authentic. Given this reality, here I find it most expedient to proceed by first addressing how late the texts could plausibly be if we suppose pseudo-Pauline authorship. Then I consider the passages (1 Tim. 5:18; 2 Tim. 4:20; Titus 1:5) that make it virtually impossible to situate the Pastoral Epistles within Paul's career as known from Acts. Finally, I ask where they would most likely be situated within Paul's hypothetical post-Acts career, if indeed they are Pauline compositions.

External Attestation

The earliest incontestable citation of the Pastoral Epistles comes from Irenaeus.[58] It seems more likely than not that both Ignatius and Polycarp knew our 1 and 2 Timothy.[59] As we saw from our discussion of the Johannine Epistles, Polycarp's *Letter to the Philippians* could potentially date as late as 150, and although Ignatius's letters are typically dated to Trajan's reign (98–117), they could potentially date into the mid-second century. Cumulatively, we should be wary of dating 1 and 2 Timothy later than 150, and Titus later than 175.

The Problem of Luke's Gospel (1 Tim. 5:18)

If 1 Timothy is authentic, then Timothy was located in Ephesus when this letter was written, and Paul had at some time in the relatively recent past charged him to stay there as he set out for Macedonia.[60] This could correlate well with Acts 20:1, where Paul does indeed set out for Macedonia from Ephesus. As argued above, this departure should be dated to 56. By early 57, Timothy was apparently back with Paul in Greece (cf. Acts 20:4). The narrow window between Paul's departure from Ephesus in perhaps early 56 through to his departure from Greece in early 57 is by far the best range within which to situate 1 Timothy, if it is to be situated within Paul's career as known from Acts. Indeed, it is virtually the only place within Paul's career in Acts that we could place the composition of 1 Timothy. Robinson dates the letter at this point in Paul's career, for exactly this reason.[61] There is, however, some difficulty in doing so.

First Timothy 5:18 reads, "For the scripture says, 'You shall not muzzle an ox while it is treading out the grain,' and, 'The laborer deserves to be paid.'" The first quote is from Deuteronomy 25:4, and the latter is found verbatim only in Luke 10:7. Yet we have already argued that Luke's Gospel should be dated to sometime after Paul and Luke travel together to Jerusalem in 57. As such, a ca. 56 date for 1 Timothy would place the letter prior to Luke's Gospel. Can Pauline authorship of 1 Timothy during Paul's career as known from Acts be reconciled with our already proposed date for Luke's Gospel? Robinson

---

58. Cf. Irenaeus, *Haer.* 1 Praef. 1; 1.16.3; 2.14.7; 3.14.1.

59. Cf. P. Foster, "Epistles of Ignatius," esp. 170–72; Holmes, "Polycarp's *Letter to the Philippians*," esp. 215–18.

60. 1 Tim. 1:3.

61. Robinson, *Redating*, 82–83.

fails to address this issue, although insofar as he declines to be particularly precise in dating the Synoptic Gospels, it is admittedly not as urgent for his chronology as it is for mine.

One possible path forward is found in Matthew 10:10, which is close to but not quite identical with Luke 10:7. For explicative purposes, we quote these first in Greek and second in an awkward translation that seeks to be as word for word as possible.

axios gar ho ergatēs tēs trophēs autou (Matt. 10:10).

For the worker is worth the food of him.

axios gar ho ergatēs tou misthou autou (Luke 10:7).

For the worker is worth the pay of him.

The two passages are virtually identical, except Matthew has *tēs trophēs* (the food) where Luke has *tou misthou* (the pay). We have already dated Matthew's Gospel as early as 45. Yet it is hardly impossible that someone might quote Matthew's Gospel while using a form that is in fact a Lukan variant. This is especially the case with someone like Paul, whom we know was a companion of Luke. Under such a scenario, Paul would be quoting Matthew 10:10, but reflecting the same variant of the tradition that we see in Luke 10:7. Along similar lines, we might suggest that Paul is quoting neither Matthew's Gospel nor Luke's but a now-lost source text (for which Q would present as the best candidate). The reference to "the writing" (i.e., *hē graphē*, "the Scripture") in 1 Timothy 5:18 makes it unlikely that the writer has oral tradition in mind, although a reference to now-lost oral tradition is for our purposes functionally indistinct from a reference to now-lost written tradition.

Although we certainly cannot rule out a reference to either Matthew 10:10 or now-lost tradition in 1 Timothy 5:18, it seems much more parsimonious to conclude that 1 Timothy 5:18 is quoting Luke 10:7. With that granted, we could consider dating Luke's Gospel earlier than 57–59, as did John Wenham.[62] Yet Wenham places too much weight upon 2 Corinthians 8:18, which refers to "the brother whose praise is in the gospel."[63] Wenham identifies this brother with Luke, arguing that this fame came from

---

62. Wenham, *Redating Matthew, Mark and Luke*, 229–38.
63. Translation follows Wenham, *Redating Matthew, Mark, and Luke*, 230.

his composition of the Third Gospel. He thus argues that Luke's Gospel must date prior to 55. Though I admit that this is possible, I am less than inclined to think it sufficiently probable as to justify lowering the date of Luke's Gospel. And insofar as the Pauline authorship of the Pastorals is disputable, I am also not inclined to date Luke's Gospel earlier in order to better accommodate 1 Timothy. As such, I think it preferable to date 1 Timothy later than 59, and thus to situate it within Paul's hypothetical second career.

The Problem of Trophimus (2 Tim. 4:20)

Although 2 Timothy 4:20 reports that Paul left Trophimus ill in Miletus, Acts makes clear that Trophimus traveled with Paul from Greece through Miletus to Jerusalem.[64] In principle, it is possible that Luke is simply mistaken on the matter, but this seems unlikely. The data regarding Trophimus's arrival in Jerusalem by way of Miletus come from the we-passages. If indeed the we-passages indicate the presence of the author, then it is precisely in such sections of Acts that one should expect Luke to be most accurate. Moreover, according to Acts, Trophimus's presence with Paul and Luke in Jerusalem is not a minor detail but rather the immediate catalyst for Paul's arrest. The arrest in turn sets up the major concerns of the last quarter of the book. Are we to believe that Luke blundered so spectacularly regarding events to which he was a partial witness and to which he ascribes such significance?

Pursuant to the above, we should consider whether there are other possible explanations that would allow us to situate 2 Timothy within Paul's career as can be reconstructed from Acts. For instance, one might argue that 2 Timothy 4:20 has suffered textual corruption. On such an argument, instead of referring to Miletus (*Milētos*), 2 Timothy 4:20 originally referred to Malta (*Melitē*), precisely where Acts 28:1 tells us that Paul was shipwrecked on his way to Rome.[65] On such an argument, Paul would have left Trophimus not in Miletus on his way to Jerusalem but rather in Malta on his way to Rome. This is not impossible, and we do have instances within the manuscript tradition of *Milētos* appearing in Acts 28:1 in lieu of *Melitē*.[66]

---

64. Acts 20–21, esp. 20:4 and 21:29.
65. Cf. Dibelius and Conzelmann, *Pastoral Epistles*, 125.
66. Most notably, in Vaticanus and the Vulgate.

Nonetheless, I am not aware of any variant wherein 2 Timothy 4:20 refers to Malta instead of Miletus. Given this lack of manuscript evidence, I am reluctant to affirm that 2 Timothy 4:20 originally referred to Malta, although neither can I rule it out.

Alternatively, one might argue that Paul need not have been physically present in Miletus when he "left" Trophimus there, but rather that he did not direct him to go elsewhere. This is Robinson's preferred solution, which allows him to date 2 Timothy to Paul's Caesarean imprisonment.[67] The verb in question here is *apoleipō*, and unfortunately for his argument, this reading does not seem altogether consistent with the range of semantic possibilities evinced for the word elsewhere. Without stronger evidence that *apoleipō* could indicate that Paul was not present physically when he left Trophimus, I am reluctant to affirm this hypothesis.

Another possibility considers the geography of Paul's trip to Rome. According to Acts 27:7, Paul and his companions sailed north and then west along the Asian coast as far as Cnidus. Miletus is only about 120 km further up the coast from Cnidus. The distance could be traversed with just over a day's travel. It is highly probable that by the late 50s Miletus boasted a Christian community with close ties to the church in Ephesus.[68] If he was ill, it could have been decided that although he had not the strength for the voyage to Rome, he did have the strength to reach coreligionists or relations in Miletus. Paul and company would thus have arrived in Rome without Trophimus, who was left behind in Miletus. Although such a reading is not impossible, I am reluctant to affirm this hypothesis given the more obvious interpretation of 2 Timothy 4:20—namely, that Paul and Trophimus were together when Paul left Trophimus in Miletus.

Given the above, if 2 Timothy is a genuine Pauline composition, then it almost certainly must date to Paul's hypothetical post-Acts career, during which time Paul and Trophimus parted company in Miletus.

The Problem of Crete (Titus 1:5)

In Titus 1:5, Paul says to Titus, "I left you behind in Crete for this reason, so that you should put in order what remained to be done, and should

---

67. Robinson, *Redating*, 76–77. Robinson is much influenced by Bo Reicke here. Cf. Reicke's more recent articulation of this argument in his *Re-Examining Paul's Letters*, 69–70.
68. Cf. Acts 20:17–38.

appoint elders in every town, as I directed you." Yet Acts makes no mention of missionary activity on Crete. Acts does report that Paul visited Crete on his first trip to Rome.[69] Yet because Paul was in custody and his captors in a rush because they set out so late in the shipping season, it is doubtful that he had much chance to undertake missionary work at that time. One might theorize that Paul discovered Christian communities on Crete in need of leadership and left Titus to do that task. It is not certain whether such a scenario does justice to the language of Titus 1:5. The order that Titus should build upon the work that was begun in Crete suggests something closer to a missionary journey than a layover while being transported as a prisoner.

Alternatively, much as with Trophimus in 2 Timothy 4:20, one could argue that when Paul claims to have "left" Titus on Crete, he was not physically present but rather did not direct Titus to go elsewhere. This again is Robinson's preferred solution.[70] As we already saw in the case of 2 Timothy 4:20, this does not seem to be the best reading of Paul's language. The letter would seem to most fully envision that Paul and Titus engaged in missionary work together on Crete, and then Paul at that time left Titus there. As such, it seems probable that if Titus is to be considered a genuinely Pauline composition, it should date to Paul's hypothetical post-Acts career.

Paul's Hypothetical Post-Acts Career

The Acts narrative ends with Paul in Rome in 62. For his life and career after this point, we are left without the guidance of an early biographical work. First Clement 5.7 tells us that Paul reached the "farthest limits of the West."[71] From this, we have good reason to think that Paul did in fact fulfill his aim— stated in Romans 15:28—of going to Spain. We can imagine that Paul was in Spain the balance of 62 and probably into, if not through, 63. The earliest that we can imagine he was back in the eastern Mediterranean is likely late 63. Before writing 1 Timothy, he likely spent time with Timothy in Ephesus and then traveled to Macedonia.[72] Before writing to Titus, he likely spent time with him on Crete.[73] Such travels likely would have taken at least one year, possibly

---

69. Acts 27:8–12.
70. Robinson, *Redating*, 76–77, 81–82. Cf. also Reicke, *Re-examining Paul's Letters*, 69–70.
71. 1 Clem. 5.7, trans. Holmes, *Apostolic Fathers*, 53.
72. 1 Tim. 1:3.
73. Cf. Titus 1:5.

more. As such, the earliest we can reasonably expect him to have returned to Rome is ca. 64. In that city he was likely executed, probably no later than the death of Nero in 68.

The Composition of 1 Timothy and Titus

There is little indication that Paul was in prison while writing 1 Timothy and Titus. According to Titus 3:12, he planned on wintering in Nicopolis, which suggests some freedom of movement when he wrote at least that letter. Thus, I am inclined to judge it probable that he wrote both 1 Timothy and ·Titus before his final imprisonment in Rome, during a hypothetical fourth missionary journey. His itinerary during this mission is unclear. My own suspicion, however, is that he visited Crete first: an itinerary from Crete north by northeast to Ephesus and then from there northwest on to Macedonia seems to make better sense than an itinerary from Ephesus northwest to Macedonia and then back south to Crete. This would make good sense of his decision to winter at Nicopolis, which would have been on the way back west to Rome. Given such an itinerary, I am inclined to think that Paul wrote both 1 Timothy and Titus from Macedonia, or perhaps from Achaia on his way toward Nicopolis. Given the above projection, I suggest that each was written sometime in 63 or 64.

The Composition of 2 Timothy

For its part, 2 Timothy was almost certainly written from Rome while Paul was undergoing his second imprisonment there. According to 2 Timothy 1:16–17, Onesiphorus sought Paul in Rome and found him. Robinson observes that nothing in 2 Timothy 1:16–17 says that Onesiphorus found Paul *in Rome*.[74] He thus argues that Onesiphorus went to Rome expecting to find Paul there, and upon realizing that Paul was not there, he made inquiries that led him to Caesarea. This is hardly an impossible reading. Nonetheless, Robinson's argument for a Caesarean origin seems notably less parsimonious than that of the argument for a Roman one. Moreover, as we have seen, a Caesarean origin does not adequately deal with the problem of Trophimus. I thus argue that Paul likely wrote 2 Timothy in Rome, no earlier than 64 and no later than 68.

---

74. Robinson, *Redating*, 75–76.

Conclusion to the Pastoral Epistles

Insofar as it is the case that

- on the basis of external attestation, we should be wary of dating 1 and 2 Timothy later than 150 and Titus later than 175;
- 1 Timothy 5:18 is most intelligible after the composition of Luke's Gospel ca. 57 through 59 and thus cannot be readily situated within Paul's career as can be reconstructed from Acts;
- 2 Timothy 4:20 is most intelligible following a visit to Miletus with Trophimus, subsequent to Paul's career as can be reconstructed from Acts;
- Titus 1:5 is most intelligible following Pauline missionary activity on Crete subsequent to Paul's career as can be reconstructed from Acts;
- Paul plausibly had a "post-Acts" career that ran from ca. 62 through 68; and
- 1 Timothy and Titus were plausibly written after a visit to Spain in 62–63 and during subsequent ministry in the eastern Mediterranean,

we conclude that 2 Timothy was plausibly written during a second Roman imprisonment; if they are Pauline, 1 Timothy and Titus were written in 63 or 64, and 2 Timothy no earlier than 64 and no later than 68. If these texts are pseudo-Pauline, then 1 and 2 Timothy could date as late as 150 and Titus as late as 175. If pseudo-Pauline, the Pastoral Epistles were likely not written before Paul became a known Christian writer. As such, I suggest that they were written no earlier than 60.

Including absolute dates relevant for our purposes as we have thus far discussed and established in this chapter, our cumulative chronological framework can be summarized in the following table (with dates of composition shown in bold):

Event	Date
Crucifixion of Jesus	ca. 29–34
Conversion of Paul	no earlier than late 29
Paul's visit to Jerusalem of Acts 9 // Gal. 1:18	no earlier than late 31
Paul's first missionary journey	40–45
Paul's visit to Jerusalem of Gal. 2:1–10	no earlier than 42

Event	Date
Death of Herod Agrippa	44
Paul's visit to Jerusalem of Acts 12	prior to 45
Galatians	**47–52**
Paul's visit to Jerusalem of Acts 15	48
Paul's Corinthian sojourn	50–52
1 Thessalonians	**50–52**
2 Thessalonians	**50–52**
Gallio's tenure in Corinth	mid-51–mid-52
Paul's probable visit to Jerusalem of Acts 18	late 52
Paul's Ephesian sojourn	54–56
Paul's possible imprisonment in Ephesus	55 or 56
1 Corinthians	**early 56**
Paul leaves Ephesus for Macedonia and then on to Greece	56
2 Corinthians	**late 56**
Romans	**winter of 56/57**
Paul's visit to Jerusalem of Acts 21	57
Paul's imprisonment in Caesarea	57–59
Ephesians, Colossians, Philemon, and Philippians	**57–59**
The succession from Felix to Festus	59
Paul's first imprisonment in Rome	60–62
One or more earthquakes strike the Lycus Valley	60–64
Paul ministers in Spain	62–63
Paul possibly returns to the eastern Mediterranean; travels to Crete, Ephesus, Macedonia	63 and 64
1 Timothy	**if Pauline: 63 or 64** **if pseudo-Pauline: 60–150**
Titus	**if Pauline: 63 or 64** **If pseudo-Pauline: 60–175**
2 Timothy	**If Pauline: 64–68** **If pseudo-Pauline: 60–150**

Cumulative Conclusion to Chapter 6:
The Compositional Dates of the Pauline Corpus

Insofar as it is the case that

- 1 and 2 Thessalonians most likely were written during Paul's Corinthian sojourn;
- the Corinthian sojourn most likely dates to 50 through 52;
- 1 Corinthians most likely was written near the final year of Paul's Ephesian sojourn;
- the Ephesian sojourn likely dates to 54 through 56;
- 2 Corinthians most likely was written just before Paul's final recorded journey to Greece, which took place in the latter part of 56;
- 2 Corinthians 1–9 and 10–13 either are both original to 2 Corinthians or were written during an ongoing interaction between Paul and the Corinthians in the latter part of 56;
- Romans most likely was written from Corinth, just prior to Paul's final recorded journey to Jerusalem;
- the integrity of Romans is more probable than not;
- correlation between Acts and Galatians favors a date for Galatians either of 47 or 48 (Acts 12 theory) or of 48 through 52 (Acts 15 theory);
- the Letter to Philemon was most likely written to Colossae at the same time as the Letter to the Colossians;
- the Letter to the Ephesians was most likely written at the same time as the Letter to the Colossians;
- Ephesians, Colossians, and Philemon were most likely written during Paul's imprisonment in Caesarea ca. 57 through 59;
- Philippians most likely was written from Caesarea during Paul's imprisonment there;
- the integrity of Philippians is more probable than not;
- on the basis of external attestation, we should be wary of dating 1 and 2 Timothy later than 150 and Titus later than 175;
- 1 and 2 Timothy and Titus are most intelligible subsequent to Paul's career as can be reconstructed from Acts; and

- 1 Timothy and Titus were plausibly written after a visit to Spain in 62–63 and during subsequent ministry in the eastern Mediterranean,

we conclude that Galatians was written sometime from 47 through 52; 1 and 2 Thessalonians, no earlier than 50 and no later than 52; 1 Corinthians, in early 56; 2 Corinthians, in late 56; Romans, in winter of 56/57; Ephesians, Colossians, Philemon, and Philippians, no earlier than 57 and no later than 59; 1 Timothy, 63 or 64 if Pauline, no earlier than 60 and no later than 150 if pseudo-Pauline; Titus, in 63 or 64 if Pauline, no earlier than 60 and no later than 175 if pseudo-Pauline; 2 Timothy, no earlier than 64 and no later than 68 if Pauline, and no earlier than 60 and no later than 150 if pseudo-Pauline.

We can summarize the likely compositional dates of the Pauline Epistles along with other works thus far investigated in this study via the following table:

Text	Date
Gospel of Mark	42–45
Gospel of Matthew	45–59
Galatians	**47–52**
1 Thessalonians	**50–52**
2 Thessalonians	**50–52**
1 Corinthians	**early 56**
2 Corinthians	**late 56**
Romans	**winter of 56/57**
Ephesians, Colossians, Philemon, and Philippians	**57–59**
Gospel of Luke	59
Gospel of John	60–70
1 and 2 John	60–100
Acts of the Apostles	62
1 Timothy	**if Pauline: 63 or 64 if pseudo-Pauline: 60–150**
Titus	**if Pauline: 63 or 64 if pseudo-Pauline: 60–175**

Text	Date
2 Timothy	**if Pauline: 64–68** **if pseudo-Pauline:** **60–150**
Revelation	68–70
3 John	before 100

Hebrews and the Letters of James, Peter, and Jude

7

Hebrews and James

Part 4 aims to establish the most probable dates for Hebrews, James, 1 and 2 Peter, and Jude.[1] These are grouped together in part because—apart from Hebrews—they are typically termed the "General" or "Catholic" Epistles. Although 1, 2, and 3 John are also typically considered General Epistles, it was most expedient to treat them as part of the larger Johannine tradition. Chapter 7 will treat Hebrews and James; chapter 8 will treat 1 and 2 Peter and Jude.

In both chapters, we consider each letter in turn, returning to our broader pattern of using synchronization, contextualization, and authorial biography as a central organizing rubric. This chapter concludes that Hebrews was most likely written no earlier than 50 and no later than 70, and James no later than 62.

Hebrews

This section aims to establish the most likely date of composition for the Letter to the Hebrews. Our approach will be the reverse of that which we

---

1. In developing this chapter, I found the following commentaries particularly useful: Achtemeier, *1 Peter*; Allison, *James*; Attridge, *Hebrews*; Koester, *Hebrews*; Lane, *Hebrews*; Laws, *James*; Martin, *James*; Mitchell, *Hebrews*.

took to the Pauline Letters. Whereas regarding the Pauline Epistles, the data compelled us to move with relative speed through the work of synchronization and contextualization to then labor at length on the work of authorial biography, with Hebrews, synchronization will offer the vast majority of data available to us. This is the case because Hebrews lacks any indication of a putative author. Although early Christians attributed the letter to Paul more than to any other figure, they were hardly universal in this judgment. More to the point, modern scholarship quite rightly recognizes Pauline authorship to be a nonstarter. For its part, judicious attention to the work of contextualization demonstrates that it offers little assistance in narrowing down the date of Hebrews. The cumulative data are such that whereas most scholars date Hebrews to the 80s and 90s, this study concludes that Hebrews was written from ca. 50 to ca. 70.

Synchronization

In this section, we consider (1) external attestation, (2) the question of persecution, (3) the death of Peter, (4) the significance of the year 70, and (5) the reference to Timothy in Hebrews 13:23. Through the work of synchronization, we conclude it to be probable that Hebrews was written sometime after 50 and sometime before 70.

External Attestation

Hebrews appears in $\mathfrak{P}^{46}$, which has been dated variously between the late first century and the mid-third century.[2] Clement of Alexandria is certainly aware of Hebrews in the late second century. Writing earlier, the author of 1 Clement is more likely than not also aware of Hebrews.[3] First Clement could potentially date as late as 150, which permits J. V. M. Sturdy to date Hebrews to 110.[4] That being said, few would date 1 Clement later than 100. External attestation thus virtually excludes a date for Hebrews much later than 150 and should make us wary of dating it much later than 100.

---

2. For a late first-century date, cf. Kim, "Dating of $\mathfrak{P}^{46}$." For an early second-century date, cf. Comfort and Barrett, *Earliest New Testament Greek Manuscripts*, 1:183–87. For a third-century date, cf. Orsini and Clarysse, "New Testament Manuscripts."

3. Cf. esp. 1 Clem. 36.2–5 with Heb. 1:3–13. Cf. Gregory, "*1 Clement* and the Writings," esp. 152–53.

4. Sturdy, *Redrawing the Boundaries*, 72. On the date of 1 Clement, see the discussion in chap. 9 below.

The Question of Persecution (Heb. 10:32–34; 12:4)

The Letter to the Hebrews contains several references to persecution. Those of potentially greatest relevance read as follows:

> But recall those earlier days when, after you had been enlightened, you endured a hard struggle with sufferings, sometimes being publicly exposed to abuse and persecution, and sometimes being partners with those so treated. For you had compassion for those who were in prison, and you cheerfully accepted the plundering of your possessions, knowing that you yourselves possessed something better and more lasting. (Heb. 10:32–34)

> In your struggle against sin you have not yet resisted to the point of shedding your blood. (Heb. 12:4)

If these passages reference a known course of persecution, immediately three candidates come to mind: the Domitianic persecution of the 90s, the Neronian persecution of the 60s, and the expulsion from Rome, likely ca. 49. The Domitianic persecution is a virtual nonstarter for the primary reason that there was likely not a Domitianic persecution.[5] Perhaps the strongest argument supporting a reference to the Neronian persecution is the suggestion in Hebrews 10:33 that some among the readers were subjected to public abuse. This could constitute a reference to the public humiliations that, according to Tacitus, were inflicted upon the Christians under Nero.[6] But Hebrews 12:4 states that the readers have not yet resisted sin to the point of shedding blood. It seems somewhat difficult to reconcile this statement with the hypothesis that they have suffered something as violent as the Neronian persecution was remembered to have been. Indeed, even John Robinson recognized that this makes a reference to the Neronian persecution here unlikely, despite his persistent tendency to frame the New Testament in relation to Nero.[7] If Hebrews 10:32–34 references the Neronian persecution, then we are probably well warranted in thinking that Tacitus has exaggerated the sufferings inflicted upon Christians at that time. However, insofar as one must adjust one's view of the Neronian persecution to fit Hebrews, one also weakens the argument that Hebrews must be referencing that event.

---

5. Cf. the discussion in the introduction to this volume.
6. Cf. Tacitus, *Ann.* 15.44.
7. Cf. Robinson, *Redating*, 211.

The expulsion from Rome in ca. 49 presents as a more likely candidate for the referent of Hebrews 10:32–34 than either a putative Neronian or Domitianic persecution.[8] Suetonius tells us that Claudius expelled "the Jews" from Rome due to disturbances instigated by a certain "Chrestus."[9] The majority of scholars identify this "Chrestus" with "Christ," infer from Suetonius's report that under Claudius there were disturbances in Rome regarding the establishment of Christianity in that city, and associate the resulting expulsions with those that Acts 18:2 reports forced Priscilla and Aquila to leave Rome. Those expelled could easily have experienced these disturbances as public mockery and persecution, as per Hebrews 10:33, and expulsion could have resulted in the loss of property, as per Hebrews 10:34. Moreover, there is little evidence of significant violence during the disturbances and the expulsion, which resonates well with 12:4. Overall, if 10:32–34 is referencing a known course of persecution, the expulsion from Rome is probably the most likely candidate.

Potentially strengthening a reference in 10:32–34 to the expulsion under Claudius is 13:24, which tells us, "Those from Italy [apo tēs Italias] send their greetings." This has at times been taken as an indication that the text was written from Italy, or more specifically, from Rome. While not impossible, it does not seem to be a natural turn of phrase for an author present *in* Italy to refer to those *from* (apo) Italy.[10] It seems more likely that the author was writing from outside Italy while in the company of Italian Christians. One further notes with interest that Acts 18:2 describes Priscilla and Aquila as having come apo tēs Italias (from Italy). This is precisely the same expression that we find in Hebrews 13:24. The possibility that Hebrews 13:24 references persons expelled from Rome ca. 49 is tantalizing. Robinson, I think, too quickly dismisses the hypothesis on the basis that it does not likely refer specifically to Priscilla and Aquila.[11] It is entirely plausible that it refers to other Christians expelled from Rome under Claudius; if this is affirmed, we might want to date the letter closer to 50 than 100. Nonetheless, that Hebrews 13:24 references persons expelled from Rome ca. 49 remains no more than a possibility. Ultimately, we should join with

---

8. On the date of the expulsion, see Jewett, *Chronology of Paul's Life*, 36–38; Lüdemann, *Paul, Apostle*, 164–71; Riesner, *Paul's Early Period*, 157–204.

9. Cf. Suetonius, *Claud.* 25.

10. Robinson quite rightly rejects this (*Redating*, 206).

11. Robinson, *Redating*, 206.

Robinson in holding that it cannot be used to reinforce the probability either that Hebrews 10:32–34 references the expulsion, or that the letter dates closer to 50 than to 100.

Cumulatively, the most we can say is that if Hebrews 10:32–34 references a known course of persecution, then it is most likely the expulsion under Claudius reported by Suetonius and Acts 18:2. Nonetheless, there is sufficient evidence that Christians suffered mistreatment in their first decades that we should be reluctant to correlate references to persecution too closely with any known historical example without a compelling reason. Moreover, even if Hebrews is referencing the expulsion of 49, the text could have been written much later. The question of persecution should be considered nonprobative with regard to establishing the date of Hebrews.

Quo Vadis? (Heb. 6:6)

Robinson makes much of Hebrews 6:6, which, including verses 4–5, reads as follows:

> For it is impossible to restore again to repentance those who have once been enlightened, and have tasted the heavenly gift, and have shared in the Holy Spirit, and have tasted the goodness of the word of God and the powers of the age to come, and then have fallen away, since on their own they are crucifying again the Son of God and are holding him up to contempt. (Heb. 6:4–6)

Robinson argues that Hebrews 6:6 is referring to the *Quo Vadis?* legend preserved in the Acts of Peter 35.[12]

> But while they made these plans Xanthippe discovered her husband's conspiracy with Agrippa and sent and told Peter, so that he might withdraw from Rome. And the rest of the brethren together with Marcellus entreated him to withdraw. But Peter said to them, "Shall we act like deserters, brethren?" But they said to him, "No, it is so that you can go on serving the Lord." So he assented to the brethren and withdrew by himself, saying "Let none of you retire with me, but I shall retire by myself in disguise." As he went out of the gate he saw the Lord entering Rome; and when he saw him he said, "Lord, whither (goest thou) here [*quo vadis*]?" And the Lord said to him, "I am coming to Rome to be crucified." And Peter said to him, "Lord, art thou being crucified again?" He said to him,

12. Robinson, *Redating*, 214.

"Yes, Peter, I am being crucified again." And Peter came to himself; and he saw the Lord ascending into heaven; then he returned to Rome rejoicing and giving praise to the Lord, because he said, "I am being crucified"; (since) this was to happen to Peter.[13]

The phrase "being crucified again" in both passages is sufficiently close that we should probably imagine some sort of connection, whether Hebrews knew Acts of Peter, Acts of Peter knew Hebrews, or both drew upon common tradition. Robinson argues that Hebrews 6:6 betrays a familiarity with this legend and thus must postdate Peter's death.[14] While this is not impossible, neither is it particularly probable. It is more likely that Hebrews predates Acts of Peter; thus we should be wary of using a text found in the latter as background for the former. Indeed, it seems significantly more probable that if there is any direct connection between the two passages, Hebrews 6:6 served as a source for Acts of Peter 35. Robinson's argument is indeed sufficiently weak that I almost did not include discussion of it in this study. We should consider Hebrews 6:6 and the death of Peter to be nonprobative with regard to the date of the Letter to the Hebrews.

Would Not the Sacrifices Have Ceased? (Heb. 10:1–3)

Robinson begins his discussion of the date of Hebrews with the statement that "apart from the prophecies of the fall of Jerusalem in the synoptic gospels, there is no other piece of New Testament literature that raises so acutely as does the epistle to the Hebrews the question of its relation to the events of 70."[15] This rather overstates the case: we have already seen that the matter of 70 is also of decisive importance for thinking about the date of John's Gospel and the Revelation of John. Unsurprisingly, Robinson further engages in a problematic argument from silence in advancing his argument. He emphasizes this line of argumentation from silence by comparing Hebrews with Epistle of Barnabas 16.4, which explicitly references the Jewish War and the destruction of the temple.[16] The comparison is interesting and potentially even instructive, but it does not establish that Hebrews should evince a comparable awareness if written post-70.

13. Acts Pet. 35, trans. Schneemelcher, "Acts of Peter," 314.
14. Robinson, *Redating*, 214. Here Robinson follows Edmundson, *Church in Rome*, 153.
15. Robinson, *Redating*, 200.
16. Robinson, *Redating*, 204. Cf. the discussion of Barn. 16.4 in chap. 10 below.

Nonetheless, there is a positive argument to be made for a pre-70 date from the text of Hebrews. The relevant passage here is Hebrews 10:1–3:

> Since the law has only a shadow of the good things to come and not the true form of these realities, it can never, by the same sacrifices that are continually offered year after year, make perfect those who approach. Otherwise, would they not have ceased being offered, since the worshipers, cleansed once for all, would no longer have any consciousness of sin? But in these sacrifices there is a reminder of sin year after year.

Hebrews here speaks of the temple in the present tense. This could be taken as a historical present, such as we find elsewhere in reference to the temple after 70.[17] As such, the present tense itself does not establish that Hebrews 10:1–13 was written before 70. Nonetheless, Hebrews here asks a question that would seem to make stronger rhetorical sense before 70. If in 85 I were to ask, "Would not the sacrifices have ceased being offered?" you likely would respond, "But they have!" It might be objected that sacrifices continued to be offered at the site of the former temple for some time after 70, and thus the window of probable dates must be extended upward.[18] That there continued to be some sacrifices at the site of the former temple cannot be excluded, although neither can it be shown. Surely there was some disruption in the operations of the cult ca. 70, a reality that stands in some variance with Hebrews's emphasis upon its undisrupted continuity.

Consequent to the above, it might be best said that while Hebrews 10:1–3 does not exclude the possibility of a post-70 date, it is more readily intelligible if written before 70. As such, without evidence that necessitates a post-70 date for the letter, we should favor a pre-70 one.

Our Brother, Timothy (Heb. 13:23)

Consistent with but not necessitating a pre-70 date is the reference to "our brother, Timothy" in 13:23. However, because we have established a pre-70 date to be more likely than a post-70 one, this datum allows us to potentially narrow down the range during which Hebrews was most likely

---

17. Cf. Josephus, *Ant.* 4.6.1–8 §§102–50; 4.7.1–7 §§151–87; 4.9.1–7 §§224–57. Cf. also discussions in Attridge, *Hebrews*, 8; Lane, *Hebrews*, 1:lxiii. Note that this differs from the case of John 5:2, where there are reasons to exclude a historical present.

18. Cf. the argument in Clark, "Jerusalem Temple after A.D. 70."

written. Acts 16:1–2 indicates that Timothy was already active in Christian ministry by ca. 49. According to Acts 16:2, when deciding to take him along in his ministry, Paul relied upon the testimony of the believers in Lystra and Iconium. According to Acts 14:18–19, Paul had himself been active in the area just a few years earlier. Thus, given that Paul had limited personal knowledge of Timothy ca. 49, we can reasonably infer that Timothy either was not a believer at that earlier time, or was a believer but had not yet assumed a leadership role. We should thus be wary of dating Hebrews much earlier than 50.

Yet Hebrews 13 is sometimes considered to be secondary to our epistle. William Lane helpfully lists three major reasons for seeing Hebrews 13 this way: (1) "The chapter begins abruptly, without apparent link with what precedes"; (2) "The form of chap. 13 is without parallel in earlier chapters," as "the exhortation suddenly gives way to a series of catechetical precepts"; and (3) "The content of chap. 13 clearly distinguishes this section from the remainder of the document."[19] None of these reasons are particularly compelling, either on their own or cumulatively. Nonetheless, the admitted possibility that Hebrews 13 is secondary does somewhat vitiate the evidentiary value of 13:23. Likewise, we cannot exclude the possibility that the reference to Timothy is part of a pious fiction aimed to associate the letter with Paul.[20] Equally, we cannot exclude the possibility that Hebrews 13:23 references another man named Timothy altogether. Still, the reference to Timothy in Hebrews 13:23 does seem to be more intelligible after he entered Christian ministry ca. 50 than earlier.

Conclusion to Hebrews: Synchronization

Insofar as it is the case that

- the data of external attestation allow a date for Hebrews as late as 140, although we should probably be wary of a date much later than 100;
- the references to persecution within Hebrews are nonprobative for establishing the date of composition;

19. Lane, *Hebrews*, 2:496.
20. An understanding of Hebrews argued at length by Rothschild, *Hebrews as Pseudepigraphon*.

- the death of Peter is nonprobative with regard to the date of the Letter to the Hebrews;
- the rhetoric of Hebrews 10:1–3 is more intelligible if the temple yet stood; and
- the reference to Timothy in Hebrews 13:23 is more intelligible after he entered Christian ministry ca. 50 than earlier,

we conclude that Hebrews was written no earlier than 50 and no later than 70.

Contextualization

In this section, we will consider whether Hebrews 2:3 and 13:7 refer to a postapostolic context. We conclude that while this is possible, it is not sufficiently probable to overturn the conclusion reached on the basis of synchronization.

Hebrews 2:3 reads as follows: "How can we escape if we neglect so great a salvation? It was declared at first through the Lord, and it was attested to us by those who heard him." From this one might infer that Hebrews was written at a time when some but not many of those who heard the earthly Jesus remained yet alive. Such inference overstates the evidence. Hebrews 2:3 necessitates only that the speaker and the recipients consist mostly (but not necessarily primarily or exclusively) of persons who had not heard the earthly Jesus. Such a condition is intelligible from 40 onward. On the one hand, by the 50s at the latest, we find in the person of Paul a significant Christian leader who did not know the earthly Jesus. Indeed, the number of Christians who had seen or heard the earthly Jesus would likely have been a distinct minority by 40. The author could conceivably be writing at least as early as 50 and yet use such language as we find in Hebrews 2:3. On the other hand, the language of Hebrews 2:3 hardly supposes that those who attested to the earthly Jesus did so only by spoken word. The author could quite conceivably be writing well into the second century and yet use such language as we find in 2:3. As such, Hebrews 2:3 is nonprobative for purposes of establishing the date of our letter.

Hebrews 13:7 admonishes the readers, "Remember your leaders, those who spoke the word of God to you; consider the outcome of their way of life, and imitate their faith." As "those who spoke the word of God to you," the leaders in question were likely those who founded the community. Since they are to be remembered, they are likely deceased. The difficulty is that we do not know who these leaders were and thus when they might have died. Moreover, we certainly know that major leaders of the first Christian generation had died by 70. Hence, Hebrews 13:7 does not suffice for us to prefer a date later than 70. Hebrews 13:7 might incline one to prefer a date closer to 70 than to 50, but given the chronological ambiguities around the passage, we should prefer to say more generally that Hebrews was written ca. 50 through ca. 70.

Conclusion to Hebrews: Contextualization

Insofar as it is the case that

- on the basis of synchronization we can with reasonable confidence date Hebrews no earlier than 50 and no later than 70;
- Hebrews 2:3 necessitates only that the speaker and the recipients consist largely of persons who had not heard the earthly Jesus—a condition intelligible from 40 onward; and
- Hebrews 13:7 provides insufficient data to determine when the "leaders . . . who spoke the word of God to you" had passed away,

we conclude that Hebrews was written no earlier than 50 and no later than 70.

Authorial Biography

The Letter to the Hebrews has frequently been associated with Paul and his circle. Indeed, $\mathfrak{P}^{46}$, which we have noted is the earliest extant collection of Paul's writings, includes the Letter to the Hebrews. Already in the second century, however, readers recognized difficulties with the Pauline attribution. Clement of Alexandria, for instance, suggested that Paul had written the work in Hebrew and that Luke had then translated it into Greek.[21] Such reticence surrounding the Pauline attribution has led to a veritable cottage industry aimed at identifying the author. Figures as diverse as Apollos, Barnabas, Clement of Rome, Luke himself (and not as a translator), and Priscilla and Aquila have been suggested. None of these can be excluded

21. According to Eusebius, *Hist. eccl.* 6.14.2.

with certainty, but neither do any rise above the level of possibility. Origen's famous quip that only God knows the author probably contains more truth than error.[22] The most we might say is that the widespread tendency to attribute Hebrews to a companion of Paul could reflect a memory that the author was a contemporary of the apostle. It is far from certain that we can say even that.

Conclusion to Hebrews: Authorial Biography

Insofar as it is the case that

- on the basis of synchronization and contextualization we can with reasonable confidence date Hebrews no earlier than 50 and no later than 70; and
- the author of Hebrews is unknown, and as such the work of authorial biography contributes little to establishing the compositional date of the epistle,

we conclude that Hebrews was written no earlier than 50 and no later than 70.

Cumulative Conclusion to Hebrews

Insofar as it is the case that

- the data of external attestation allow a date for Hebrews as late as 140, although we should probably be wary of a date much later than 100;
- the rhetoric of Hebrews 10:1-3 is more intelligible if the temple yet stood; and
- the reference to Timothy in Hebrews 13:23 is more intelligible after he entered Christian ministry ca. 50,

we can with reasonable confidence date Hebrews no earlier than 50 and no later than 70.

---

22. According to Eusebius, *Hist. eccl.* 6.25.14.

James

This section aims to establish the most probable date of composition for the canonical Epistle of James. Unlike other New Testament books, it is difficult to define a majority opinion on the date of James's letter.[23] Dale Allison suggests that there are two basic schools of thought with regard to James: "Either James the brother of the Lord stands behind our text, or it is a pseudepigraphon written in his name."[24] Those who suppose that James the brother of the Lord stands behind the text tend to date the letter prior to 62, the most likely year of James's death. Those who suppose that it is a pseudonymous work tend to date the letter after 70. This study argues that indeed James the brother of the Lord stands behind our text; thus we conclude that the Epistle of James was written no later than 62.

Synchronization

In this section, we consider (1) external attestation, (2) the letter's relationship with the broader New Testament Jesus tradition, (3) its relationship to the Letters of Paul, and (4) the possible relevance of the Birkat Haminim. On the basis of synchronization, we conclude that the Epistle of James probably was written no later than 125.

External Attestation

The Epistle of James lacks unequivocal attestation prior to Origen in the third century.[25] There are certainly points of similarity among 1 Peter, 1 Clement, or Shepherd of Hermas on the one hand and the Epistle of James on the other. Nonetheless, in none of these cases is the evidence clear enough to establish whether these texts betray knowledge of the Epistle of James, whether James betrays knowledge of these texts, or whether they collectively betray knowledge of shared, nonextant traditions (oral or written) or a common milieu. Given only the data of external attestation, then, we cannot with certainty exclude a date for James as late as 200. Nonetheless, the later one dates the letter after 100, the more instances of possible

---

23. Cf. the survey of proposed dates in Allison, *James*, 27–29.
24. Allison, *James*, 4.
25. For this section, cf. the relatively recent overview of the evidence relevant for early attestation in Allison, *James*, 13–18.

attestation one needs to discount. As such, one should probably be wary of dating the Epistle of James much later than the first quarter of the early second century—that is, 125.

Relationship to the Broader New Testament Jesus Tradition

There is a dense set of relationships between Jesus tradition in James on the one hand and Jesus tradition in other New Testament writings, especially the Gospel of Matthew. John Kloppenborg helpfully identifies a number of models by which to account for this relationship: the first denies that there is any Jesus tradition in the Epistle of James, positing that the two lone references to Jesus (1:1; 2:1) are secondary interpolations; the second likewise denies that there is Jesus tradition in the Epistle of James but does not consider the references to Jesus to be interpolations; the third posits that the Epistle of James knows and utilizes one or more Synoptic Gospels as a source for Jesus tradition; the fourth posits that, as the brother of Jesus, the author is dependent upon his own eyewitness memories; the fifth posits that the Jesus tradition common to the Jacobean and Synoptic material results from common oral tradition; the sixth posits that the Jesus tradition common to the Jacobean and Synoptic texts results from common written material, with an emphasis upon the hypothetical Q text.[26] For our purposes, we might group these six models into two broad categories: independence theories, which encompass all but the third model, and dependence theories, which encompass the third as well as the logically possible if not empirically probable hypothesis that the Epistle of James constituted a source of Jesus tradition for one or more Synoptic Gospels. Given the number of documents involved, one could in principle imagine that there is much truth to both categories.

We need not ultimately resolve this matter for our purposes. Rather, we need only recognize that the complexity of the data resists a clear resolution to the question of how the Jesus tradition in the Epistle of James relates to that found in the balance of the New Testament, especially the Synoptic Gospels. As such, we should probably consider this matter to be nonprobative for establishing the date of the Epistle of James.

---

26. Cf. Kloppenborg, "Jesus Tradition in James." Cf. the history of scholarship in P. Foster, "Q and James."

Relationship to the Letters of Paul

It is often supposed that the Epistle of James is responding to Paul, especially his Letters to the Romans and the Galatians. James 2:14–24 is typically considered the locus classicus for reading our letter as a Jacobean or pseudo-Jacobean response to Paul. We begin with James 2:14–19:

> What good is it, my brothers and sisters, if you say you have faith but do not have works? Can faith save you? If a brother or sister is naked and lacks daily food, and one of you says to them, "Go in peace; keep warm and eat your fill," and yet you do not supply their bodily needs, what is the good of that? So faith by itself, if it has no works, is dead.
>
> But someone will say, "You have faith and I have works." Show me your faith apart from your works, and I by my works will show you my faith. You believe that God is one; you do well. Even the demons believe—and shudder.

There can be little doubt that in this passage the author is engaged with one or more putative interlocutors. The data, however, are not friendly to the hypothesis that these putative interlocutors include Paul. Let us begin with James 2:14. Does that passage suggest that the Epistle of James is responding to someone, and is that person surely not Paul? Let us consider. The conditional nature of the phrase "if you say you have faith" (*ean pistin legē tis echein*) suggests that we are dealing with hypothetical speech: not necessarily with what has been said, but with what might be said. As such, perhaps the writer knows of an actual interlocutor who is saying this, or perhaps not. This does not seem sufficient to demonstrate that the Epistle of James is responding to an actual interlocutor, let alone that the interlocutor is Paul.

At casual glance, perhaps more promising for the hypothesis that the epistle is responding to Paul is 2:18a. Is not the author surely presenting the words of a hypothetical interlocutor? Yes, surely. Is not this hypothetical interlocutor surely Paul? Probably not, for if the hypothetical interlocutor is Paul, then James is presenting Paul as one who will say that he has works rather than faith! For its part, James 2:18b seems more likely a response to Paul. Here the Epistle of James enjoins the reader, "Show me your faith apart from your works, and I by my works will show you my faith." We can certainly grant that this could be a response to Paul. Equally, it might not be; I am wary to affirm 2:18b as a response to Paul when 2:18a so clearly is not.

This brings us to James 2:20–24:

> Do you want to be shown, you senseless person, that faith apart from works is barren? Was not our ancestor Abraham justified by works when he offered his son Isaac on the altar? You see that faith was active along with his works, and faith was brought to completion by the works. Thus the scripture was fulfilled that says, "Abraham believed God, and it was reckoned to him as righteousness," and he was called the friend of God. You see that a person is justified by works and not by faith alone.

This passage is frequently read alongside Romans 4:1–5 and Galatians 3:6–18. Certainly, James and Paul each present what we might loosely describe as "Christian midrash" upon the Abraham tradition from Genesis, with a shared interest in especially Genesis 15:6 (cf. Rom. 4:3; Gal. 3:6; James 2:23). For our purposes, the question is whether such shared interest most likely results from the Epistle of James using either Romans or Galatians as sources. As often is the case with such situations, the data do not permit us to rule out either that Romans and Galatians are responding to the Epistle of James, or that both Paul and the Epistle of James gain this shared interest from common oral or written discourses and traditions no longer extant.

Cumulatively, we are left with a statement (James 2:14) that may or may not be responding to an actual interlocutor; a statement (2:18a) that declares the opposite of the Pauline position against which the author is putatively arguing; a passage (2:18b) that could but need not be a response to Paul; and an interest in Abrahamic tradition—especially Genesis 15:6 (James 2:20–24)—that could but need not be a response to Paul. Such ambiguity stands in marked contrast to what we find in Galatians, wherein Paul explicitly tells us that he has had dealings with a certain James and with people associated with (presumably) that same James.[27] Even if we do not judge the historical James brother of the Lord to have been the author of our letter, it remains true that Paul is demonstrably familiar with someone named James in a way that the Epistle of James is not demonstrably familiar with Paul. Moreover, Paul demonstrates this familiarity precisely in one of the letters that evinces the greatest resonances with the Epistle of James. Such awareness on Paul's part inclines us toward the position that if there is any dependence between the Epistle of James and Galatians, it

---

27. Cf. Gal. 1:19; 2:9; 2:12.

seems more likely that Paul in Galatians is responding to the Epistle of James than that the Epistle of James is responding to Paul.

That having been said, it remains far from clear that Paul must be responding to James or James to Paul. Robinson advances the possibility that Paul is not responding to the Epistle of James but rather to distorted Jacobean teaching.[28] More specifically, he outlines a narrative by which the Epistle of James represents James's authentic teachings; these teachings were intended for Jewish persons, but "persons from James" (cf. Gal. 2:12), acting without instructions (cf. Acts 15:24), extended these teachings to gentile Christians; the actions of these unauthorized representatives provoked the controversy that led to the Jerusalem Council (Acts 15); and Galatians responds to these extended teachings rather than to the Epistle of James. This is to say, Paul is responding to teaching that was uttered in James's name and extended James's own teaching but that did not in fact issue from James himself. Robinson's narrative is tantalizing, yet we should be wary of considering it any more than possible. Ultimately, we should conclude that the relationship between the Epistle of James and the Epistles of Paul is nonprobative, although if it is probative, James likely predates Paul's Epistles.

The Birkat Haminim (James 3:9-10)

We have already established that the Jewish benediction known as the Birkat Haminim is irrelevant for establishing the compositional date of the Gospel of John.[29] Many of the same reasons that render the Birkat Haminim irrelevant for the Gospel of John make it equally irrelevant for establishing the compositional date of the Letter of James. Nonetheless, a recent, quite prominent commentator on the Epistle of James has argued that James 3:9–10 most likely betrays knowledge of the Birkat Haminim and that the letter was therefore likely written after 70.[30] Adverting to our earlier discussion of the Birkat Haminim, we can advance the following reasons for thinking otherwise.

First, there is the question of whether James 3:9–10 does in fact betray knowledge of the Birkat Haminim. Beginning at verse 8, the passage reads as follows:

28. Robinson, *Redating*, 128.
29. Cf. the discussion in chap. 3 above.
30. Cf. the discussions in Allison, *James*, 29, 552–53.

But no one can tame the tongue—a restless evil, full of deadly poison. With it we bless the Lord and Father, and with it we curse those who are made in the likeness of God. From the same mouth come blessing and cursing. My brothers and sisters, this ought not to be so. (James 3:8–10)

We can certainly grant that James 3:9–10 could be referring to the Birkat Haminim, where indeed heretics (*minim*) and in some versions Christians (*notserim*) are cursed. We must also acknowledge that there is little to connect this passage with the Birkat Haminim. Indeed, the passage need not be read as more than just a general, perhaps proverbial, recognition that the mouth can both bless and curse. Allison argues for a connection since "James uses καταρώμεθα [*katarōmetha*] and κατάρα [*katara*]," and "in apparent references to the benediction against heretics, Justin Martyr [in *Dial*. 16.4] uses that very verb and that very noun."[31] We should, however, emphasize the word "apparent" here: it is not self-evident that Justin is referencing the Birkat Haminim in *Dialogue with Trypho* 16.4.[32] It is possible—perhaps even probable—that with the words *katarōmetha* and *katara* James intends to reference identical practices as does Justin. It is also possible—perhaps even probable—that Justin is referencing the Birkat Haminim. But the cumulative uncertainty in both those propositions should give us pause before determining that James is referencing the Birkat Haminim here.

There is a further chronological issue. Allison leans upon Joel Marcus's then-recent work on the origins of the Birkat Haminim.[33] He correctly notes that Marcus's work significantly increases the possibility that the Birkat Haminim existed in the late first century.[34] Marcus, however, also argues that the Birkat Haminim might have antecedents already as early as Jesus's lifetime. As such, even if we grant that indeed James 3:9–10 is referencing the Birkat Haminim or something much like it, this would not preclude a date for the letter potentially as early as the 30s. Cumulatively, given that it is far from certain that James 3:9–10 betrays knowledge of the Birkat Haminim or its antecedents, and given that the Birkat Haminim or its antecedents could plausibly predate even Jesus's ministry, we should consider the Birkat Haminim to be nonprobative for establishing the date of the Epistle of James.

31. Allison, *James*, 552.
32. Cf. also Justin Martyr, *Dial*. 47.2; 96.2; 137.2.
33. Cf. Joel Marcus, "Birkat ha-Minim Revisited."
34. Cf. Allison, *James*, 552.

Conclusion to James: Synchronization

Insofar as it is the case that

- external attestation should leave us wary of dating the Epistle of James later than 125;
- the Epistle of James's relationship to the New Testament Jesus tradition is such that we cannot determine with precision which if any of these texts utilized James, or which if any were utilized by James;
- the Epistle of James's relationship to the Letters of Paul is such that we cannot determine whether the author knew Paul's writings, whether Paul knew the Epistle of James, or whether both are mutually independent, although Paul's knowledge of the Epistle of James is more likely than the Epistle of James's knowledge of Paul; and
- the date of the Birkat Haminim is irrelevant for establishing the date of the Letter of James,

we conclude that the Epistle of James was written no later than 125.

Contextualization

In this section, we will consider (1) the writing's Jewish matrix, (2) the reference to the recipients' synagogue in James 2:2, (3) the absence of what is normally considered to be distinctive Christian language, and (4) the ecclesiology supposed by the letter. On the cumulative basis of synchronization and contextualization, we conclude that the Epistle of James was written no later than 125.

The Jewish Matrix

As with Hebrews, there is little doubt that the Epistle of James is immersed in imagery and Scriptures drawn from the Jewish tradition. The Wisdom tradition seems to have been particularly influential. Jewish imagery and Scriptures broadly and the Wisdom tradition more specifically continued to influence Christianity from the earliest period up through the second century.[35] Immersion in imagery and Scriptures drawn from the Jewish tradition does little to narrow down the date of the Epistle of James.

---

35. Cf. Allison, who has argued that James's Jewish matrix indicates a second-century Ebionite origin (*James*).

Of related interest are the suggestions that the Epistle of James originated in Palestine and was written to the diaspora. The strongest evidence for this is that the letter is written to "the twelve tribes in the diaspora."[36] This prima facie suggests a Palestinian origin and a diasporic destination for the text. Certainly, a text deeply immersed within the Jewish tradition and written from Palestine to the diaspora would be consistent with a lower date, not to mention Jacobean authorship. Nonetheless, although the evidence for "Jewish Christianity" within Palestine decreases after 70, there is not an absence of evidence.[37] In the introduction we have already seen a report from Eusebius telling us that Domitian had members of Jesus's extended family arrested.[38] We might add to this another report from Eusebius—namely, that members of Jesus's family traveled throughout the land expounding upon genealogical matters.[39] Eusebius offers a list of bishops of Jerusalem up through the Bar Kokhba revolt (132–135), most of whom have names more likely to belong to Jewish than to gentile persons.[40] Thus, there are some hints that what we might loosely call Jewish Christianity continued within Palestine at least through Domitian's reign and up through 135.

Given the above considerations, the certain Jewish matrix and probable Palestinian origin should individually and cumulatively be considered nonprobative for establishing the date of the Epistle of James.

Into Your Synagogue (James 2:2)

In James 2:2 the author refers to people coming "into your assembly," or more literally, "into your synagogue" (eis synagōgēn hymōn). Early Christians did not frequently use synagōgē to reference their own assemblies. "Infrequent" is not identical with "never," however. The Shepherd of Hermas and Ignatius's Letter to Polycarp both use synagōgē to reference Christian gatherings.[41] Ignatius is almost certainly a second-century work, and the Shepherd is most

---

36. James 1:1.
37. With specific regard to Palestine, cf. the overview of the relevant evidence in Broadhead, *Jewish Ways*, 80–90. Cf. the various discussions in Skarsaune and Hvalvik, *Jewish Believers*. On the difficulties of defining Jewish Christianity and identifying its remains archaeologically, cf. esp. Broadhead, *Jewish Ways*, 6–58; Carleton Paget, "Definition of the Terms"; and Skarsaune, "Jewish Believers"; Strange, "Archaeological Evidence?"
38. Eusebius, *Hist. eccl.* 3.19.1–3.20.7.
39. Eusebius, *Hist. eccl.* 1.7.14.
40. Eusebius, *Hist. eccl.* 4.5.3–4. Cf. also Epiphanius, *Pan.* 66.1–2.
41. Herm. Mand. 11.9, 13, 14 (43.9, 13, 14); Ign. *Pol.* 4.2.

frequently dated after 100.[42] This might lead one to conclude that the Letter of James is probably a second-century or at least a post-70 composition. Nonetheless, insofar as *synagōgē* was also a term current among Jewish groups in the pre-70 era, and insofar as early Christianity remained heavily Jewish during that period, James 2:2 seems just as intelligible in this earlier period. Hence, James 2:2 should be considered nonprobative for purposes of establishing the compositional date.

James's Conspicuous Silences

This section addresses what Allison has felicitously described as "James' conspicuous silences."[43] By this term, Allison refers to the reality that "everything that we think of as being characteristically Christian remains [in the letter] at best tacit."[44] When one reads the Epistle of James, one is struck by both its failure to explicitly address the readers as followers of Jesus and its general lack of christological statements. Such distinctive language is, to a large extent, evident already in the Pauline corpus, which makes the absence of that language all the more conspicuous when we read the Epistle of James. This would be even more striking if the Epistle of James is responding to Paul.[45] Not surprisingly, Robinson wants to make much of such silences.[46] Yet as with any argument from silence, the absence of such distinctive language is of limited probative value. One can indeed plausibly explain this absence by stating that the Epistle of James predates the development of such language. Alternatively, one can argue that the Epistle of James dates relatively late, issuing from a sector of Christianity that had not yet adopted such characteristic language.[47]

Yet there is some reason to favor the hypothesis that the Epistle of James represents a relatively early text that largely predates the Christian distinctives and second-century concerns discussed above, rather than a relatively late text issuing from a sector of Christianity in which these were generally absent. These distinctives and concerns are evident among those Christian groups and persons who over the course of the second century developed the initial outlines of what became the New Testament canon. Precisely to the extent that

---

42. On the date of the Shepherd of Hermas, see chap. 10 below.
43. Allison, *James*, 36.
44. Allison, *James*, 37.
45. Cf. the discussion above.
46. Cf. Robinson, *Redating*, 119–20.
47. Again, cf. Allison, *James*.

one presents the Epistle of James as the product of a Christianity distant from the Christians who were responsible for developing the distinctive Christian language evident throughout the balance of the canon, to that extent one will have difficulty accounting for why it came to be included in that canon at all. This problem largely disappears the moment we affirm that the Epistle of James originated relatively early, during a time before Christianity had yet to develop much of the distinctive language on display in other New Testament texts or an interest in the concerns evident in second-century Christian writings.

It must be stressed, however, that while such considerations might give us some reason to favor a lower rather than a higher date on the basis of contextualization, it does not suffice to render lower dates probable or higher ones improbable. Moreover, we should as always be wary of affirming any argument predicated upon silence. As such, I am inclined to consider James's conspicuous silences to be tantalizing but ultimately of limited value for establishing the date of the letter.

Ecclesiology

The Epistle of James evinces explicit awareness of two "positions" or roles within the church: teachers and elders.[48] If these were indeed the only roles known to the author, then we might well have reason to prefer lower and middle over higher dates. Certainly, the later we date the Epistle of James into the second century, the more we should expect to see some reference to bishops. Here, however, we must give the following caveats. First, we must remember that ecclesiology did not necessarily develop at a uniform pace across the ancient world. Second, we must always be wary of arguments from silence. We cannot rule out the possibility that the author is aware of but does not mention other ecclesiastical positions. Nonetheless, given the letter's ecclesiology, we should probably be wary of dating the letter much later than 125.

Conclusion to James: Contextualization

Insofar as it is the case that

- on the basis of synchronization, the Epistle of James was written no later than 125;

---

48. James 3:1; 5:14.

- Christian immersion within Jewish imagery and Scripture continued through the first and second centuries and thus cannot narrow down the compositional date of the Epistle of James;
- James 2:2 could here reference Christian assemblies as early as the 30s and into the second century;
- the lack within James of distinctive Christian language found elsewhere in the New Testament might lead us to favor an earlier rather than a later date, but that lack cannot do so decisively; and
- the ecclesiology of the Epistle of James is wholly intelligible within the first century and does not require, yet does not exclude, a second-century provenance,

we conclude that the Epistle of James probably was written no later than 125.

Authorial Biography

The previous two sections demonstrated that little in the way of synchronization or contextualization militates against a date for the Epistle of James as early as the 30s or as late as 200. As such, we must turn to the data of authorial biography. In what follows, I ask which James likely authored our letter and where we might be able to date the text within his career. Judging the author to be James brother of the Lord, I argue that the Epistle of James likely dates no later than his death in 62.

James 1:1 explicitly identifies the author of the letter as James. The New Testament contains a multitude of persons named James: James son of Zebedee; James son of Alphaeus; James son of Mary, brother of Joseph; James brother of the Lord (a.k.a. James the Just); James "the lesser" or "the younger," son of Mary, brother of Joseph; James son of Mary; James father of Judas (not Iscariot).[49] Most probably, all three persons identified as James

---

49. • James son of Zebedee, brother of John, is referenced explicitly by this name in Matt. 4:21; 10:2; Mark 1:19; 3:17; 5:37; 10:35; Luke 5:10; Acts 12:2. He is presumably included in the phrase "sons of Zebedee" in Matt. 20:20; 27:56. He is the probable referent in Matt. 17:1; Mark 1:29; 9:2; 10:41; 13:3; 14:33; Luke 6:15; 8:51; 9:28, 54.
• James son of Alphaeus is referenced in Matt. 10:3; Mark 3:18; Luke 6:15; Acts 1:13.
• James brother of the Lord, is referenced in Matt. 13:55; Mark 6:3. He is the probable referent in Acts 12:17; 15:13; 21:18; 1 Cor. 15:7; Gal. 1:19; 2:9; 2:12; Jude 1.
• James son of Mary and brother of Joseph is mentioned in Matt. 27:56.

son of Mary are the same. This man could potentially also be identified
with James son of Alphaeus. As such, there are most likely four—possibly
five—persons named James in our New Testament. This probably reflects
the reality that James represents one of the most common male names in
Palestine at the time.[50] Fortunately for our discussion, only James son of
Zebedee and James brother of the Lord are ever identified simply as "James,"
without qualification. Given the absence of such qualification here, our letter
likely intends for us to identify one of these two men as the putative author.

James son of Zebedee was executed under Herod Agrippa, no later than
the latter's death in 43.[51] James brother of the Lord was executed in 62.[52] If
the son of Zebedee were the author, then the Epistle of James could date no
later than the early 40s; if the brother of the Lord, no later than the early
60s. Because the early 40s is usually considered too early for the Epistle of
James, there has emerged a general agreement that the putative author is
James brother of the Lord. Against this general agreement one could raise
three challenges. First, thus far we have found nothing to exclude a date for
the Epistle of James in the early 40s or even the 30s, and thus James son of
Zebedee remains a possible author. Second, if the Epistle of James is pseudonymous, then it could potentially be attributed to James son of Zebedee
and yet date decades after his death. Third, we cannot exclude the possibility
that the James of 1:1 is James son of Alphaeus, James son of Mary, James
the lesser, or indeed an otherwise unattested James. These qualifications notwithstanding, it does seem more likely that James brother of the Lord is the
putative author, whether the letter is authentic or pseudonymous. The present
study will proceed on that basis.

We should, however, consider some of the more prevalent arguments
against reading the Epistle of James as an authentic Jacobean work. It is
often objected that James brother of the Lord could not have composed the
Epistle of James, as he would have lacked the necessary fluency in Greek.
Such argumentation risks committing the ecological fallacy, wherein one
supposes that James could not have written such a letter since most people

---

- James "the lesser," son of Mary and brother of Joseph, is mentioned in Mark 15:40.
- James son of Mary is mentioned in Mark 16:1; Luke 24:10.
- James father of Judas is referenced in Luke 6:16; Acts 1:13.

50. Cf. the discussion in Bauckham, *Jesus and the Eyewitnesses*, 67–92.

51. Cf. Acts 12 and the discussions in Jewett, *Chronology of Paul's Life*, 33–34; Riesner,
Paul's Early Period, 117–23.

52. Cf. Josephus, *Ant.* 20.9.1 §200.

from his sort of background would not have been able to do so.[53] Insofar as "most" is not synonymous with "all," the fallacious character of such argumentation is evident. This is not mere sophistry: the very fact that James and Peter were key leaders in one of the ancient world's most successful religious movements means that they were not typical persons. If anyone is an exception to a generalization that admits of exceptions, it is the demonstrably exceptional person.

In addition to the above, we must consider the possibility that James had assistance from scribes with the skills necessary to write our Epistle of James. Bart Ehrman has argued stridently against the hypothesis that scribes could and did contribute substantially to the shape of the texts that they helped write, at least in texts such as those found in the New Testament.[54] Ehrman examines those known texts in which scribes contributed to the shape of the texts that they helped to write. He argues that these come from persons of much higher class than were the authors of early Christian writings. He further argues that insofar as Christian literature was produced by less affluent persons, their scribes would have lacked the skill needed to contribute to the texts on which they labored. This is an argument from a silence that does not really even exist: it holds if and only if one grants that the practices of a Cicero cannot be thought to be comparable to that of a Paul. This is likely a non sequitur. After all, skill is relative. Tertius (cf. Rom. 16:22) might not have been as skilled a writer as those scribes who aided Cicero (although this is not a given), but he did demonstrably have some skill. At the very least, the possible contributions of scribes are such as to allow for the possibility that James had a greater or lesser degree of assistance in writing the canonical letter attributed to him. Thus, the argument that James could not have written this letter fails.

As discussed during the work of synchronization (above), there is no unambiguous external evidence for the Epistle of James prior to the early third century. Such lack of clear, early attestation might be taken as evidence that our Epistle of James is pseudo-Jacobean.[55] Such argumentation is less than convincing, most notably because it is an argument from silence. Given the fragmentary character of our evidence, it should hardly be unexpected if

53. On the ecological fallacy in historical investigation, cf. Fischer, *Historians' Fallacies*, 119–20.
54. Ehrman, *Forgery and Counterforgery*, 218–22.
55. Cf. the recent argument to this effect in Allison, *James*, 19–24.

certain first-century texts go unattested until the third century. The relatively late date of attestation should thus be considered nonprobative with regard to authorship.

Through my study of the Epistle of James, I have found nothing persuading me that we solve a greater number of problems by positing pseudonymous authorship than by positing Jacobean authorship. As such, I am reasonably confident in concluding that the Epistle of James dates no later than 62, the year in which James the brother of the Lord died.

Conclusion to James: Authorial Biography

Insofar as it is the case that

- the cumulative work of synchronization and contextualization permits a date as late as 125 for the Letter of James; and
- the probable author of the Epistle of James is James the brother of Jesus,

we conclude that the Epistle of James was written no later than 62, the year of James's death.

Cumulative Conclusion to James

Insofar as it is the case that

- external attestation should leave us wary of dating the Epistle of James later than 125;
- the Epistle of James's relationship to the New Testament Jesus tradition is such that we cannot determine with precision which if any of these texts utilized James or which if any were utilized by James;
- the Epistle of James's relationship to the Letters of Paul is such that we cannot determine whether the author knew Paul's writings, Paul knew the Epistle of James, or both are mutually independent, although Paul's knowledge of the Epistle of James is more likely than the Epistle of James's knowledge of Paul;
- the date of the Birkat Haminim is irrelevant for establishing the date of the Letter of James;

- Christian immersion within Jewish imagery and Scripture continued through the first and second centuries and thus cannot narrow down the compositional date of the Epistle of James;
- James 2:2 could here reference Christian assemblies as early as the 30s and into the second century;
- within James the lack of distinctive Christian language found elsewhere in the New Testament might lead us to favor an earlier rather than a later date but cannot do so decisively;
- the ecclesiology of the Epistle of James is wholly intelligible within the first century and does not require, but does not exclude, a second-century provenance; and
- the probable author of the Epistle of James is James the brother of Jesus,

we conclude that the Epistle of James was written no later than 62.

Cumulative Conclusion to Chapter 7:
The Letters of Hebrews and James

This chapter has argued that Hebrews was likely written between 50 and 70 and the Epistle of James prior to 62. We can thus summarize the likely compositional dates of the texts considered thus far in this study via the following table:

Text	Date
Gospel of Mark	42–45
Gospel of Matthew	45–59
Galatians	47–52
1 Thessalonians	50–52
2 Thessalonians	50–52
Hebrews	**50–70**
1 Corinthians	early 56
2 Corinthians	late 56
Romans	winter of 56/57

Text	Date
Ephesians, Colossians, Philemon, and Philippians	57–59
Gospel of Luke	59
Gospel of John	60–70
1 and 2 John	60–100
James	**before 62**
Acts of the Apostles	62
1 Timothy	if Pauline: 63 or 64 if pseudo-Pauline: 60–150
Titus	if Pauline: 63 or 64 if pseudo-Pauline: 60–175
2 Timothy	if Pauline: 64–68 if pseudo-Pauline: 60–150
Revelation	68–70
3 John	before 100

8

1 and 2 Peter and Jude

Chapter 8 will consider the probable dates for 1 and 2 Peter and Jude. Since both 1 and 2 Peter are attributed to the same putative author, it is expedient to consider them together; and because 2 Peter and Jude share a significant amount of material in common, it is equally expedient to consider them together. This chapter argues that 1 Peter was written ca. 60–69; Jude prior to 96; and 2 Peter ca. 60–69 if Petrine, and ca. 60–125 if pseudo-Petrine.

1 Peter

This section aims to establish the most probable date of composition for 1 Peter.[1] Probably a majority of New Testament scholars working today judge 1 Peter to be a pseudo-Petrine work of the last quarter of the first century or perhaps the early years of the second. That notwithstanding, this chapter argues that 1 Peter was most likely written no earlier than 60 and no later than 69.

Synchronization

In this section, we consider (1) external attestation, (2) source-critical concerns, (3) the geographic spread of Christianity, and (4) a possible relationship between the text and the Neronian persecution. On the basis of

---

1. In developing this chapter, I found the following especially useful: Achtemeier, *1 Peter*; Bauckham, *Jude and 2 Peter*; Bigg, *St. Peter and Jude*; Elliott, *1 Peter*; D. Harrington, *1 Peter, Jude, 2 Peter*; Kelly, *Epistles of Peter and Jude*; Michaels, *1 Peter*; Neyrey, *2 Peter, Jude*.

synchronization, we conclude that 1 Peter was most likely written no earlier than 57 and no later than 69.

External Attestation

The first explicit citations of 1 Peter appear in the late second century, particularly in the writings of Clement of Alexandria, Irenaeus, and Tertullian.[2] On the basis of these data alone, a date for 1 Peter as late as 175 is permissible. Earlier in the second century, a number of passages in Polycarp's *Letter to the Philippians* betray a notable degree of similarity to 1 Peter.[3] Moreover, Eusebius explicitly informs us that Polycarp made use of 1 Peter.[4] As we have already seen, it is possible that Polycarp's *Letter to the Philippians* dates as late as 150.[5] Moving potentially into the first century, there is reason to think that 1 Clement might have made use of 1 Peter. As noted in our discussion of Hebrews, 1 Clement could date as late as 150.[6] On the basis of external attestation, then, we should be wary of dating 1 Peter much later than 135.

In 2 Peter 3:1, the author informs the recipients that this is the second letter that he is writing to them.[7] Unfortunately for our purposes, in this verse the description of the earlier letter is sufficiently vague that we cannot establish with confidence that it is 1 Peter. Moreover, the date of 2 Peter remains unsettled and (as we will see) is even more difficult to establish than that of 1 Peter. Thus, we should consider 2 Peter 3:1 to be nonprobative with regard to the date of 1 Peter, although it will need to be considered at greater length when we consider the date of 2 Peter.

Source Criticism

In his extensive tabulation of overlaps between 1 Peter and other first- and second-century literature, Ora Delmer Foster concludes with near certainty that 1 Peter knew Romans and Ephesians.[8] He further concludes that it is likely that

---

2. Cf. the extensive tabulation of possible relations between 1 Peter and first- and second-century Christian literature in O. Foster, "Literary Relations."

3. Cf. Pol. *Phil.* 1.3 with 1 Pet. 1:8; Pol. *Phil.* 2.1 with 1 Pet. 1:13, 21; Pol. *Phil.* 8.1 with 1 Pet. 2:22, 24. Cf. the discussion in Holmes, "Polycarp's *Letter to the Philippians*," esp. 220–23.

4. Eusebius, *Hist. eccl.* 4.14.8–9.

5. Harrison, *Polycarp's Two Epistles.*

6. Cf. the extended discussion in chap. 9 below.

7. Cf. further discussion of this passage in the section on 2 Peter and Jude below.

8. Cf. O. Foster, "Literary Relations," 424–55.

either 1 Peter knew Hebrews or vice versa.[9] There is a long-standing tradition that 1 Peter was written from Rome; interestingly, among the early Christian texts demonstrating the greatest overlaps with 1 Peter, several have connections with Rome. Romans was written to that city; as we saw above, Hebrews 13:24 could indicate that this letter was also written to Rome; and 1 Clement was certainly written from Rome.[10] Given that Romans and Hebrews were written *to* Rome and 1 Clement *from* Rome, I find it quite attractive to imagine that they helped shape the common milieu current among Roman Christians, which is then reflected in 1 Peter and 1 Clement as they were written from Rome. If Romans dates from 57 and Hebrews from sometime in 50–70, then I am inclined to treat 57 as the earliest probable date for 1 Peter.

Geographic Spread of Christianity

First Peter 1:1 addresses the letter to "the exiles of the Dispersion in Pontus, Galatia, Cappadocia, Asia, and Bithynia." From this we can infer that the letter dates from a time when Christianity had already spread to these regions. There is evidence suggesting that Christians were in at least four and plausibly all five of these regions by the early 50s.[11]

Acts 2:9 reports that persons from Cappadocia, Pontus, and Asia were present at Pentecost, which opens the possibility that there were already persons from these regions who had heard the Christian message sometime in the 30s. In the case of Pontus, Aquila is explicitly identified as a native of this region.[12] It is unclear exactly when and where Aquila joined the Christian movement. Nonetheless, Aquila seems to have already been a Christian before moving to Corinth, given how quickly he and his wife, Priscilla, took up with Paul. Moreover, he and Priscilla were likely among those who had to leave Rome ca. 49 as a result of the disturbances over "Chrestus."[13] Turning specifically to Galatia, there is the classic question of whether 1 Peter is referring to North Galatia or South Galatia.[14] If 1 Peter is referring to North Galatia, then Paul likely ministered there ca. 49, shortly after the Jerusalem Council of 48.[15] If

9. Cf. O. Foster, "Literary Relations," 480–91.
10. On 1 Peter's Roman provenance, cf. 1 Pet. 5:13, as well as the discussion below.
11. Cf. the discussion of the relevant evidence in Schnabel, *Early Christian Mission*, 1:819–52.
12. Acts 18:2.
13. Cf. the discussion of the expulsion in chap. 7.
14. Cf. the discussion of North and South Galatia in chap. 6.
15. Acts 16:6.

1 Peter is referring to South Galatia, then Paul likely ministered there prior to the council. In the case of Asia, Priscilla and Aquila set up shop in Ephesus probably ca. 52.[16] Shortly thereafter, they encountered Apollos.[17] Luke appears convinced that Apollos was already a Christian and that he came to Ephesus independent of the Pauline mission. Similarly, Paul not long thereafter encounters another set of believers in Ephesus.[18] There are no comparable early references to spread into Bithynia, and the only New Testament reference to the region outside 1 Peter 1:1 explicitly states that Paul did not minister there.[19] That having been said, our knowledge is potentially vitiated by the fact that this region and Pontus were united into a single province.

Ultimately, although we cannot be certain when the first Christian communities emerged in these regions, in each case but Bithynia we have very good reason to think that this had occurred by ca. 50, and conceivably as early as the 30s in the cases of Pontus, Cappadocia, and Asia. Further, only an argument from silence excludes the possibility that there were Christian communities in Bithynia prior to 50. Cumulatively, the address to Pontus, Galatia, Cappadocia, Asia, and Bithynia is probably nonprobative for purposes of establishing the date of 1 Peter.

A Fiery Ordeal (1 Pet. 4:12)

There is no question that 1 Peter is greatly concerned with the matter of suffering because of one's faith. Of particular interest is 1 Peter 4:12: "Beloved, do not be surprised at the fiery ordeal that is taking place among you to test you, as though something strange were happening to you." John Robinson wants to connect the language especially of a "fiery ordeal" with the Neronian persecution.[20] Such a connection is dubious. The phrase "fiery ordeal" is sufficiently imprecise that it could reference a persecution other than that by Nero. This is especially the case given that we do not know of every instance when Christians suffered in the first hundred or so years after Jesus's death. Moreover, although the Neronian persecution appears to have been limited to Rome, the author states that this

16. Cf. the discussion of the Corinthian and Ephesian sojourns in chap. 6. Notably, according to Acts 18:18–19, when Paul set out from Corinth at the end of that sojourn (likely in 52), Priscilla and Aquila accompanied him as far as Ephesus and settled there.
17. Acts 18:24.
18. Acts 19:1–7.
19. Acts 16:7.
20. Robinson, *Redating*, 159.

fiery ordeal is something experienced by the readers in Asia Minor. This all but precludes reference to the Neronian persecution. Therefore, 1 Peter 4:12 is too imprecise for us to affirm that it refers to the Neronian persecution.

Conclusion to 1 Peter: Synchronization

Insofar as it is the case that

- external attestation allows for a date as late as 175 for 1 Peter but tends to militate against one much later than 150;
- source-critical matters militate against a date for 1 Peter much earlier than 57;
- the known geographic spread of Christianity is such that by ca. 50 Christians were most likely in at least four of the five areas addressed by 1 Peter and were plausibly in the fifth; and
- the persecution supposed by 1 Peter 4:12 cannot be linked specifically to the Neronian persecution,

we conclude that 1 Peter was written no earlier than 57 and no later than 135.

Contextualization

In this section, we consider (1) the discussion of gentiles in 1 Peter, (2) ecclesiology supposed by the letter, and (3) the use of the term "Christian." We conclude that 1 Peter was likely written no earlier than 57 and no later than 135.

Before the Gentile Mission? (1 Pet. 2:12; 4:3)

Both 1 Peter 2:12 and 4:3 refer to gentiles in such a way that we might infer that the audience is primarily, if not exclusively, Jewish. In such a reading, the author would be saying to his readers that whereas they—although Jewish—once lived as non-Jews, they must now live otherwise. From this one might infer that 1 Peter predates the full flourishing of the gentile mission. That being said, it seems equally likely that by "gentile" the author means something like "pagan"—that is, persons who practice neither Judaism nor Christianity.[21] In

---

21. Cf. 1 Cor. 5:1; 12:2; 1 Thess. 4:5.

any case, the possibilities are sufficiently well balanced that we cannot build any chronological conclusions on the hypothesis that the readers were primarily Jewish. Moreover, as we saw with the Epistle of James, a primarily Jewish audience would be consistent with an earlier date, but it would not militate against a later one. We should consider these references to gentiles to be nonprobative for purposes of establishing the date of 1 Peter.

Ecclesiology

In 1 Peter 5:1, the author refers to himself as an elder. Much as with the Epistle of James, if the author knows only of elders and not of bishops, then we might have reason to prefer lower and middle over higher dates. As with the Epistle of James, we must remember that ecclesiology did not necessarily develop at a uniform pace across the ancient world and further be wary of arguing from silence. Therefore, it is probably best to conclude that our epistle's ecclesiology does not require a second-century date, but neither does it exclude one.

The Name "Christian" (1 Pet. 4:16)

First Peter 4:16 employs the term "Christian" (*christianos*) to refer to Christians. One might argue that this indicates a date toward the end of the first century or even into the second. It is true that *christianos* occurs infrequently in the first century and in references to that century. Rare, however, is not quite the same as nonexistent. To get a stronger sense of how this word's usage developed, we do well to cite the most relevant texts on the matter.

> Yet if any of you suffers as a Christian, do not consider it a disgrace, but glorify God because you bear this name. (1 Pet. 4:16)

> It was in Antioch that the disciples were first called "Christians." (Acts 11:26)

> Agrippa said to Paul, "Are you so quickly persuading me to become a Christian?" (Acts 26:28)

> During [Nero's] reign many abuses were severely punished and put down. . . . Punishment was inflicted on the Christians [Lat. *Christianos*], a class of men given to a new and mischievous superstition.[22]

22. Suetonius, *Nero* 16.2 (Rolfe).

Therefore, to scotch the rumour [that he started the Great Fire], Nero substituted as culprits, and punished with the utmost refinements of cruelty, a class of men, loathed for their vices, whom the crowd styled Christians [Lat. *Christiani*]. Christus, the founder of the name, had undergone the death penalty in the reign of Tiberius, by sentence of the procurator Pontius Pilatus, and the pernicious superstition was checked for a moment, only to break out once more, not merely in Judaea, the home of the disease, but in the capital itself, where all things horrible or shameful in the world collect and find a vogue.[23]

These passages at least potentially attest to the first-century usage of the term "Christian." In Acts 11:26, we are told that the believers were first called "Christians" in Antioch. It is not clear exactly when Luke envisions that this usage began. In 11:19 his narration returns briefly to the period just prior to Paul's conversion and recounts, through to the beginning of Herod Agrippa I's reign, the activities of Christians scattered by the Pauline persecution. In this context he states that they were first called "Christians." This suggests that Luke thinks the appellation "Christian" was already current in the 30s. One gets the impression from Acts 11:26 that "Christian" began as something that others called the believers, rather than as a self-description. Interestingly, the only time the word "Christian" appears in direct speech within the New Testament is on the lips of an outsider: Herod Agrippa II.[24] In *Annales* 15.44, Tacitus likewise informs us that already at the time of Nero, a group was known by "the crowd" as "Christians." Luke situates Herod Agrippa II's statement in almost certainly 59. As Tacitus is talking of Nero's actions following the Great Fire of Rome in 64, he situates the use of "Christian" in the mid-60s. Suetonius also makes explicit reference to "Christians" in the context of Nero's reign, but he fails to specify whether this word was being used by persons internal or external to the movement. Nonetheless, cumulatively these texts render it quite plausible that by the 60s—and potentially already in the 30s—"Christian" was being used by persons external to the movement, perhaps in a derisive sense.

Such usage seems to continue through Trajan's reign (98–117) and possibly beyond. Around 112, Pliny the Younger corresponded with Trajan regarding the appropriate treatment of Christians in Bithynia and Pontus.[25] Moreover, Pliny explicitly asks the emperor whether the name (*nomen*) "Christian" is sufficient

23. Tacitus, *Ann.* 15.44 (Moore and Jackson).
24. Acts 26:28.
25. Pliny the Younger, *Ep.* 10.96. Cf. also Trajan's response in *Ep.* 10.97.

to warrant punishment. Further, as we have seen, both Suetonius (ca. 121) and Tacitus (ca. 115) use the term "Christian" derisively. The usage in 1 Peter 4:16 similarly evinces an awareness that the term "Christian" could be used derisively, even as the basis for harassment. Pliny's correspondence with Trajan evinces a remarkable parallel with 1 Peter's emphasis upon suffering for the name "Christian." Given that both are concerned in part with Christianity in Bithynia and Pontus as well as with persecution due to the name "Christian," one is tempted to suppose that the Pliny-Trajan correspondence speaks to the same situation as that described in 1 Peter. Alternatively, Pliny the Younger reports that as many as twenty-five years earlier some of those whom he investigated renounced Christianity. As such, one could argue that 1 Peter speaks to earlier persecutory activities that occurred perhaps as early as 87. While the similarities are tantalizing, they do not establish that 1 Peter should be situated ca. 87 or 112.

As we see from the discussion above, the term "Christian" is more fully documented starting from the reign of Trajan. This on its own would provide warrant for dating 1 Peter toward the end of the first or perhaps in the early second century. Yet there is evidence that the term was used earlier, perhaps as early as the 30s. Although the data thus far suggest a middle or higher date for 1 Peter, we have yet to consider the matter of authorial biography.

Conclusion to 1 Peter: Contextualization

Insofar as it is the case that

- we can, on the basis of synchronization, judge it likely that 1 Peter was written no earlier than 57 and no later than 135;
- the references to gentiles in 1 Peter 2:12 and 4:3 are nonprobative for purposes of establishing the date of 1 Peter;
- the ecclesiology of 1 Peter is wholly intelligible within the first century and neither requires nor excludes a second-century provenance; and
- the usage of the term "Christian" as found in 1 Peter 4:16 is plausible from the 30s through to at least 120, yet became more common after 100,

we conclude that 1 Peter was written no earlier than 57 and no later than 135.

Authorial Biography

Unlike the Epistle of James, there is little question regarding the identity of the putative author. He can be only Simon Peter, follower of the earthly Jesus and frequent spokesperson for the twelve apostles. For its part, Simon/Simeon appears to have been the single most common Jewish male name in Palestine at the time.[26] Consequently, the New Testament is glutted with persons named Simon/Simeon.[27] "Peter," however, was a nickname associated with only Simon Peter.

As with the Epistle of James, I am generally persuaded that 1 Peter is authentic. There are really only two cogent arguments against reading 1 Peter as a Petrine document: the first, that it must postdate 70; the second, that Peter lacked the language skills to produce such a text. We have already dispensed with the first argument by showing through the work of synchronization and contextualization that 1 Peter could date as early as 57. The second can be dispensed with by reminding the reader of our earlier discussion regarding James's literacy. To this, we might add a few additional notes pertinent specifically to 1 Peter. The strongest evidence that Peter lacked such proficiency comes from Papias's report that Peter required an interpreter or translator.[28] But this report is a double-edged sword, for it also tells us that Peter worked at times with just such an interpreter or translator, identified as Mark. In 1 Peter 5:13, for example, the author indicates that someone named Mark is present with him as he writes. Admittedly, Papias's report that Mark served as Peter's interpreter or translator could be an inference from 1 Peter 5:13. Further, 1 Peter never states that Mark was involved in writing the letter, an observation that cuts both ways: it vitiates the argument that Papias's report is an inference from 1 Peter 5:13, but equally it vitiates the likelihood that Mark was indeed involved in writing 1 Peter. Nonetheless, 1 Peter does mention a person (Mark) reported elsewhere as having assisted Peter's efforts to communicate, and this name is associated with the production of a major piece of early Christian literature, the Gospel of Mark. Further, John Mark

---

26. Cf. the discussion in Bauckham, *Jesus and the Eyewitnesses*, 67–92.

27. In addition to Simon Peter, we find references to Simon the Zealot (Matt. 10:4; Mark 3:18; Luke 6:15; Acts 1:13); Simon brother of Jesus (Matt. 13:55; Mark 6:3); Simon the leper (Matt. 26:6; Mark 14:3); Simon of Cyrene (Matt. 27:32; Mark 15:21; Luke 23:26); Simeon, who blessed the infant Jesus (Luke 2:25–35); Simeon, ancestor of Joseph (Luke 3:30); Simon Iscariot, father of Judas (John 6:71; 13:2, 26); Simon Magus (Acts 8:9–24); Simon the tanner (Acts 9:43; 10:6); and Simeon Niger (Acts 13:1).

28. According to Eusebius, *Hist. eccl.* 3.9.15.

is identified in Acts 13:5 as a *hypēretēs* (ὑπηρέτης), a term that elsewhere can refer to the *khazan* (חזן). The *hypēretēs/khazan* was responsible for taking care of the scrolls in an ancient synagogue.[29] It is not certain, however, that the Mark of 1 Peter 5:13 is John Mark.[30]

First Peter 5:12 also mentions Silvanus, whom we should probably identify with the person by the same name who appears in the Pauline literature and likely also the person named Silas who appears in Acts.[31] Here the author further claims to be writing through (*dia*) Silvanus.[32] More likely than not, 1 Peter 5:12 means to state that Silvanus is carrying the letter to its recipients rather than that he participated in its composition. Nonetheless, the reference to Mark in 1 Peter 5:13 makes it plausible that Peter could have had assistance in writing his letter. The evidence for such potential aid significantly decreases the argument that Peter lacked access to the language skills requisite to produce 1 Peter.

Insofar as I consider it likely that 1 Peter is a Petrine composition, this section argues that it most likely was written no earlier than 57 and no later than 69.[33] We do need to consider the evidence of a Roman origin, however.

A Dispatch from Babylon (1 Pet. 5:13)

In 1 Peter 5:13, the author informs the reader, "Your sister church in Babylon, chosen together with you, sends you greetings; and so does my son Mark." Writing in the second century, Clement of Alexandria identified "Babylon" here as a coded reference to Rome.[34] In our discussion of Revelation, we have already seen that such a coded use of the word "Babylon" need not indicate a post-70 date.[35] Yet 1 Peter 5:13 remains relevant for our purposes since it has typically led those who accept the letter as authentically Petrine to suppose that the letter was written when Peter was in Rome during the 60s. In chapter 2, we argued that we can plausibly place Peter and Mark together in Rome in the 40s. This, however, does not exclude the possibility that they were

29. Cf. the discussion of the חזן in Levine, *Ancient Synagogue*, 434–42.
30. Cf. the discussion in chap. 2 above.
31. Acts presents Silas as accompanying Paul on the so-called second missionary journey, including the first missions to Macedonia and Greece; he is first introduced in Acts 15:22, accompanies Paul on his journeys from 15:40 through 17:15, and then at 18:5 rejoins Paul in Corinth. Paul mentions Silvanus at 2 Cor. 1:19; 1 Thess. 1:1; and 2 Thess. 1:1.
32. Cf. Ign. *Phld.* 11.2, where Ignatius states that he is writing *dia* Burrhus.
33. Cf. the discussion of Peter's death in chap. 3 above.
34. Cf. Eusebius, *Hist. eccl.* 2.15.2.
35. Cf. the discussion in chap. 4 above.

together in Rome again later. Given the indications that 1 Peter dates no earlier than 57, I am inclined to situate its composition during Peter's time in Rome during the 60s. We should probably consider 60 the earliest date for 1 Peter.

In chapter 6, we argued that Paul wrote 2 Timothy during his second Roman imprisonment. Given that in 2 Timothy 4:11 Paul asks Timothy to bring Mark to him in the capital, we might date 1 Peter no earlier than the beginning of Paul's second Roman imprisonment, ca. 64.[36] Nonetheless, given uncertainties regarding the identity of the Mark of 1 Peter 5:13 and the Mark of 2 Timothy 4:11, I am wary of considering this datum in making a chronological judgment here. Cumulatively, we conclude that the Roman provenance is consistent with a compositional date no earlier than 60.

Conclusion to 1 Peter: Authorial Biography

Insofar as it is the case that

- we can, on the basis of synchronization and contextualization, judge it likely that 1 Peter was written no earlier than 57 and no later than 135; and
- Petrine authorship of 1 Peter with a Roman provenance would be consistent with a compositional date likely no earlier than 60 and no later than 69 (the latest possible year of Peter's death),

we conclude that 1 Peter was written no earlier than 60 and no later than 69.

Cumulative Conclusion to 1 Peter

Insofar as it is the case that

- source-critical matters militate against a date for 1 Peter much earlier than 57; and
- Petrine authorship with a Roman provenance is consistent with a compositional date likely no earlier than 60,

we conclude that 1 Peter was written no earlier than 60 and no later than 69.

36. Cf. 2 Tim. 4:11.

2 Peter

This section aims to establish the most probable date of composition for 2 Peter. As with the Pastoral Epistles, the legitimate questions regarding Petrine authorship are such that I will offer two date ranges: one if the letter is an authentic Petrine composition, a second if pseudo-Petrine. Although most New Testament scholars would probably date 2 Peter to ca. 70 through ca. 125, this study argues that 2 Peter was written no earlier than 60 and no later than 69 if it is Petrine, and no earlier than 60 and no later than 125 if pseudo-Petrine.

Synchronization

In this section, we consider (1) external attestation, (2) the reference to an earlier letter in 2 Peter 3:1–2, and (3) the reference to "all of Paul's letters" in 2 Peter 3:15b–16. On the basis of synchronization, we conclude that 2 Peter was most likely written no earlier than 60 and no later than 125, although in principle we cannot exclude dates as early as the 30s or as late as 180.

External Attestation

Earliest attestation is difficult to determine for 2 Peter. Origen states that "Peter, on whom the Church of Christ is built, against which the gates of Hades shall not prevail, has left one acknowledged epistle, and, it may be, a second also; for it is doubted."[37] Origen more than likely betrays knowledge of 2 Peter here. Eusebius reports that Clement of Alexandria knew "the Catholic epistles."[38] It is unclear, however, whether that includes 2 Peter or not. Numerous second-century texts prior to Clement of Alexandria contain material that looks like it could be from 2 Peter.[39] Unfortunately, we cannot say with confidence that any of the writings in question know 2 Peter. Cumulatively, on the basis of attestation, 2 Peter could be dated into the fourth quarter of the second century, although the later one dates the letter after 100, the more instances of possible attestation one needs to discount. Thus, one should be wary of dating 2 Peter much later than the first quarter of the second century. A compositional date for 2 Peter prior to 125 thus seems warranted.

---

37. According to Eusebius, *Hist. eccl.* 6.25.8.
38. According to Eusebius, *Hist. eccl.* 6.14.1.
39. These are collected conveniently by Bigg, *St. Peter and Jude*, 204–10.

A First Letter (2 Pet. 3:1–2)

In 2 Peter 3:1–2, the author writes the following:

> This is now, beloved, the second letter I am writing to you; in them I am trying to arouse your sincere intention by reminding you that you should remember the words spoken in the past by the holy prophets, and the commandment of the Lord and Savior spoken through your apostles.

Probably most scholars assume that if 2 Peter is the second letter, then 1 Peter must be the first. Yet this is far from certain. Most notably, the description of the two letters in 2 Peter 3:1b–2 does not particularly sound like what we find in 1 Peter. As such, alternatives have been suggested, such as a now-lost letter, 2 Peter 1 (taken as an earlier letter incorporated into our 2 Peter), or the Epistle of Jude.

Here we should attend to Robinson's argument that the material common to 2 Peter and Jude results from common authorship.[40] Robinson builds his argument in part upon Jude 3, in which the author writes, "While eagerly preparing to write to you about the salvation we share, I find it necessary to write and appeal to you to contend for the faith that was once for all entrusted to the saints." Robinson proceeds to argue that what the author of Jude was eagerly preparing to write was none other than 2 Peter, while the earlier letter referenced in 2 Peter 3:1 is the Epistle of Jude. The author, he goes on to suggest, is actually Jude: Jude was preparing to write 2 Peter at Peter's behest and in his name; he paused to write a shorter letter in his own name; thus Jude naturally drew upon the material that he had already prepared for our 2 Peter; then, when he was writing 2 Peter, Jude referred back to the Epistle of Jude as his first letter. If accepted, then two implications would follow: 2 Peter would slightly postdate Jude, although perhaps by only a matter of days or weeks, and both would predate the death of Peter.

There is admittedly a certain elegance to Robinson's hypothesis. It would readily explain the similarities between the texts while also explaining why 2 Peter is attributed to Peter and Jude to Jude. Unfortunately, there are empirical difficulties. Most notably, it requires us to suppose that in 2 Peter 3:1, Jude not only broke character from Peter's voice to speak in his own but also expected his audience to recognize the shift in authorial voice. This difficulty

---

40. Robinson, *Redating*, 193–95. Cf. the further discussion below.

is not necessarily fatal to Robinson's hypothesis, but neither does it seem particularly friendly to it. In light of this, combined with the reality that it is far from certain that the "first letter" of 2 Peter 3:1–2 is Jude, I find myself unable to affirm Robinson's hypothesis.

Cumulatively, 2 Peter 3:1–2 is sufficiently ambiguous that we must consider it nonprobative for purposes of establishing the compositional date of the letter.

All of Paul's Letters (2 Pet. 3:15b-16)

Second Peter 3:15b–16 contains an explicit reference to Paul's Letters.

> So also our beloved brother Paul wrote to you according to the wisdom given him, speaking of this as he does in all his letters. There are some things in them hard to understand, which the ignorant and unstable twist to their own destruction, as they do the other scriptures.

Strictly speaking, this passage requires only that 2 Peter knew of two or more Pauline Letters. It does not require knowledge of or access to a collection of Paul's Letters, or even to extant Pauline Letters. In theory, Paul could have converted as early as 29, the earliest probable year for Jesus's crucifixion. As such, a date for 2 Peter in the 30s cannot be excluded on the basis of this passage. Yet the reference to "all his letters" likely refers to more than just two letters, and it seems likely that the author is referring at least in part to letters later preserved in the Pauline corpus. Hence, on the basis of this verse, I am wary of dating 2 Peter any earlier than the latter part of Paul's letter-writing career.

It might be objected that Paul's Letters could not have been described as "scripture" as early as his own lifetime or that of Peter's. This argument is not as strong as it might initially appear. The Greek word in question, γραπή (*graphē*), is less specialized than the English word "scripture" suggests. For English readers, "scripture" tends to mean something formally recognized as canonical. *Graphē*, however, has a more basic sense of "writing." Nonetheless, given that 2 Peter 3:16 describes how people twist Paul's words to their own destruction, we can reasonably suppose that his letters were considered by many to be of special significance. This significance should once again incline us to date 2 Peter no earlier than the latter part of Paul's letter-writing career. In considering 2 Peter 3:15–16, we need to be wary of dating 2 Peter earlier than 60.

> ### Conclusion to 2 Peter: Synchronization
>
> Insofar as it is the case that
>
> - external attestation cannot exclude a date as late as the last quarter of the second century but tends to militate against a date much later than 125;
> - we cannot with confidence identify the "first letter" of 2 Peter 3:1-2; and
> - the reference to "all of Paul's letters" in 2 Peter 3:15b-16 should leave us wary to date 2 Peter earlier than 60,
>
> we conclude that 2 Peter was written no earlier than 60 and no later than 125.

Contextualization

Regarding 2 Peter, the primary contextual matter to consider is its reference to "ancestors" in 2 Peter 3:4. Cumulative with the work of synchronization, we judge that 2 Peter likely dates no earlier than 60 and no later than 125. In 2 Peter 3:3–7, we read the following:

First of all you must understand this, that in the last days scoffers will come, scoffing and indulging their own lusts and saying, "Where is the promise of his coming? For ever since our ancestors died, all things continue as they were from the beginning of creation!" They deliberately ignore this fact, that by the word of God heavens existed long ago and an earth was formed out of water and by means of water, through which the world of that time was deluged with water and perished. But by the same word the present heavens and earth have been reserved for fire, being kept until the day of judgment and destruction of the godless.

It is tempting to suppose that this passage, especially in verse 4, refers to the death of the apostolic generation. In such a case, this passage would likely reflect the same sort of anxiety regarding the delay of the parousia as we find in 1 Thessalonians 4:13–17. This, however, necessarily supposes that the "ancestors" (literally, "the fathers," *hoi pateres*) in verse 4 are deceased Christian ancestors. While possible, this is not certain. Indeed, the reference back to creation and to a radical transformation of the world at the time of Noah suggests a greater temporal depth. Indeed, it is possible that the author has in mind Adam as the first of the fathers envisioned here. Given this exegetical ambiguity, I am inclined to consider 2 Peter 3:4 to be nonprobative with regard to establishing the compositional date. That said, if 2 Peter 3:4 is probative for purposes of establishing the date of the letter, then it would tend to militate against a particularly low date. Again, we should be wary of dating 2 Peter earlier than 60.

Conclusion to 2 Peter: Contextualization

Insofar as it is the case that

- the work of synchronization should incline us toward a compositional date for 2 Peter no earlier than 60 and no later than 125; and
- the reference to the "ancestors" in 2 Peter 3:4 could indicate that the letter was written after much of the first Christian generation had passed away,

we conclude that 2 Peter was written no earlier than 60 and no later than 125.

Authorial Biography

Central to the question of authorial biography is whether the author of 1 Peter is also the author of 2 Peter. The style and content of the letters are sufficiently distinct that most contemporary scholars are inclined to judge common authorship unlikely. The further tendency is to judge 2 Peter to be a pseudo-Petrine work, whether 1 Peter is accepted as authentically Petrine or not. Gene Green opts against using 2 Peter to reconstruct Peter's own theology, a task for which he is prepared to use even the Gospel of Mark.[41] Insofar as there are a greater number of indicators in 2 Peter that are difficult (although not impossible) to reconcile with a lower date, I am likewise inclined to judge that if only one of these texts can be a Petrine composition, than 1 Peter is the better candidate. Indeed, 2 Peter is probably the strongest candidate for pseudonymous authorship in the New Testament corpus.

41. Green, *Vox Petri*, 32–46, 96–98.

Given such considerations, I am wary of supposing that 2 Peter must date from Peter's lifetime. At the same time, neither is the data such as to exclude the possibility that 2 Peter originated during Peter's final years, nor that Peter was in some way involved in its production (even if only to authorize someone else to write it in his name). Consequently, I am inclined to date 2 Peter to ca. 60–125, but I recognize that if the text is an authentic Petrine writing, it was likely written no earlier than 60 and almost certainly predates Peter's death no later than 69.

Conclusion to 2 Peter: Authorial Biography

Insofar as it is the case that

- the cumulative work of synchronization and contextualization indicates that 2 Peter was likely written sometime between 60 and 125; and
- 2 Peter is the strongest candidate for pseudonymous authorship in the New Testament corpus,

we conclude that 2 Peter was written no earlier than 60 and no later than 69 if Petrine; and no earlier than 60 and no later than 125 if pseudo-Petrine.

Cumulative Conclusion to 2 Peter

Insofar as it is the case that

- external attestation cannot exclude a date as late as the last quarter of the second century but tends to militate against a date much later than 125;
- the reference to "all [of Paul's] letters" in 2 Peter 3:15b–16 should leave us wary to date 2 Peter earlier than 60; and
- 2 Peter is the strongest candidate for pseudonymous authorship in the New Testament corpus,

we conclude that 2 Peter was written no earlier than 60 and no later than 69 if Petrine; and no earlier than 60 and no later than 125 if pseudo-Petrine.

Jude

This section aims to establish the most probable date of composition for Jude. Although most scholars would probably date Jude earlier than 2 Peter but still between 70 and 125, this study argues that Jude was most likely written no later than 96.

Synchronization

In this section, we consider (1) external attestation and (2) the relationship between 2 Peter and Jude. We conclude that Jude was written no later than 125.

External Attestation

The earliest explicit references to Jude come from Clement of Alexandria and Tertullian.[42] Like 2 Peter, there is second-century material that looks as though it could have come from the Epistle of Jude.[43] Much as is the case with 2 Peter, Jude could be dated into the fourth quarter of the second century, although the later one dates the letter into the second century, the more instances of possible attestation one needs to discount. Thus, one should be wary of dating Jude much later than 125.

The Relationship between 2 Peter and Jude

The similarities between 2 Peter and the Epistle of Jude are sufficiently strong for most scholars to agree that there must be some sort of literary relationship. As with any other such literary relationship between two texts, there are three basic configurations it can take: the author of 2 Peter used the Epistle of Jude as a source; the author of the Epistle of Jude used 2 Peter as a source; or each author used a common, no longer extant, third source. The majority position on the relationship between 2 Peter and Jude is that the author of 2 Peter utilized the Epistle of Jude. This is based upon the supposition that a writer would more likely incorporate parts of a smaller letter into his writing than create a text that consists in large part of extracts from an earlier composition. If there is indeed direct dependence moving in either direction, then I am inclined to agree with this judgment. Overall,

42. In Clement of Alexandria, cf. *Paed.* 3.44–45; *Strom.* 3.2.11. In Tertullian, *Cult. fem.* 1.3.
43. Cf. the evidence collected in Bigg, *St. Peter and Jude*, 307–10.

I find it is easier to imagine 2 Peter as an "expansion" of Jude than to read Jude as an "abbreviation" of 2 Peter. Absent other considerations, we should be wary of dating Jude later than 2 Peter. After concluding that 2 Peter was written no earlier than 60 and no later than 125, and lacking grounds to exclude a pre-60 origin for Jude, we should be inclined to date our letter sometime prior to 125.

Conclusion to Jude: Synchronization

Insofar as it is the case that

- external attestation cannot exclude a date for Jude as late as the last quarter of the second century but tends to militate against a date much later than 125; and
- Jude is likely dependent upon 2 Peter, which we have suggested probably dates no later than 125,

we conclude that Jude was written no later than 125.

Contextualization

In this section, we must consider the reference in Jude 3 to (1) "the faith that was once for all entrusted" and (2) the identity of Jude's opponents. This section concludes that we should incline toward a compositional date for Jude no later than 125.

The Faith That Was Once for All Entrusted (Jude 3b)

Jude 3b is sometimes considered to indicate a middle or higher date for the letter.

> I find it necessary to write and appeal to you to contend for the faith that was once for all entrusted to the saints. (Jude 3)

This passage could suggest a middle or higher date if we suppose that "the faith that was once for all entrusted to the saints" is a fixed deposit of inalterable doctrine and that such a fixed deposit was impossible before 70 but later became possible. Richard Bauckham sums up the difficulties with this line of argumentation succinctly, rightly observing that "the contrast set up between Jude and the Christianity of the first generation generally results from (1) underestimating the role of tradition in Christianity from the first, and (2) exaggerating the extent to which Jude's language implies a fixed body of formal doctrine."[44] Already we have Paul in the 50s speaking about doctrines that were passed on to him.[45] Jude seems to suppose nothing more fixed or formal than does Paul. Nonetheless, although Jude 3 would not be out of place before 70, neither would it be out of place in the later first or early second centuries. We should consider this passage nonprobative for purposes of establishing the date of Jude.

Jude's Opponents

The Letter of Jude is concerned with responding to false teachings and teachers. For instance, he is concerned with licentious conduct (cf. vv. 4, 8, 16), denial of Jesus (v. 4), rejection of authority (v. 8), slander against the angels (vv. 8–10), possibly persons who use Christian ministry (perhaps specifically prophecy) to enrich themselves at the communities' expense (vv. 11–12), and possibly denial of the Holy Spirit (v. 19). It would potentially advance our purpose here if we could place these teachings and teachers in time. Certainly, many of these concerns find echoes in the Pauline corpus, especially 1 and 2 Corinthians, while at the same time there is nothing to specifically tie the material to the second century. Nonetheless, these are general concerns that continue throughout the later first and early second centuries. As such, they should be considered nonprobative for purposes of establishing the date of the Letter of Jude.

Conclusion to Jude: Contextualization

Insofar as it is the case that

- on the basis of synchronization, we should incline toward a compositional date for Jude no later than 125;
- the reference to the "faith that was once for all entrusted" in Jude 3 is nonprobative for purposes of establishing the date of Jude; and

---

44. Bauckham, *Jude and 2 Peter*, 32.
45. 1 Cor. 15:2–3.

> • the false teaching countered by Jude is nonprobative for purposes
> of establishing the date of Jude,
>
> we conclude that Jude was written no later than 125.

Authorial Biography

The previous two sections demonstrated that the work of synchronization and contextualization suggests a date for Jude no later than 125. We now turn to the work of authorial biography to narrow this down. In seeking to do so, we consider the identity of the putative author and whether the letter might date from his lifetime. This section concludes that Jude likely dates no later than 96.

Jude 1a introduces the putative author as "Jude, a servant of Jesus Christ and brother of James." As with James himself, there are several persons named Jude (or Judas) in our New Testament and roughly coeval Christian writings: Judas Iscariot; Judas brother of Jesus and James (the Just); Judas son of James, a member of the Twelve; Judas the Galilean; Judas of Damascus, to whose home Paul went immediately after he was struck blind on the road to Damascus; Judas called Barsabbas; and Jude, also known as Didymus or Thomas.[46] Of these, we can rule out Judas Iscariot, who was remembered as a traitor to the movement and who died shortly after Jesus's own death, and Judas the Galilean, who was a Jewish rebel active ca. 6 CE. Of the remaining candidates, the best is Judas brother of Jesus and James. We have already discussed how only James son of Zebedee and James brother of Jesus are typically mentioned without any further identification. The absence of such qualification in Jude 1a makes it virtually certain that one of these two Jameses is intended, and only James brother of Jesus is known to have also had a brother named Jude.

As noted in our discussion of 2 Peter, I am not convinced by Robinson's argument that Jude wrote both 2 Peter and the Epistle of Jude. Nonetheless,

---

46. Judas Iscariot is mentioned in Matt. 10:4; 26:14, 25, 47; 27:3; Mark 3:19; 14:10, 43; Luke 6:16; 22:3, 47–48; John 6:71; 12:4; 13:26, 29; 18:2–5; Acts 1:15–19, 25. Judas brother of Jesus and James is mentioned in Matt. 13:55; Mark 6:3. Judas son of James, one of the Twelve, is mentioned in Luke 6:16; probably John 14:22; Acts 1:13. Judas the Galilean is mentioned in Acts 5:37. Judas of Damascus is mentioned in Acts 9:11. Judas called Barsabbas is mentioned in Acts 15:22, 27. The Gospel of Thomas identifies itself as containing the teachings of Jude, otherwise known as Didymus or Thomas. Most likely the apostle Thomas's given name was "Jude," but he received "Didymus" and "Thomas," which both mean "twin," as nicknames.

I am persuaded that Jude was responsible for the letter bearing his name. As such, we need to consider whether the Letter of Jude could issue from the historical Jude's lifetime. The answer to this is yes, for we have already seen that the letter could date anytime prior to 125. Robinson argues that the absence of reference to the historical James the Just's passing should incline us to date the Letter of Jude earlier than 62.[47] As with any argument from silence, we should be wary of affirming this. We are thus left to consider when Jude most likely passed away. Unfortunately, we lack a clear year of death. As James's brother, he was obviously his contemporary. One suspects a younger contemporary, because James's greater role in the early church probably makes best sense if he was Jesus's oldest surviving brother (or at least the oldest who joined the Christian movement). In this study we have already seen Eusebius's report that Domitian ordered the execution of members of Jesus's family; this report explicitly identifies those family members as Jude's grandsons.[48] Regardless of the veracity of this story, the fact that it singles out Jude's grandsons rather than Jude himself probably means he passed away no later than the end of Domitian's reign. Thus, I am disinclined to date the Letter of Jude later than 96.

Conclusion to Jude: Authorial Biography

Insofar as it is the case that

- on the basis of synchronization and contextualization, we should incline toward a compositional date for Jude no later than 125; and
- the historical Jude was most likely deceased by the end of Domitian's reign,

we conclude that the compositional date for Jude is no later than 96.

Cumulative Conclusion to Jude

Insofar as it is the case that the historical Jude was most likely deceased by the end of Domitian's reign, Jude was written no later than 96.

---

47. Cf. Robinson, *Redating*, 197–98.
48. Eusebius, *Hist. eccl.* 3.19.1–20.1.

Cumulative Conclusion to Chapter 8: 1 and 2 Peter and Jude

This chapter has argued that 1 Peter was written ca. 60 through 69; Jude prior to 96; and 2 Peter ca. 60 through 69 if Petrine, and ca. 60 through ca. 125 if pseudo-Petrine. We can thus summarize the likely compositional dates of those texts considered thus far in this study via the following table:

Text	Date
Gospel of Mark	42–45
Gospel of Matthew	45–59
Galatians	47–52
1 Thessalonians	50–52
2 Thessalonians	50–52
Hebrews	50–70
1 Corinthians	early 56
2 Corinthians	late 56
Romans	winter of 56/57
Ephesians, Colossians, Philemon, and Philippians	57–59
Gospel of Luke	59
1 Peter	**60–69**
2 Peter	**if Petrine: 60–69** **if pseudo-Petrine: 60–125**
Gospel of John	60–70
1 and 2 John	60–100
James	before 62
Acts of the Apostles	62
1 Timothy	if Pauline: 63 or 64 if pseudo-Pauline: 60–150
Titus	if Pauline: 63 or 64 if pseudo-Pauline: 60–175
2 Timothy	if Pauline: 64–68 if pseudo-Pauline: 60–150
Revelation	68–70
Jude	**before 96**
3 John	before 100

Early Extracanonical Writings

9

I Clement and the Didache

Part 5 aims to establish the probable date of several select, early extracanonical Christian writings: 1 Clement, the Didache, the Epistle of Barnabas, and the Shepherd of Hermas.[1] The criteria by which these were selected for treatment is determined by the penultimate chapter in John Robinson's *Redating the New Testament*, titled "A Post-apostolic Postscript." In this chapter, Robinson treats these four texts at some length.[2] Insofar as the present volume serves as something of a spiritual successor to *Redating the New Testament*, it seems appropriate to address the compositional dates of these four texts. Chapter 9 considers the compositional dates of 1 Clement and the Didache, and chapter 10 those of the Epistle of Barnabas and the Shepherd of Hermas. The present chapter argues that 1 Clement was most likely written ca. 64–70, and the Didache ca. 45–125.[3]

1 Clement

The aim of this section is to establish the most probable date for the letter known as 1 Clement. This letter was written from Rome to Corinth and is

---

1. As elsewhere throughout this study, I follow translations by Holmes, *Apostolic Fathers*.
2. Robinson, *Redating*, 312–35.
3. In developing this chapter, I found the following studies particularly useful: Erlemann, "Datierung des ersten Klemensbriefes"; Gregory, "Disturbing Trajectories"; Herron, *Clement and the Early Church*; Herron, "Most Probable Date"; Lightfoot, *Apostolic Fathers*, pt. 1, 1:346–58; Merrill, *Early Christian History*, 216–41; Milavec, *Didache*; Niederwimmer, *Didache*; Welborn, "Date of First Clement"; Wilhelm-Hooijbergh, "View of Clemens"; Wilhite, *The Didache*.

traditionally attributed to a Roman church leader known as Clement. Being a Roman Christian, the author is often called "Clement of Rome" to distinguish him from the later Clement of Alexandria. In this letter, Clement (or Pseudo-Clement, if the traditional authorship is rejected) seeks to intervene on behalf of one side in an ecclesiastical struggle within the Corinthian church. In this section it is argued that although most scholars date 1 Clement to ca. 95, a date ca. 64–70 is to be preferred.

Synchronization

In this section, we consider (1) external attestation, (2) source-critical matters, (3) the reference to "repeated misfortunes" in 1.1, (4) the reference to the deaths of Peter and Paul in 5.4–7, (5) the reference to the church of Corinth as "ancient" in 47.6, (6) the reference in 63.3 to blameless men who have lived from "youth" to "old age" among the Roman Christians, (7) the reference to Fortunatus in 65.1, and (8) the matter of 70, with specific regard to chapters 40–44. On the basis of synchronization, it is concluded that 1 Clement was most likely written ca. 64–70.

External Attestation

Hegesippus appears to have read our 1 Clement in Corinth.[4] Hegesippus's journey to Corinth appears to have been during, or perhaps slightly before, the Roman episcopacy of Anicetus (ca. 155–166).[5] It is typically supposed that Polycarp's *Letter to the Philippians* betrays knowledge of 1 Clement. Even those who challenge the degree to which Polycarp is influenced by 1 Clement usually suppose that Polycarp knew 1 Clement.[6] As we saw in previous discussions, Polycarp's *Letter to the Philippians* could date as late as 150. Given the combination of data from Hegesippus and Polycarp, we should be wary of dating 1 Clement much later than 150.

Source Criticism

First Clement 47.1 explicitly references a letter written by Paul to the Corinthians, 47.2 very plausibly quotes Philippians 4:15, and 47.3 provides a

---

4. According to Eusebius, *Hist. eccl.* 3.16.1.
5. Cf. Hegesippus's self-reported itinerary, as preserved by Eusebius, *Hist. eccl.* 4.22.1–4.
6. Cf., for instance, Berding, "Polycarp's Use of *1 Clement*."

précis that quite adequately describes 1 Corinthians.[7] First Clement likely also knows Romans and Hebrews.[8] A middle date for Hebrews has especially fueled the tendency to date 1 Clement to the mid-90s. Yet this study has argued that Hebrews should instead be dated ca. 50–70. This does not necessitate but certainly permits a lower date for 1 Clement. There are also parallels with the Synoptic material, although it is more likely that Clement knows this material from extracanonical sources.[9] Even if this material comes from our Synoptic Gospels, this study has argued that these were likely completed not much later than Romans or 1 Corinthians. Cumulatively, given that 1 Clement likely knows both Romans and 1 Corinthians, we can confidently exclude a date for the letter any earlier than 57.

Repeated Misfortunes (1 Clem. 1.1)

Related to the middle chronology's tendency to situate 1 Clement ca. 95 is 1 Clement 1.1, which refers to "sudden and repeated misfortunes and reverses that have happened to us [i.e., the Roman church]."[10] This has been taken as a reference to the putative Domitianic persecution.[11] We have already in this study considered the reasonable doubts regarding whether such a persecution ever took place.[12] More concretely, there is good reason to doubt whether 1 Clement 1.1 refers to any persecution at all. It has been argued that such apologies for delays were a common rhetorical strategy in writings that aimed at conciliating two opposed factions.[13] This raises the very real possibility that 1 Clement 1.1 is not referencing any actual events, let alone persecution, let alone any persecution known to us, let alone the putative Domitianic persecution.

Nevertheless, if we affirm that 1 Clement 1.1 references actual and known events that befell the Roman church, we would still need to engage with arguments that seek to identify the "sudden and repeated misfortunes" with the chaos immediately following Nero's death—that is, the Year of Four

---

7. Cf. Gregory, "*1 Clement* and the Writings," esp. 144–48; and Hagner, *Testaments in Clement*, 195–213.

8. On the use of Romans, cf. Gregory, "*1 Clement* and the Writings," 148–51; Hagner, *Testaments in Clement*, 214–20. On the use of Hebrews, cf. Gregory, "*1 Clement* and the Writings," 152–53; Hagner, *Testaments in Clement*, 179–95.

9. Gregory, "*1 Clement* and the Writings," 131–39; and Hagner, *Testaments in Clement*, 135–78.

10. 1 Clem. 1.1, trans. Holmes, *Apostolic Fathers*, 45.

11. Cf. Lightfoot, *Apostolic Fathers*, pt. 1, 1:350–52.

12. Cf. the discussion in the introduction.

13. Welborn, "Date of First Clement," 46–47.

Emperors (July 68–July 69). Robinson not surprisingly prefers to see in 1.1 a reference to these events.[14] Certainly such a theory would have something to commend it over and against associating 1.1 with the Domitianic persecution, for the simple reason that we can be confident that the so-called Year of Four Emperors actually happened. However, since it is unclear whether 1 Clement 1.1 references any actual or known event, we do best to consider this passage nonprobative for purposes of dating the letter.

Deaths of Peter and Paul (1 Clem. 5.4–7)

First Clement 5.4–7 reports the deaths of Peter and Paul. As we have already seen, the earliest likely year of Peter's death is 55.[15] We have also recognized that Paul was certainly alive as late as 62, the probable end of his first two years of imprisonment in Rome, and probably alive as late as at least 64, following his likely "post-Acts" trip to Spain, renewed work in the eastern Mediterranean, and return to Spain.[16] Given 1 Clement 5.4–7 and what we know about the deaths of Peter and Paul, it thus seems likely that the letter was written no earlier than 64.

The Ancient Church (1 Clem. 47.6)

First Clement 47.6 reads as follows:

> It is disgraceful, dear friends, yes, utterly disgraceful and unworthy of your conduct in Christ, that it should be reported that the well-established and ancient church of the Corinthians, because of one or two persons, is rebelling against its presbyters.

Much has been made of the reference to the church in Corinth as "ancient" (*archaian*). There were certainly Christians present in Corinth no later than Paul's arrival there ca. 50.[17] Certainly, if the church in Corinth was founded ca. 50, then by ca. 70 it would be at most twenty years old—hardly "ancient." But then again, if founded ca. 50, the same church would be approximately forty years old by 90, and fifty by 100. One wonders how much more "ancient"

---

14. Cf. Robinson, *Redating*, 327–34. Here Robinson follows Edmundson, *Church in Rome*, 188–202.
15. Cf. the discussion in chap. 3 above.
16. Cf. the discussion in chap. 6 above.
17. Cf. Acts 18:1–3.

forty and fifty years are than twenty. Perhaps one could make the case that by 150 the Corinthian church would more appropriately be described as "ancient," but that in large part would turn upon what is meant by *archaian*.

Proponents of a lower date for 1 Clement often look at early Christian usage of *archaian*. In 1 Clement 47.6 they read an allusion to Paul's words in Philippians 4:15, "You Philippians indeed know that in the early days of the gospel [*en archē tou euangeliou*], when I left Macedonia, no church shared with me in the matter of giving and receiving, except you alone." First Clement plausibly references Philippians 4:15 just a few verses earlier (47.2), when he asks, "What did he [Paul] first write to you in the 'beginning of the gospel' [*en archē tou euangeliou*]?"[18] Perhaps of even greater relevance, Acts 15:7 refers to the early period of the Christian movement as "early days" (*hēmerōn archaiōn*), and Acts 21:16 refers to Mnason as an "early disciple" (*archaios mathētēs*). Given such usage, *archaiōn* in 47.6 might be better translated as something like "archaic," in the sense of something that stems from an early period. Even "early" likely captures the sense here better than "ancient." Indeed, in a movement that by ca. 70 had been around no longer than forty years, the Corinthian community would probably have existed for at least half that time. The sense that the Corinthian community stems from a relatively early period in ecclesiastical history would make eminent sense under such conditions. Given the vagaries of the term "ancient," 1 Clement 47.6 should probably be reckoned as nonprobative for the compositional date of our letter.

Blameless Men (1 Clem. 63.3)

First Clement 63.3 states that the Roman church has sent with the letter "trustworthy and prudent men who from youth [*neotēs*] to old age [*gēras*] have lived blameless lives among us, who will be witnesses between you and us." It might be argued that this excludes a lower date for 1 Clement, for that would not have allowed enough time for any Christian to have lived from youth to old age among the relatively young Roman church. To evaluate this claim, we must consider first the antiquity of the Roman church. In Romans 15:20, Paul reports that he was delayed in visiting Rome because Christianity already had a foundation in the city. If Romans 15:20 is original to Romans (cf. the discussion in chap. 6 above), then this suggests that the

---

18. Cf. Edmundson, *Church in Rome*, 198; Herron, "Most Probable Date," 115; Robinson, *Redating*, 332.

Roman church existed prior to 57. Such dating coheres with Acts 18:2, which suggests that Christian leaders such as Priscilla and Aquila were operating in Rome no later than 49.[19] In this study we have already considered evidence that Peter traveled to Rome in ca. 42.[20] Acts 2:10 reports that Jewish and proselyte pilgrims and immigrants from Rome heard the gospel preached in Jerusalem just a few weeks after Jesus's death. This raises the possibility that Christians were present in Rome as early as the 30s, which is potentially confirmed by Romans 16:7, where Andronicus and Junia are said to have become Christians before Paul. Once again, however, Romans 16:7 is potentially secondary to Romans; even if original, it does not establish when Andronicus and Junia began to reside in Rome.[21] The various qualifications given above notwithstanding, we can judge it virtually certain that some Christians were in Rome no later than the mid-50s, very probable that there were Christians in Rome by 50, plausible that there were Christians in Rome by 42, and possible that there were Christians in Rome not long after the first Christian Pentecost, ca. 29–34.

Even more significant than the antiquity of the Roman church, however, are the meanings of *neotēs* and *gēras*. In the *Iliad*, Odysseus notes to Agamemnon that they have been at war "since youth to old age" (*ek neotētos . . . es gēras*).[22] Surely we are not to suppose that Odysseus and Agamemnon went off to war the moment they were born. Closer to 1 Clement temporally and culturally, 1 Timothy 4:12 refers to Timothy as a *neotēs* while envisioning him as a leader in the Ephesian church. Presumably the author of 1 Timothy does not have in mind a juvenile, but rather someone in at least their twenties if not their thirties. On the other end, Lightfoot argues that *gēras* must refer to someone at least sixty years old.[23] If indeed there was a Christian community in Rome already in the 30s, a man then in his twenties could easily have been in his sixties by 68; conversely, a man in his sixties in 120 would have been born ca. 65. In light of the very real possibility that by 70 the Roman church was already upward of forty years old and the vagaries surrounding the precise meaning of "youth" and "old age," 1 Clement 63.3 seems nonprobative regarding the date of 1 Clement.

19. Regarding the date of the expulsion, cf. the discussions in Jewett, *Chronology of Paul's Life*, 36–38; Lüdemann, *Paul, Apostle*, 164–71; Riesner, *Paul's Early Period*, 157–204.

20. Cf. the discussion in chap. 2. The relevant primary literature consists of: Eusebius, *Hist. eccl.* 2.14.6; Helm, *Die Chronik*, 179; Jerome, *Vir. ill.* 1.

21. Cf. the discussion in chap. 6 above.

22. Homer, *Il.* 14.86. Cf. the discussion in Wilhelm-Hooijbergh, "View of Clemens," 275.

23. Lightfoot, *Apostolic Fathers*, pt. 1, 1:27.

Fortunatus (1 Clem. 65.1)

In 65.1, the Roman church tells the Corinthian Christians, "Now send back to us without delay our messengers, Claudius Ephebus and Valerius Bito, together with Fortunatus." Robinson thinks that Fortunatus is not one of the messengers but in fact a member of the Corinthian church; that this is probably the same Fortunatus that we find mentioned in 1 Corinthians 16:17; and that if Fortunatus was already active in Christian ministry in the mid-50s, then it was unlikely that he was yet active in the mid-90s.[24] This line of argumentation is less than compelling. Certainly, it is quite plausible that Fortunatus was a Corinthian Christian. It is perhaps even probable, given that he is set off from the Roman messengers. It is not impossible but far from certain or even probable that he is to be identified with the person of the same name mentioned in 1 Corinthians 16:17. Moreover and more crucially, even if granted that this is the same Fortunatus, we do not know how old he was in the 50s. If he was in his twenties or even early thirties, then it is altogether plausible that he was still active forty years later. The identification is too tenuous and the still-permissible range of dates still too great for us to draw any chronological judgments from this passage. The most we can probably say is that if 1 Clement dates toward the earlier end of the range from 64 to 140, this would significantly increase the probability that the Fortunatus of 65.1 is to be identified with that of 1 Corinthians 16:17—although even under those conditions the identification would hardly approach probability.

Once Again, 70 (1 Clem. 40-44)

In 1 Clement 40–44 the author invokes the temple administration in order to demonstrate a divine preference for liturgical and institutional order. In this text, 1 Clement uses the present tense to describe the temple administration. As always, this is not sufficient to demonstrate that the temple still stood at the time of writing. The text's rhetoric nonetheless poses some difficulties for a post-70 date.[25] According to 1 Clement, just as God ordained the temple order (40–41), so too did God ordain the emergent ecclesiastical order (42–44.3). Thus, it is unjust to remove from ministry those appointed by the

---

24. Robinson, *Redating*, 333. Robinson here follows Edmundson, *Church in Rome*, 199.

25. Cf. comparable arguments in Herron, *Clement and the Early Church*, 14–16; Herron, "Most Probable Date," 108–10; Robinson, *Redating*, 329–30.

apostles and their successors (44.3–6). If written after 70, the audience could quite reasonably object that if this earlier divine temple order was overturned by human agents, then so too could be the current ecclesial one. While his readers knew that the temple had in recent memory been destroyed violently, how plausibly could 1 Clement 40.4, in the midst of speaking of the temple administration, declare that "those, therefore, who make their offerings at the appointed times are acceptable *and blessed*, for those who follow the instructions of the Master cannot go wrong"?[26] Such explicit declaration, that just as the temple administration is blessed because it abides by divine ordinances so too are ecclesiastical administrations, makes much greater sense before rather than after 70. Although this datum cannot exclude a post-70 date, we should probably be inclined to favor a pre-70 one.

Conclusion to 1 Clement: Synchronization

Insofar as it is the case that

- external attestation permits a date as late as 150 for 1 Clement;
- 1 Clement's use of Romans and 1 Corinthians excludes a date earlier than 56;
- the reference to repeated misfortunes in 1 Clement 1.1 is nonprobative for purposes of establishing the date of 1 Clement;
- the reference to the deaths of Peter and Paul in 1 Clement 5.4-7 exclude a date earlier than 64;
- the description of Corinth as an "ancient church" in 1 Clement 47.6 is nonprobative for purposes of establishing the date of 1 Clement;
- the references to blameless men who lived among the Roman Christians from "youth" to "old age" in 1 Clement 63.3 are nonprobative for purposes of establishing the date of 1 Clement;
- the reference to Fortunatus in 1 Clement 65.1 is nonprobative for purposes of establishing the date of 1 Clement; and
- 1 Clement 40-44 is more intelligible before 70 than after,

we conclude that 1 Clement was written no earlier than 64 and no later than 70.

---

26. 1 Clem. 40.4, trans. Holmes, *Apostolic Fathers*, 99 (emphasis added).

Contextualization

In this section, we are here concerned with (1) the reference to apostles and those who knew them in 1 Clement 44.2–3 and (2) the ecclesiology of the letter. This section concludes that cumulative with synchronization, 1 Clement was most likely written no earlier than 64 and no later than 70.

Which Generation? (1 Clem. 44.2-3)

First Clement 44.2–3 reads as follows:

> For this reason, therefore, having received complete foreknowledge, they [i.e., the apostles] appointed the officials mentioned earlier and afterwards they gave the offices a permanent character; that is, if they should die, other approved men should succeed to their ministry. Those, therefore, who were appointed by them or, later on, by other reputable men with the consent of the whole church, and who have ministered to the flock of Christ blamelessly, humbly, peaceably, and unselfishly, and for a long time have been well spoken of by all—these men we consider to be unjustly removed from their ministry.[27]

One might read the report of "those, therefore, who were appointed by them" being removed from office as an indication that at the time the letter was written there were yet persons active in ministry who were personally appointed by the apostles. But the letter need not be read as suggesting that there remained at the time of composition direct apostolic appointees active in the ministry. Rather, 44.3 could be read as suggesting that either apostolic appointees or those appointed by apostolic appointees were among those unjustly removed from their ministry in Corinth.[28] It really depends upon who the "them" are in this phrase. Turning to absolute dates, Polycarp apparently knew either John son of Zebedee or John the Elder, both of whom were disciples of the earthly Jesus.[29] Insofar as Polycarp was active as late as the 150s, it is entirely conceivable that persons only two degrees of ecclesial separation from the apostles could have been active as late as the mid-second century.

27. 1 Clem. 44.2–3, trans. Holmes, *Apostolic Fathers*, 103–5.
28. Contra Welborn, who on the basis of 44.3 assumes that not only apostolic appointees but also the appointees of apostolic appointees must have already passed away ("Date of First Clement," 37).
29. Cf. Irenaeus's *Letter to Florinus*.

It might be argued that the time span from 50 to 70 does not, on a lower date, allow enough time for the ecclesial successions reported in 44.2–3. This is less than compelling. First Clement is writing about apostolic operations more generally, not just those in Corinth. This widens the time frame significantly. By 70, upward of four decades would have elapsed since the first Christian communities had been founded, and there would have been more than sufficient time not only to appoint successors but also for questions to emerge about who should succeed the initial appointees and even their successors in turn. Moreover, such questions about succession could quite conceivably have occurred within a matter of years as posts became vacant through resignation, illness, and death. Thus, Robinson rightly observes that even twenty years should suffice for such questions of succession to have arisen.[30] Consequently, 44.2–3 should be considered nonprobative for purposes of establishing the compositional date of 1 Clement.

Ecclesiology

First Clement evinces no awareness of a monarchical bishop in either Rome or Corinth. Rather, it seems to suppose presbyterial rule throughout. In this regard, we suggest that the ecclesiology of 1 Clement is closer to that evidenced from Philippians 1:1, with its address to Philippian bishops in the parallel, than to that of Ignatius of Antioch, whose letters strongly emphasize the singularity of the bishop. One does not want to push the chronological significance of this observation too far, and indeed Robinson pushes it further than I prefer.[31] As noted throughout this study, our evidence for the development and, more importantly, the regional diversity and rate of change in late first- and early second-century ecclesiastical structures is relatively thin. As often is the case, rates of change are sufficiently unclear as to largely obviate the argument from development. That having been said, the ecclesiology of the letter should make us wary of dating it much later than 125.

Conclusion to 1 Clement: Contextualization

Insofar as it is the case that

- the work of synchronization leads us to date 1 Clement no earlier than 64 and no later than 70;

30. Robinson, *Redating*, 331.
31. Robinson, *Redating*, 328.

- the reference to leaders appointed by the apostles or their successors in 44.2-3 is nonprobative for purposes of establishing the date of 1 Clement; and
- the ecclesiology of 1 Clement is such that we should be wary of dating the letter much later than 125,

we conclude that we should date 1 Clement no earlier than 64 and no later than 70.

Authorial Biography

In this section, we consider whether (1) the author of our epistle should be identified with the Clement of Philippians 4:3 and (2) whether our letter should be dated to Clement's term as bishop of Rome.

Clement in Philippians 4:3

In Philippians 4:3, Paul refers to a person named "Clement." It is possible that this Clement is in fact Clement of Rome, the putative author of our letter. Nonetheless, though not impossible, it is far from probable. Moreover, even if we allow that it is the same person, then depending upon Clement's year of birth we could not exclude a date for 1 Clement into the early second century. The uncertainty regarding the identity of these figures renders Philippians 4:3 nonprobative for establishing the date of 1 Clement.

Bishop of Rome

Influential in supporting a ca. 95 date for the letter is the supposition that it must have been written when Clement was bishop of Rome (likely in the 90s). In response to this supposition, one can raise several challenges. Most radically, one can argue against ascribing 1 Clement to the "historical Clement of Rome," meaning the bishop putatively active toward the end of the first century. This would have little effect on when to date the letter. Alternatively, one might argue that the historical Clement was indeed responsible for the letter but at some point other than during his putative episcopate. This is Robinson's position.[32] Such a position coheres strongly with certain internal

---

32. Cf. Robinson, *Redating*, 328, 333.

and external data. Internally, it coheres with the letter's tendency to speak in the first-person plural as well as the absence of reference to a monepiscopacy. Externally, it coheres with Hermas, Vision 2.4.3 (8.3), which states that a certain Clement was responsible for sending letters to other cities.[33] These data have together led to a tendency to portray Clement more as a "foreign secretary" than a monarch.[34] It also coheres with Dionysius's letter to Bishop Soter of Rome, in which Dionysius refers to the Roman church having written what is likely our 1 Clement "through" (διά) Clement.[35] Cumulative to the above discussion, the dates of Clement's supposed episcopate are thus nonprobative for our purposes.

Conclusion to 1 Clement: Authorial Biography

Insofar as it is the case that

- the work of synchronization and contextualization lead us to date 1 Clement no earlier than 64 and no later than 70;
- uncertainty in identifying the Clement of Philippians 4:3 with Clement of Rome is such that this matter is nonprobative for purposes of establishing the date of 1 Clement; and
- Clement's role in the early church is nonprobative for purposes of establishing the date of 1 Clement,

we conclude that 1 Clement was written no earlier than 64 and no later than 70.

Cumulative Conclusion to 1 Clement

Insofar as it is the case that

- the reference to the deaths of Peter and Paul in 1 Clement 5.4–7 exclude a date earlier than 64;

---

33. Cf. the discussion below.

34. The use of the term "foreign secretary" in this connection comes from Lightfoot, *Apostolic Fathers*, pt. 1, 1:348. Cf. further discussion of this passage when we consider the date of the Shepherd below.

35. According to Eusebius, *Hist. eccl.* 4.23.11.

- the description of Corinth as an "ancient church" in 1 Clement 47.6 is nonprobative for purposes of establishing the date of 1 Clement; and
- 1 Clement 40–44 is more intelligible before 70 than after,

we conclude that 1 Clement was written no earlier than 64 and no later than 70.

The Didache

The aim of this section is to establish the most probable date for the early church manual known as the Didache. The only Greek copy of the Didache known to contemporary scholarship is found in Codex Hierosolymitanus (hereafter abbreviated H), which Philotheos Bryennios discovered in 1873 and published in 1883.[36] Because the H text dates to 1054, the exact relationship between this text and the Didache as it stood in the first or second century is debatable. The present study follows Christopher Tuckett in "presum[ing] that 'the *Didache*' is the text substantially represented in H," while recognizing that this "do[es] not of course apply to the detailed wording of the H text" since "no one would pretend to claim that the wording of the text can have been handed down in pristine purity over a period of almost a thousand years."[37] Concretely, this means that we will take the H text as that of the Didache, but we will note wherever necessary relevant text-critical issues that could affect our argument.

Clayton Jefford helpfully divides Didache scholarship into three broad "schools": the French, the German, and the British/American.[38] He reports that the French "school" tends to suppose that the Didache is a product of the first century, while the German tends to favor later dates, often in the second century. Jefford further argues that the British/American "school" does not demonstrate as clear a tendency on the matter as either the French or the German, although from his survey it seems there is a general preference for dates around the turn of the second century. Using the schema of lower, middle, and higher chronologies developed in this book, we suggest that French scholarship tends to favor lower dates for the Didache, British/American scholarship middle dates, and German scholarship higher

36. Bryennios, Διδαχὴ τῶν δώδεκα ἀποστόλων.
37. Tuckett, "*Didache* and the Writings," 85.
38. Jefford, *Sayings of Jesus*, 3–19; cf. also the helpful histories of research in Draper, "*Didache* in Modern Research"; and more recently Wilhite, "Thirty-Five Years Later."

dates. This study argues that, unfortunately, the data are such that we cannot readily adjudicate between lower, middle, and higher dates for the Didache. Thus, we argue that the Didache (in a form similar to but not identical with that found in the H text) was completed no earlier than 45 and no later than 125.

Synchronization

In this section, we consider (1) external attestation and (2) source-critical matters. We conclude from the work of synchronization that the Didache (in a form similar to but not identical with that found in the H text) was completed no earlier than 45 and no later than 400.

External Attestation

A host of material from the late second through the fourth centuries looks quite similar to the Didache.[39] Thus a papyrus (P.Oxy.XV 1782) contains Greek fragments of Didache 1.3c–1.4a and 2.7b–3.2a, although it should be acknowledged that these could have come from an independently circulated copy of the "Two Ways" tradition found in Didache 1–5. Bernard P. Grenfell and Arthur S. Hunt dated this papyrus to the late fourth century while allowing for the possibility that it could date to the early fifth.[40] Also in the fourth century we find our earliest probable references to the Didache, with both Eusebius and Athanasius mentioning texts that they designate the "so-called" Teachings (*Didachai*) of the Apostles.[41] On the grounds exclusively of textual and reception criticism, it seems reasonable to judge that the Didache (in a form similar to but not identical with that found in the H text) existed by the end of the fourth century. External attestation allows no greater precision than this.

Source Criticism

In terms of source criticism, the Didache contains material that relates in some fashion to material found in the Epistle of Barnabas, the Shepherd of Hermas, and the Synoptic Gospels (especially but not exclusively

---

39. On the textual- and reception-critical data regarding the Didache, cf. the overview in Niederwimmer, *The Didache*, 4–30; Wilhite, *Didache*, 10–18.

40. Cf. Grenfell and Hunt, *Oxyrhynchus Papyri*, 12–15.

41. Athanasius, *Ep. fest.* 39 §11; and Eusebius, *Hist. eccl.* 3.25.4.

Matthew's).[42] For our purposes, we need not define these relationships precisely, but we can speak in generalities. With regard to Barnabas and Hermas, contemporary scholarship seems to favor shared source theories as opposed to dependence theories. At least the data are such that the relationships between the Epistle of Barnabas and the Shepherd on the one hand and the Didache on the other hand cannot be used to determine a relative ordering of these texts.

Determining the precise relationship between the Didache and the Synoptic Gospels is complicated by textual-critical issues. As Tuckett notes, where Didache 1.3c–1.4a and 2.7b–3.2a parallel Matthew's Gospel and Luke's, the readings in H are closer to the Gospel texts than the readings in P.Oxy.XV 1782.[43] From this evidence, Tuckett argues that the Didache's text has become assimilated to that of the Gospels. If such assimilation is affirmed, then we should probably anticipate that a similar process occurred throughout the text. Thus, it is not unreasonable to suppose that the Didache of the first century resembled the Synoptic Gospels to a lesser extent than H alone suggests. Hence, we should hardly be surprised to discover that on this issue contemporary scholarship also seems inclined to favor shared-source theories to explain the relationship to the Synoptics, although there is a notable openness to envisioning the Didache as being dependent on at least Matthew's Gospel. Even Alan Garrow—who argues that the Didache was a source for Matthew's Gospel—is forced to argue that the references in the Didache (8.2; 11.3; 15.3–4) to a "gospel" represent a late redaction layer that supposes the existence of Matthew's Gospel.[44] Didache 8.2, which introduces as Gospel material a version of the Our Father very close to that of Matthew 6:9–13, seems especially more intelligible if dependent upon Matthew's Gospel than if independent. Yet the probability that the eleventh-century Didache was closer to the Matthean text than was the first-century Didache negates a high degree of confidence in this matter. Nonetheless, we should probably be wary of dating the Didache earlier than Matthew's Gospel.

---

42. On source-critical data regarding the Didache, cf. Niederwimmer, *Didache*, 42–52; Tuckett, "*Didache* and the Writings"; Wilhite, *Didache*, 30–59.

43. Tuckett, "*Didache* and the Writings," 87.

44. Garrow, *Matthew's Dependence upon the Didache*, 129–41.

Conclusion to the Didache: Synchronization

Insofar as it is the case that

- on the basis of external attestation, the Didache (in a form similar to but not identical with that found in the H text) existed by the end of the fourth century; and
- the Didache, in something resembling (but probably not identical with) the form found in H, probably knows the Gospel of Matthew, which we have already dated in this study to ca. 45 through 59,

we conclude that the Didache (in a form similar to but not identical with that found in the H text) was completed no earlier than 45 and no later than 400.

Contextualization

In this section, we are here concerned with (1) the Jewish matrix of the text, (2) the concern with food sacrificed to idols in Didache 6.3, and (3) the Didache's ecclesiology. This section concludes that, cumulative with synchronization, the Didache (in a form similar to but not identical with that found in the H text) was likely completed no earlier than 45 and no later than 125.

At the outset of our discussion of contextualization, we need to consider the unity of the text. That the Didache represents a composite text seems likely. If the composition took place over a considerable span of time—such as centuries—then it is quite conceivable that it contains data indicating a diversity of temporal provenances. Jean-Paul Audet and Robinson, however, both suggest that the composition of the Didache could have spanned as few as twenty years.[45] If for heuristic purposes we treat twenty years as the shortest likely compositional duration, then it remains altogether conceivable that the Didache could have been largely completed by ca. 50. Indeed, given that twenty years could conceivably be an overestimate of compositional duration, we cannot on such grounds rule out a date as early as the 40s for the Didache (in a form similar to but not identical with that found in the H text). Only if it proves impossible to situate the Didache within a single,

---

45. Audet, *La Didachè*, 219; Robinson, *Redating*, 323.

intelligible temporal provenance should we appeal to a diversity of temporal provenances to account for the data.

A Jewish Matrix

As we have noted regarding other works in this study, there is little question that the Didache is immersed in imagery and Scriptures drawn from the Jewish tradition. As noted with regard to those other works, this in and of itself tells us little. Such immersion is evident already in Paul's writings and continued well beyond the New Testament period. There were indeed Jewish or Judaizing Christian (or perhaps "Christianizing Jewish") groups such as the Nazoreans into the fourth century.[46] Thus, while the Didache's Jewish matrix is certainly consistent with a lower or middle date, it cannot be used to rule out a higher one either.

Food Sacrificed to Idols (Did. 6.2–3)

Didache 6.2–3 is concerned with matters that correlate closely with debates otherwise most fully attested from the late 40s through the 60s.

> For if you are able to bear the whole yoke of the Lord, you will be perfect. But if you are not able, then do what you can. Now concerning food, bear what you are able, but in any case keep strictly away from meat sacrificed to idols, for it involves the worship of dead gods.

As discussed in chapter 4 with regard to Revelation, the 40s through 60s of the first century are the only time in Christian history that we have good reason to think that the movement was preoccupied with the extent to which believers—gentile or Jewish—should avoid eating food sacrificed to idols.[47] Indeed, Jefford has gone as far as to argue that Didache 6.2–3 might well represent an early form of the apostolic decree recorded in Acts 15:23–29.[48] Although Jefford's source-critical argument might well push the relationship between Didache 6 and Acts 15 somewhat further than the data allow, his work does help elucidate the extent to which this material is most fully intelligible within the context of the 40s through 60s.

46. Cf. Kinzig, "The Nazoreans."
47. Cf. Acts 15:20, 29, which is set ca. 48; 1 Cor. 8:4–13. Cf. the discussion in chap. 4 above.
48. Jefford, "Tradition and Witness."

Yet as discussed in chapter 4, we cannot exclude the possibility that such debates continued beyond the 60s. Hence, we should be wary of insisting that 6.2–3 must date to these decades. Nonetheless, insofar as we lack other indicators regarding when to best date the Didache, 6.2–3 can at least help us anchor the text a bit more solidly to a specific temporal context. At the very least, the later one wants to date the Didache after 100, the more that Didache 6.2–3 begins to look out of place. Cumulative to the above discussion, I am inclined to date the Didache no later than 125.

Ecclesiology (Did. 11-13; 15.1)

The ecclesiology of the Didache is also consistent with that of the 40s through 60s. Didache 11–13 dwells at length on the regulation of traveling teachers, apostles, and prophets. All three of these roles are amply demonstrated from this period, and in 1 Corinthians 9 Paul betrays knowledge of policies on the matter of itinerant leaders remarkably similar to those found in Didache 11–13. Perhaps most significantly, Didache 15.1 refers to the bishops and deacons—*episkopoi kai diakonoi*—exactly the same formulation as found in Philippians 1:1. Nonetheless, as with other texts in this study, we should be wary of supposing that ecclesiological development was uniform. Again, the later one dates the Didache after 100, the more Didache 11–13 and 15.1 begin to look out of place. Cumulative to the above discussion, I am inclined to date the Didache no later than 125.

Conclusion to the Didache: Contextualization

Insofar as it is the case that

- on the basis of synchronization we can conclude that the Didache (in a form similar to but not identical with that found in the H text) was completed no earlier than 45 and no later than 400;
- the Jewish matrix of the text permits dates as early as 45 and as late as 400;
- the concern with gentile inclusion evidenced in Didache 6.2–3 parallels developments most fully associated with the 40s–60s and would begin to look increasingly out of place by ca. 125; and
- the concern with regulating traveling teachers, apostles, and prophets in Didache 11-13 and the reference to bishops and

> deacons in 15.1 parallel developments most fully associated with the 40s–60s and would begin to look significantly out of place by ca. 125,
>
> we conclude that the Didache (in a form similar to but not identical with that found in the H text) was completed no earlier than 45 and no later than 125.

Authorial Biography

Like many first- or second-century Christian texts, the Didache is often treated as an anonymous work. Nonetheless, in its longer title the Didache is designated "The Lord's Teaching through the Twelve Apostles to the Gentiles" (*Didachē kyriou dia tōn dōdeka apostolōn tois ethnesin*). Insofar as the Didache could date centuries later than the putative authors, there is greater justification for scholars to treat the Didache as a pseudonymous work than is the case with virtually any other text in the New Testament and the Apostolic Fathers. Given legitimate uncertainties regarding the relationship (if any) between the Twelve and the text of the Didache, we should consider this putative attribution to be nonprobative for purposes of establishing the compositional date of the text.

Conclusion to the Didache: Authorial Biography

Insofar as it is the case that

- on the cumulative basis of synchronization and contextualization the Didache, in something resembling (but probably not identical with) the form found in H, was likely completed between 50 and 125; and
- the putative attribution to the "Twelve Apostles" should be considered nonprobative for purposes of establishing the compositional date of the Didache,

we conclude that the Didache (in a form similar to but not identical with that found in the H text) was completed no earlier than 45 and no later than 125.

Cumulative Conclusion to the Didache

Insofar as it is the case that

- on the basis of external attestation the Didache (in a form similar to but not identical with that found in the H text) existed by the end of the fourth century;

- the writers of the Didache, in something resembling (but probably not identical with) the form found in H, probably knew the Gospel of Matthew, which we have already dated in this study to ca. 45 through 59;

- the concern with gentile inclusion evidenced in Didache 6.2–3 parallels developments most fully associated with the 40s–60s and begins to look increasingly out of place by ca. 125; and

- the concern with regulating traveling teachers, apostles, and prophets in Didache 11–13 and the reference to bishops and deacons in 15.1 parallel developments most fully associated with the 40s–60s and begin to look significantly out of place by ca. 125,

we conclude that the Didache (in a form similar to but not identical with that found in the H text) was completed no earlier than 45 and no later than 125.

Cumulative Conclusion to Chapter 9: 1 Clement and the Didache

Chapter 9 argued that 1 Clement was most likely written ca. 64-70, and the Didache ca. 45-125. We can thus summarize the likely compositional dates of the texts considered thus far in this study via the following table:

Text	Date
Gospel of Mark	42–45
Gospel of Matthew	45–59
The Didache	**45–125**
Galatians	47–52
1 Thessalonians	50–52
2 Thessalonians	50–52
Hebrews	50–70
1 Corinthians	early 56

Text	Date
2 Corinthians	late 56
Romans	winter of 56/57
Ephesians, Colossians, Philemon, and Philippians	57–59
Gospel of Luke	59
1 Peter	60–69
2 Peter	if Petrine: 60–69 if pseudo-Petrine: 60–125
Gospel of John	60–70
1 and 2 John	60–100
James	before 62
Acts of the Apostles	62
1 Timothy	if Pauline: 63 or 64 if pseudo-Pauline: 60–150
Titus	if Pauline: 63 or 64 if pseudo-Pauline: 60–175
2 Timothy	if Pauline: 64–68 if pseudo-Pauline: 60–150
1 Clement	**64–70**
Revelation	68–70
Jude	before 96
3 John	before 100

10

The Epistle of Barnabas and the Shepherd of Hermas

Chapter 10 considers the compositional dates of the Epistle of Barnabas and the Shepherd of Hermas.[1] It argues that the Epistle of Barnabas was written no earlier than 70 and no later than 132; and the Shepherd of Hermas no earlier than 60 and no later than 125.

The Epistle of Barnabas

The aim of this section is to establish the most probable date for the Epistle of Barnabas. Attributed putatively to Barnabas, companion of Paul, it contains one of the earliest extant discussions that explicitly addresses Jewish-Christian relations. This study argues that the Epistle of Barnabas was written no earlier than 70 and no later than 132. This is largely consistent with most opinions on the compositional date of the Epistle of Barnabas.

1. In developing this chapter, I found the following studies particularly useful: Carleton Paget, *Epistle of Barnabas: Outlook and Background*; Osiek, *Shepherd of Hermas*. As elsewhere throughout this study, for English language quotations from the Apostolic Fathers I follow translations by Holmes, *Apostolic Fathers*.

Synchronization

In this section, we consider (1) external attestation, (2) source-critical matters, (3) the "king count" of Barnabas 4.4–5, and (4) the matter of 70 for the
unity of the text. From the work of synchronization we conclude that the
Epistle of Barnabas was written no earlier than 70 and no later than 132.

External Attestation

According to Eusebius, Clement of Alexandria wrote a commentary on
this text in his *Hypotyposeis*.[2] As such, we can be reasonably confident, on
the basis of external attestation, that the Epistle of Barnabas existed no later
than the last quarter of the second century. We are thus disinclined to date
our epistle later than 175.

Source Criticism

As with many texts, we cannot with confidence demonstrate that the Epistle
of Barnabas knew any given first- or second-century text.[3] Thus, we should
be inclined to consider the matter of sources to be nonprobative for purposes
of establishing the date of the Epistle of Barnabas.

The Little Offshoot of a Horn (Barn. 4.4–5)

In Barnabas 4.4–5 we read,

> And so also says the prophet: "Ten kingdoms will reign over the earth, and
> after them a little king will arise, who will subdue three of the kings with a
> single blow." Similarly Daniel says, concerning the same one: "And I saw the
> fourth beast, wicked and powerful and more dangerous than all the beasts of
> the earth, and how ten horns sprang up from it, and from these a little offshoot
> of a horn, and how it subdued three of the large horns with a single blow."[4]

Arguments regarding the date of Barnabas often focus upon identifying the "little king"—that is, the "little offshoot of a horn" mentioned in

---

2. *Hist. eccl.* 6.14.1. Cf. the discussion in Carleton Paget, *Epistle of Barnabas: Outlook and
Background*, 249–50.
3. Cf. the discussion in Carleton Paget, "*Barnabas* and the Writings," as well as the discussion of the relationship between the Didache and the Epistle of Barnabas in chap. 9 above.
4. Barn. 4.4–5, trans. Holmes, *Apostolic Fathers*, 387–89.

4.4–5. Much as we found with regard to Revelation 17:9–11 in chapter 4 (above), such efforts to "count kings" are fraught with difficulties. On the supposition that the ten king(dom)s/horns are to be identified with Roman emperors, prime candidates include Vespasian or perhaps Nerva.[5] John Robinson strongly favors Vespasian, to the point of treating a Vespasianic date for the epistle as unassailable.[6] I am less convinced. Both Vespasian and Nerva might be said to have "subdued" three "king(dom)s"—Vespasian, by coming after the short reigns of Galba, Otho, and Vitellius; Nerva, by coming after the three emperors of the Flavian dynasty: Vespasian, Titus, and Domitian. If we count each historical emperor as a king(dom)/horn, then Vespasian was the ninth (if we begin with Augustus) or tenth (if we begin with Julius), while Nerva was the twelfth (if we begin with Augustus) or the thirteenth (if we begin with Julius). Neither would be the eleventh and thus would have difficulty corresponding with the little horn. One might adjust the king count by excluding certain emperors or including other figures, but the necessity of such ad hoc argumentation tends to undermine the correlation of the king(dom)s/horns with historical emperors. Moreover, it is not self-evident that Barnabas intended for the Danielic king(dom)s/horns to correlate precisely with historical figures, in which case efforts to build a chronology upon such correlation become fraught with doubt. Given such difficulties, we should consider Barnabas 4.4–5 to be nonprobative for purposes of establishing the compositional date of the text.

The Matter of 70 (Barn. 16.3–4)

We have seen that the Gospels of Matthew, Mark, and John—as well as Hebrews, Revelation, and 1 Clement—to one extent or another suppose that the temple and Jerusalem more generally yet stand. By contrast, the Epistle of Barnabas is unequivocally aware of the temple's destruction in 70 (cf. 16.1–5). Indeed, 16.3–4 has become a locus classicus for establishing the date of the letter.

> Furthermore, again he [the Lord] says: 'Behold, those who tore down this temple will build it themselves.' This is happening now. For because they went to war,

5. See Carleton Paget, *Epistle of Barnabas: Outlook and Background*, 13–17, for an overview of the evidence in favor of each one.
6. Robinson, *Redating*, 315.

it was torn down by their enemies, and now the very servants of their enemies will re-build it.[7]

There is a general supposition among contemporary scholars that Barnabas 16.3–4 could only have been written prior to 135, when the resolution of the Bar Kokhba revolt made rebuilding the temple quite unlikely. Although not certain, hope that the temple would be imminently rebuilt does seem more intelligible before 135 than after. The admittedly enigmatic statement that the temple will be rebuilt by "the servants of their enemies" probably should incline us to think that the epistle was written before the outbreak of the Bar Kokhba revolt (132–135): after that time we are not inclined to think that the "servants" of the Romans would be assisting the Jewish people in rebuilding the temple. Some go even farther, claiming to find evidence for increased expectation that the temple would be rebuilt during Hadrian's reign (117–138), at least prior to the second revolt.[8] The evidence is less than compelling. Nonetheless, on the basis of 16.3–4 we can say that the Epistle of Barnabas certainly postdates 70 and most likely predates 132.

Conclusion to Epistle of Barnabas: Synchronization

Insofar as it is the case that

- on the basis of external attestation, we can be confident that the Epistle of Barnabas existed by the last quarter of the second century;
- the matter of sources is nonprobative for purposes of establishing the date of the Epistle of Barnabas;
- Barnabas 4.4–5 is nonprobative for purposes of establishing the date of the Epistle of Barnabas; and
- Barnabas 16.3–4 is most intelligible after 70 but before 132,

we conclude that the Epistle of Barnabas was written no earlier than 70 and no later than 132.

---

7. Barn. 16.3–4, trans. Holmes, *Apostolic Fathers*, 431–43. Cf. discussion of this passage in Carleton Paget, *Epistle of Barnabas: Outlook and Background*, 17–30.
8. Cf. the overview of these matters in Carleton Paget, *Epistle of Barnabas: Outlook and Background*, 22–27.

Contextualization

Since we can confidently state that the Epistle of Barnabas was composed between 70 and 132, we are most concerned with any contextual material within the book that would incline us toward a date earlier or later within that range. Perhaps the only such material that might sway us in one direction or another is the text's manifest anti-Judaism. This might incline us toward a later date, after the so-called parting of the ways. The reality, though, is that this "parting" was a lengthy and involved process, one that can hardly be identified with any precision. As such, it should be considered nonprobative, and the work of contextualization offers little of value for establishing the date of the Epistle of Barnabas.

Conclusion to Epistle of Barnabas: Contextualization

Insofar as it is the case that

- we can on the basis of synchronization argue that the Epistle of Barnabas was written no earlier than 70 and no later than 132; and
- the work of contextualization offers little of value for establishing the date of the Epistle of Barnabas,

we conclude that the Epistle of Barnabas was written no earlier than 70 and no later than 132.

Authorial Biography

Through the work of synchronization and contextualization, we have concluded that the Epistle of Barnabas was written no earlier than 70 and no later than 132. It is possible that the historical Barnabas was active during the earlier part of this period. Indeed, our earliest witness to the text—Clement of Alexandria—seems to have thought that the letter was authentic.[9] Nonetheless, what we know of the historical Barnabas—a Levite who on at least one occasion sided with a more "conservative" faction regarding Jewish-gentile interactions within the emerging Christian movement (cf. Gal. 2:13)—does seem difficult to reconcile with the supersessionist Epistle of Barnabas. As such, we should probably be inclined to state that while, strictly speaking, it is

9. According to Eusebius, *Hist. eccl.* 6.14.1.

not impossible that our letter was written by the historical Barnabas, neither is it probable. Certainly the possibility is not strong enough to narrow the range of possible dates of composition.

Conclusion to Epistle of Barnabas: Authorial Biography

Insofar as it is the case that

- we can on the basis of synchronization and contextualization conclude that the Epistle of Barnabas was most likely written between 70 and 132; and
- there is insufficient possibility that it was written by the historical Barnabas to undertake the work of authorial biography,

we conclude that the Epistle of Barnabas was written no earlier than 70 and no later than 132.

Cumulative Conclusion to Epistle of Barnabas

Insofar as it is the case that Barnabas 16.3–4 is most intelligible after 70 but before 132, we conclude that the Epistle of Barnabas was written no earlier than 70 and no later than 132.

Shepherd of Hermas

The aim of this section is to establish the most probable date for the Shepherd of Hermas. Built around an occasionally startling series of visions, the Shepherd quite clearly identifies who wrote it (one Hermas) and where it was written (in and around Rome). Although most scholars tend to situate the Shepherd ca. 125–150, this study argues that it was likely completed no earlier than 60 and no later than 125.

A note is necessary regarding citations from the Shepherd of Hermas. Citing the Shepherd is sufficiently complicated that *The SBL Handbook of Style* (*SBLHS*) devotes an entire appendix to the matter. It is the only text to receive its own appendix in *SBLHS*. The complication arises from the fact that there are two numbering systems current for the Shepherd of Hermas. The older and more traditional format numbers the Visions, Mandates, and Similitudes and then provides a chapter and verse citation. The other, introduced by Molly Whittaker in 1956, numbers the whole book into 114 chapters.[10] As such, Hermas, Vision 2.4.3 in the traditional format is Hermas 8.3 in the Whittaker format. Following the recommendation of *SBLHS*, this study uses a composite format that cites the traditional format first and then provides the Whittaker numbers in parentheses: so the above example becomes Hermas, Vision 2.4.3 (8.3).

Synchronization

In this section, we consider (1) external attestation and (2) source-critical matters. From the work of synchronization, we conclude that the Shepherd was likely written no later than 175.

External Attestation

The Shepherd was well known by the last quarter of the second century, as evidenced from the writings of Clement of Alexandria and Irenaeus.[11] Given this data, we should be disinclined to date the Shepherd much later than 175.

Source Criticism

The near-total absence of explicit quotations within the Shepherd makes it difficult to determine which sources if any Hermas might have used.[12] Although it is certainly plausible that the Shepherd made use of one or more datable first- or second-century texts, in no case can we state with confidence that he did so. Thus, we should consider the matter of sources to be nonprobative for purposes of establishing the date of the Shepherd.

Conclusion to Shepherd of Hermas: Synchronization

Insofar as it is the case that

• external attestation excludes a date for the Shepherd later than 175; and

---

10. Whittaker, *Der Hirt des Hermas.*
11. On Clement of Alexandria, cf. Batovici, "Hermas in Clement." On Irenaeus, cf. Steenberg, "Irenaeus on Scripture."
12. Cf. the discussions in Osiek, *Shepherd of Hermas*, 24–27; Verheyden, "*Hermas* and the Writings."

· source-critical data are nonprobative with regard to the Shepherd,
we conclude that the Shepherd of Hermas was written no later than 175. ·

Contextualization

In this section, we are here concerned with (1) the temporal relationship of the text to the apostolic generation and (2) the ecclesiology supposed by the author. On the basis of these data, we should be wary of dating the Shepherd of Hermas much earlier than 60 or much later than 125.

The division of the Shepherd into the Visions, the Mandates (or Commandments), and Similitudes (or Parables) has led to a scholarly tendency to read the text as a composite document.[13] The Shepherd certainly details and indeed is largely structured around a series of revelations delivered over time. Indeed, Hermas, Vision 2.1.1 (5.1) explicitly states that an interval of a year had occurred between what is recorded in Vision 1 and what is recorded in Vision 2. We should probably conclude that the composition of the text took place over years, possibly even decades. As such, we need to consider the possibility that the text evinces a diversity of temporal contexts.

Those Who Sleep (Herm. Vis. 3.5.1a [13.1a]; Herm. Sim. 9.15.4 [92.4]; 9.16.5 [93.5])

We read the following in Hermas, Vision 3.5.1a (13.1a):

The stones that are square and white and fit at their joints, these are the apostles and bishops and teachers and deacons who have walked according to the holiness of God and have ministered to the elect of God as bishops and teachers and deacons with purity and reverence; some have fallen asleep, while others are still living.[14]

One is tempted to read this as evidence that Hermas was active before the last of the apostles had passed away. Robinson wants to read the passage this way.[15] If indeed the phrase "some have fallen asleep, while others are

13. Cf. the overview of scholarship in Osiek, *Shepherd of Hermas*, 8–10.
14. Herm. Vis. 3.5.1a (13.1a), trans. Holmes, *Apostolic Fathers*, 479.
15. Robinson, *Redating*, 321–22.

still living" is true of each of the four enumerated groups, then there would presumably still be some apostles yet alive when these words were written. At least two considerations give us pause, however. First, it is possible that the phrase "some have fallen asleep, while others are still living" could refer to the four categories collectively, in which case it is not necessarily the case that any apostles are still alive. Second, while Hermas speaks first of "apostles and bishops and teachers and deacons," he subsequently speaks of those "who have ministered . . . as bishops and teachers and deacons." As such, it is possible that the statement "some have fallen asleep, while others are still living" was not meant to include apostles at all. Thus, we cannot from Vision 3.5.1a (13.1a) state with any confidence that any apostles yet remained alive. Indeed, the fact that apostles are missing from the second list might also incline us toward the conclusion that Hermas was writing at a time when apostolic leadership was largely, if not entirely, a thing of the past. Cumulatively, Vision 3.5.1a (13.1a) should probably be taken as an indication that by the time the Shepherd was written, many if not all of the apostolic generation had passed away.

Turning to Hermas, Similitude 9.15.4 (92.4) and 9.16.5 (93.5), we find further reason to suspect that most if not all the apostolic generation had passed away.

"And who are the stones, sir," I said, "that came from the deep and were fitted into the building?" "The first ones," he said, "the ten that were placed on the foundations, are the first generation, and the twenty-five are the second generation of righteous men. The thirty-five are God's prophets and his ministers, and the forty are apostles and teachers of the proclamation of the Son of God."[16]

"Why, sir," I said, "did the forty stones also come up with them from the deep, when they had already received the seal?" "Because," he said, "when these apostles and teachers who preached the name of the Son of God fell asleep in the power and faith of the Son of God, they preached also to those who had previously fallen asleep, and they themselves gave to them the seal of the preaching."[17]

Carolyn Osiek suggests that the ten stones represent the generations from Adam to Noah, while the twenty-five stones represent the generations from

16. Herm. Sim. 9.15.4 (92.4), trans. Holmes, *Apostolic Fathers*, 651.
17. Herm. Sim. 9.16.5 (93.5), trans. Holmes, *Apostolic Fathers*, 653.

Noah to David.[18] She acknowledges that the parallelism breaks down when we reach the thirty-five prophets and ministers of God and forty apostles and teachers proclaiming the Son of God. Ultimately she concludes that we are likely dealing with local folklore. For our purposes, what matters most is that the apostles in Hermas, Similitude 9.15.4 (92.4) are included within a symbolic renumeration of foundational figures, without any effort to state that some of these are still active, and in 9.16.5 (93.5), they are explicitly said to have fallen asleep. Although such language is not impossible during the flourishing of the apostolic generation, it seems more intelligible either toward or after its end. Since the 60s seem to be the decade when most major figures of the apostolic generation (notably James, Peter, and Paul) passed away, I am wary of dating the Shepherd much earlier than 60.

Ecclesiology

The ecclesiology of the Shepherd seems closer to that of the first century than the second. We have already noted that Vision 3.5.1a (13.1a) writes of apostles, bishops, teachers, and deacons. This finds a close parallel in Philippians 1:1.[19] We have references to elders who preside over the church, without reference anywhere to a monarchical bishop.[20] We must, of course, remember the usual caveats—namely, that we have limited knowledge of the development of ecclesiastical offices across the late first and early second centuries and also that such developments were likely not even across all regions. Nonetheless, as with the Didache, the later in the second century that one wants to date the Shepherd, the more its ecclesiology will begin to look out of place. Cumulative to the above discussion, I am inclined to date the Shepherd of Hermas no later than 125.

Conclusion to Shepherd of Hermas: Contextualization

Insofar as it is the case that

- on the basis of synchronization, we can date the Shepherd of Hermas with reasonable confidence prior to 175;

---

18. Cf. the discussion in Osiek, *Shepherd of Hermas*, 237.
19. Cf. the discussions of Phil. 1:1 and Did. 11–13 and 15.1 in chap. 9 above.
20. Cf. the discussion of Herm. Vis. 2.4.3 (8.3) below.

- Hermas, Vision 3.5.1a (13.1a), Similitude 9.15.4 (92.4), and Similitude 9.16.5 (93.5) are more intelligible toward or after the end of the apostolic generation; and
- the ecclesiology of the Shepherd is more consistent with a first- than with a second-century date,

we conclude that the Shepherd of Hermas was composed no earlier than 60 and no later than 125.

Authorial Biography

The previous two sections gave us reason to prefer a date of 60–125 for the Shepherd of Hermas. Authorial biography gives us reason to affirm this judgment. The issues to be considered in this section include (1) the possible identity of our author with the Hermas of Romans 16:14, (2) the evidence that Hermas was a contemporary of Clement of Rome, and (3) the evidence of the Muratorian Canon.[21]

The Hermas of Romans 16:14

There is a long tradition, going back to at least Origen, of identifying the Hermas of the Shepherd with the Hermas of Romans 16:14.[22] Although not impossible, it is far from probable. Thus, the possibility that the Hermas of the Shepherd is to be identified with the Hermas of Romans cannot be used to support a specific date for the text and should, for our purposes, be considered nonprobative.

A Contemporary of Clement (Herm. Vis. 2.4.3 [8.3])

In Vision 2.4.3 (8.3), Hermas is told,

Therefore you will write two little books, and you will send one to Clement and one to Grapte. Then Clement will send it to the cities abroad, because that is his job. But Grapte will instruct the widows and orphans. But you yourself will read it to this city, along with the elders who preside over the church.[23]

21. Osiek describes these as the "three pegs upon which all theories of the date hang" (*Shepherd of Hermas*, 18).
22. Cf. the discussion in Osiek, *Shepherd of Hermas*, 18–19.
23. Herm. Vis. 2.4.3 (8.3), trans. Holmes, *Apostolic Fathers*, 469.

This text has been taken as an indication that Hermas was a contemporary of Clement of Rome, the putative author of 1 Clement.[24] In light of our discussion of 1 Clement, it is not without significance that the role assigned in Hermas, Vision 2.4.3 (8.3) coheres remarkably well with Dionysius's statement to Soter that the Roman church wrote 1 Clement to the Corinthian church through Clement.[25] That being said, such coherence could be an intentional artifice on the part of Hermas, designed to associate the Shepherd with a well-known figure of the ecclesiastical past. If this coherence between the Shepherd and Dionysius is indeed such an artifice, then Vision 2.4.3 (8.3) would likely represent an early instance in the developing legends that came to surround Clement. Against this argument for intentional artifice is the fact that it is paired with a reference to the role of one Grapte, a woman otherwise unknown to us. A more substantive objection to identifying the Clement of Vision 2.4.3 (8.3) with the historical Clement of Rome is that Clement was a quite common name. Nonetheless, the coherence between the role that we find attributed to Clement here and that described by Dionysius seems sufficient to suggest that, without evidence to the contrary, we ought to favor a date in the last third of the first century for Vision 2.4.3 (8.3), during Clement of Rome's likely floruit. It needs to be emphasized, however, that due to questions about the unity of the text, such a date for Vision 2.4.3 (8.3) does not exclude the possibility that the balance of the Shepherd was written earlier or later than this time frame.

"Pastor" and the Muratorian Canon

Potentially the strongest evidence for the author's identity comes from the Muratorian Canon, lines 73–78:

Hermas wrote the Shepherd quite lately in our time in the city of Rome, when on the throne of the church of the city of Rome the bishop Pius, his brother, was seated. And therefore it ought indeed to be read, but it cannot be read publicly in the Church.[26]

24. Cf. the discussion in Osiek, *Shepherd of Hermas*, 58–60.
25. According to Eusebius, *Hist. eccl.* 4.23.11.
26. Translation following Schneemelcher, introduction to *New Testament Apocrypha*, 1:36. The discussion of the Shepherd is located on lines 73–80 in Wilson's translation.

Pius is typically thought to have been bishop in the 140s and 150s. If we suppose that the Shepherd was written over the span of a single lifetime, that this lifetime overlapped with that of the author of 1 Clement, and that the author of 1 Clement was active as late as 100, then it is conceivable that portions of the text were written toward the end of the first century, and yet it was not completed until the 140s.

There are reasons to doubt the Canon on this matter, however. First, as we have seen, the ecclesiology of the Shepherd evinces no knowledge of a monarchical bishop and rather understands the Roman church to still be governed by presbyterial rule. While we cannot build much upon an argument from silence, it does seem a bit odd that Hermas would not be aware that the Roman church was governed by a monarchical bishop if indeed his brother occupied that position. Second, Robinson argues that Pius had a brother named Pastor and, noting that the Latin name for the Shepherd was *Liber Pastoris*, further argues that the author of the Canon has simply and wrongly supposed that it is the "Book of Pastor"—that is, Pius's brother.[27] This is possible but not necessarily probable. Although skepticism regarding the Muratorian Canon's witness is warranted, we should nonetheless be wary of any date for the Shepherd of Hermas that supposes the Muratorian Canon is in error. Insofar as Hermas could have been active ca. 125 and yet have had a brother serving as bishop in the 150s, I am inclined to continue dating the Shepherd no earlier than 60 and no later than 125.

Conclusion to Shepherd of Hermas: Authorial Biography

Insofar as it is the case that

- on the cumulative basis of synchronization and contextualization we can date the Shepherd of Hermas no earlier than 60 and no later than 125;
- the Hermas of Romans 16:14 is possibly but not probably to be identified with the Hermas who wrote the Shepherd;
- the author of the Shepherd is plausibly a contemporary of Clement of Rome; and

---

27. Cf. Robinson, *Redating*, 228. Here Robinson once again—as he too often does—follows Edmundson, *Church in Rome*, 210–12.

> • the Muratorian Canon indicates that Hermas was a brother of Pius, bishop of Rome, although there is some reason to question this testimony,
>
> we conclude that the Shepherd of Hermas was written no earlier than 60 and no later than 125.

Cumulative Conclusion to Shepherd of Hermas

Insofar as it is the case that

- Hermas, Vision 3.5.1a (13.1a), Similitude 9.15.4 (92.4), and Similitude 9.16.5 (93.5) are more intelligible toward or after the end of the apostolic generation;
- the ecclesiology of the Shepherd is more consistent with a first- than with a second-century date;
- the author of the Shepherd is plausibly a contemporary of Clement of Rome; and
- the Muratorian Canon indicates that Hermas was a brother of Pius, bishop of Rome, although there is some reason to question this testimony,

we conclude that the Shepherd of Hermas was written ca. 60–125.

Cumulative Conclusion to Chapter 10:
The Epistle of Barnabas and the Shepherd of Hermas

Chapter 9 argued that 1 Clement was most likely written ca. 64–70, and the Didache ca. 45–125. We can thus summarize the likely compositional dates of the texts considered thus far in this study via the following table:

Text	Date
Gospel of Mark	42–45
Gospel of Matthew	45–59
The Didache	45–125

Text	Date
Galatians	47–52
1 Thessalonians	50–52
2 Thessalonians	50–52
Hebrews	50–70
1 Corinthians	early 56
2 Corinthians	late 56
Romans	winter of 56/57
Ephesians, Colossians, Philemon, and Philippians	57–59
Gospel of Luke	59
1 Peter	60–69
2 Peter	if Petrine: 60–69 if pseudo-Petrine: 60–125
Gospel of John	60–70
1 and 2 John	60–100
Shepherd of Hermas	**60–125**
James	before 62
Acts of the Apostles	62
1 Timothy	if Pauline: 63 or 64 if pseudo-Pauline: 60–150
Titus	if Pauline: 63 or 64 if pseudo-Pauline: 60–175
2 Timothy	if Pauline: 64–68 if pseudo-Pauline: 60–150
1 Clement	64–70
Revelation	68–70
The Epistle of Barnabas	**70–132**
Jude	before 96
3 John	before 100

Conclusion

This study began by differentiating between three broad frameworks for thinking about the compositional dates of the New Testament texts. While all three of these frameworks agree that the undisputed Pauline Epistles should be dated to around the 50s of the first century, lower chronologies date much of the balance of the New Testament corpus prior to 70; middle chronologies date much of the balance to the period between 70 and 100; and higher chronologies date much of the balance of the New Testament to the second century. In surveying the relevant data, this study concludes that a lower chronology is most fully warranted. Our findings, compared with typical middle and higher chronologies as well as John Robinson's previous lower chronology, can be summarized as follows:

Book	Lower (Bernier)	Lower (Robinson)*	Middle (Harnack)†	Higher (Sturdy)‡
Matthew	45–59	50	70–75	130
Mark	42–45	45	65–73	80
Luke	59	60	80–95	110
John	60–70	65	80–110	140
Acts	62	62	80–95	130
Romans	winter of 56/57	57	56–57	50
1 Corinthians	early 56	55	56	50
2 Corinthians	late 56	56	56	50
Galatians	47–52	56	53	50
Ephesians	57–59	58	57–59	100

Book	Lower (Bernier)	Lower (Robinson)*	Middle (Harnack)†	Higher (Sturdy)‡
Philippians	57–59	58	57–59	50
Colossians	57–59	58	57–59	80
1 Thessalonians	50–52	50	48–49	40
2 Thessalonians	50–52	50–51	48–49	120
1 Timothy—if Pauline	63 or 64	55	n/a	n/a
1 Timothy—if pseudo-Pauline	60–150	n/a	90–110	140
2 Timothy—if Pauline	64–68	58	n/a	n/a
2 Timothy—if pseudo-Pauline	60–150	n/a	90–110	140
Titus—if Pauline	63 or 64	57	n/a	n/a
Titus—if pseudo-Pauline	60–175	n/a	90–110	140
Philemon	57–59	58	57–62	50
Hebrews	50–70	67	81–96	110
James	prior to 62	47–48	70–90	130
1 Peter	60–69	65	81–96	110
2 Peter—if Petrine	60–69	61–62	n/a	n/a
2 Peter—if pseudo-Petrine	60–125	n/a	110–120	150
1 John	60–100	60–65	80–110	140
2 John	60–100	60–65	80–110	140
3 John	prior to 100	60–65	80–110	140
Jude	prior to 96	61–62	100–130	130
Revelation	68–70	68	93–96	150
1 Clement	64–70	70	93–97	130
Didache	60–125	60	120	150
Epistle of Barnabas	70–132	75	130	140
Shepherd of Hermas	70–125	prior to 85	140	150

*Following Robinson, *Redating*, 352, with some modification. Cf. the discussion in chap. 1 above.
†Following Harnack, *Chronologie*, 717–22, with some modification. Cf. the discussion in the introduction above.
‡Following Sturdy, *Redrawing the Boundaries*, 83–86. Cf. the discussion in the introduction above.

Perhaps more important than these findings, however, is the effort to elevate the degree of methodological reflection upon how to go about making judgments regarding the compositional dates of the New Testament and other early Christian literature. The rubric of synchronization, contextualization, and authorial biography seeks to organize and better coordinate relevant evidence. It additionally assists in seeing the relative strength of different types of evidence. In principle, authorial biography is the strongest evidence, insofar as, when available, it can afford us the most precise dates (the case of Romans best exemplifies this); next is synchronization, which can rarely offer dates as precise as can authorial biography but nonetheless can often narrow down the possible range; then contextualization, which as a fundamentally analogical procedure, tends to be highly imprecise. Unfortunately, evidence relevant for the work of authorial biography often tends to be lacking, thus forcing us to rely upon synchronization and contextualization (the case of Hebrews is the most extreme example of such a situation). Such cases tend to evince the widest ranges of possible dates measurable in decades.

Much work remains to be done on establishing the compositional dates of early Christian literature. This study barely touches upon extracanonical literature, a fact that in part reflects the author's own personal research interests and expertise and in part reflects the need to keep the study to a manageable size. Nonetheless, there are many extracanonical Christian writings whose dates remain unresolved. My expectation is that highly precise dates would be impossible for many of these texts, as in so many cases we would be relying heavily upon the work of contextualization. I have a similar expectation with regard to much early Jewish literature as well. There would likely be exceptions, of course, such as the works of Ben Sira, Josephus, and Philo, which can be dated with relative precision. These, however, constitute exceptions precisely due to a relative abundance of data relevant to their authorial biography. I expect that much of the Tanakh would likewise resist precise dates, again due to a need to rely heavily upon contextualization. In the introduction, we briefly considered the difficulties involved in establishing compositional dates for the Pentateuch. Many of these difficulties would likely recur throughout efforts to date the balance of the Tanakh.

The above reflections bring us to a central point: the strategies employed to establish a compositional date must be driven in no small part by the relevant data. The rubric of synchronization, contextualization, and authorial biography helped me to ensure that the strategies I employed are generally consistent with one another, but ultimately how I approach Romans differs greatly from how I approach Hebrews because the data relevant to each differ greatly. As such, I have tried as much as possible to organize and arrange this study in such a way that even those who disagree with my conclusions find the assemblage of relevant evidence to be helpful. If you happen to think that the evidence better supports a higher date for, say, Acts, then it is my sincere hope that despite our difference of opinion on this matter you may find the way I presented the data to be helpful for your own work.

The reality is that with the publication of this work, two complete, monograph-length studies have been published since the turn of the twentieth century by professional biblical scholars who defend lower chronologies for the composition dates of the New Testament corpus, while there have been zero similar studies defending middle or higher chronologies. This puts lower chronologies in an intellectually privileged position. The best way to offset this privilege is for professional New Testament scholars to produce comparable defenses of middle or higher chronologies. I genuinely hope that this occurs, and sooner rather than later.

Bibliography

Achtemeier, Paul J. *1 Peter*. Minneapolis: Fortress, 1998.

Alexander, Loveday. *The Preface to Luke's Gospel: Literary Convention and Social Context in Luke 1:1–4 and Acts 1:1*. Cambridge: Cambridge University Press, 1993.

Allert, Craig D. *Revelation, Truth, Canon, and Interpretation: Studies in Justin Martyr's Dialogue with Trypho*. Leiden: Brill, 2002.

Allison, Dale C., Jr. *James*. London: T&T Clark, 2013.

Anderson, Paul N. *The Fourth Gospel and the Quest for Jesus: Modern Foundations Reconsidered*. London: T&T Clark, 2007.

Armstrong, Karl. *Dating Acts in Its Jewish and Greco-Roman Context*. London: T&T Clark, 2021.

Asiedu, F. B. A. *Paul and His Letters: Thinking with Josephus*. Lanham, MD: Lexington Books / Fortress Academic, 2020.

Attridge, Harold W. *Hebrews*. Minneapolis: Fortress, 1989.

Audet, Jean-Paul. *La Didachè: Instructions de apôtres*. Paris: Gabalda, 1958.

Aune, David E. *Revelation 1–5*. Dallas: Word, 1997.

———. *Revelation 6–16*. Dallas: Word, 1998.

———. *Revelation 17–22*. Dallas: Word, 1998.

Balabanski, Vicky. *Eschatology in the Making: Mark, Matthew, and the Didache*. Cambridge: Cambridge University Press, 1997.

———. "Where Is Philemon? The Case for a Logical Fallacy in the Correlation of the Data in Philemon and Colossians 1.1–2; 4.7–18." *Journal for the Study of the New Testament* 38.2 (2015): 131–50.

Barker, James W. *John's Use of Matthew*. Minneapolis: Fortress, 2015.

Barrett, C. K. *First Epistle to the Corinthians*. London: A&C Black, 1968.

———. *The Gospel according to St. John*. 2nd ed. London: SPCK, 1978.

———. *Romans*. 2nd ed. London: A&C Black, 1991.

————. *Second Epistle to the Corinthians*. London: A&C Black, 1973.

Barth, Markus. *Ephesians*. 2 vols. Garden City, NY: Doubleday, 1974.

Barth, Markus, and Helmut Blanke. *Colossians*. Translated by Astrid B. Beck. Garden City, NY: Doubleday, 1994.

Batovici, Dan. "Hermas in Clement of Alexandria." In *Clement of Alexandria: The Fourth-Century Debates*, edited by Markus Vinzent, 41–51. Vol. 14 of Papers Presented at the Sixteenth International Conference on Patristic Studies Held in Oxford 2011. Studia Patristica 66. Leuven: Peeters, 2013.

Bauckham, Richard. *Climax of Prophecy: Studies on the Book of Revelation*. Edinburgh: T&T Clark, 1993.

————, ed. *The Gospels for All Christians: Rethinking the Gospel Audiences*. Grand Rapids: Eerdmans, 1998.

————. *Jesus and the Eyewitnesses: The Gospels as Eyewitness Testimony*. 2nd ed. Grand Rapids: Eerdmans, 2017.

————. *Jesus and the God of Israel: "God Crucified" and Other Studies on the New Testament's Christology of Divine Identity*. Grand Rapids: Eerdmans, 2008.

————. *Jude and 2 Peter*. Dallas: Word, 1983.

————. *Testimony of the Beloved Disciple*. Grand Rapids: Eerdmans, 2007.

Baur, Ferdinand Christian. *The Church History of the First Three Centuries*. Edited by Peter C. Hodgson. Translated by Robert F. Brown and Peter C. Hodgson. Eugene, OR: Wipf & Stock, 2019.

————. *Paul, the Apostle of Jesus Christ: His Life and Works, His Epistles and Teachings*. Vol. 1 edited and translated by Eduard Zeller. Vol. 2 edited by Eduard Zeller and translated by Allan Menzies. London: Williams & Norgate, 1873–75.

Beasley-Murray, George R. *John*. 2nd ed. Dallas: Word, 1998.

Becker, Eve-Marie, Helen K. Bond, and Catrin H. Williams, eds. *John's Transformation of Mark*. London: T&T Clark, 2021.

Belayche, Nicole. *Iudaea-Palestina: The Pagan Cults in Rome Palestine (Second to Fourth Century)*. Tübingen: Mohr Siebeck, 2001.

Berding, Kenneth. "Polycarp's Use of *1 Clement*: An Assumption Reconsidered." *Journal of Early Christian Studies* 19.1 (2011): 127–39.

Berge, Kåre, Diana Edelman, Philippe Guillaime, and Benedetta Rossi. "Are Economics a Key to Dating *Urdeuteronium*? A Response to Sandra Lynn Richter." *Journal for the Study of the Old Testament* 45.1 (2002): 65–78.

Bernier, Jonathan. *Aposynagōgos and the Historical Jesus in John: Rethinking the Historicity of the Johannine Expulsion Passages*. Leiden: Brill, 2013.

————. *The Quest for the Historical Jesus after the Demise of Authenticity: Toward a Critical Realist Philosophy of History in Jesus Studies*. London: T&T Clark, 2016.

————. "Re-Visioning Social Values in the Emergence of Ancient Israel." *Method: Journal of Lonergan Studies* 10.2 (2019): 1–20.

———. "When Paul Met Sergius: An Assessment of Douglas Campbell's Pauline Chronology for the Years 36 to 37." *Journal of Biblical Literature* 138.4 (2019): 829–43.

Best, Ernest. *Ephesians*. London: T&T Clark, 1998.

———. *First and Second Epistles to the Thessalonians*. London: A&C Black, 1972.

Betz, Hans Dieter. *Galatians*. Philadelphia: Fortress, 1979.

Bigg, Charles. *The Epistles of St. Peter and Jude*. 2nd ed. Edinburgh: T&T Clark, 1902.

Bloch, Marc. *The Historian's Craft*. Translated by Peter Putnam. Manchester: Manchester University Press, 1954.

Blomberg, Craig. *The Historical Reliability of John's Gospel*. Downers Grove, IL: InterVarsity, 2001.

Bockmuehl, Markus. *The Epistle to the Philippians*. London: A&C Black, 1997.

Bond, Helen K. "Dating the Death of Jesus: Memory and the Religious Imagination." *New Testament Studies* 59.4 (2013): 461–75.

Bousset, Wilhelm. *Kyrios Christos: A History of Belief in Christ from the Beginnings of Christianity to Irenaeus*. Translated by John E. Steely. Waco: Baylor University Press, 2013.

Bovon, François. *Luke*. Vol. 1 translated by Christine M. Thomas. Vol. 2 translated by Donald S. Deer. Vol. 3 translated by James Crouch. Minneapolis: Fortress, 2002–13.

Bowersock, G. W. *Roman Arabia*. Cambridge, MA: Harvard University Press, 1983.

Boxall, Ian. *Revelation*. London: Continuum, 2006.

Bray, Gerald L. *The Pastoral Epistles*. London: T&T Clark, 2019.

Broadhead, Edwin K. *Jewish Ways of Following Jesus*. Tübingen: Mohr Siebeck, 2010.

Brown, Raymond E. *The Community of the Beloved Disciple: The Life, Loves, and Hates of an Individual in New Testament Times*. Mahwah, NY: Paulist Press, 1979.

———. *The Epistles of John*. Garden City, NY: Doubleday, 1982.

———. *The Gospel of John*. 2 vols. Garden City, NY: Doubleday, 1966–70.

———. *An Introduction to the Gospel of John*. Edited by Francis Moloney. New Haven: Yale University Press, 2003.

Bryennios, Philotheos. Διδαχὴ τῶν δώδεκα ἀποστόλων ἐκ τοῦ ἱεροσολυμιτικοῦ χειρογράφου νῦν πρῶτον ἐκδιδομένη μετὰ προλεγομένων καὶ σημειώσεων ἐν οἷς καὶ τῆς Συνόψεως τῆς Π. Δ., τῆς ὑπὸ Ἰωάνν. τοῦ Χρυσοστόμου, σύγκρισις καὶ μέρος ἀνέκδοτον ἀπὸ τοῦ αὐτοῦ χειρογράφου. Constantinople: Voutyra, 1883.

Bultmann, Rudolf. *The Gospel of John*. Translated by G. R. Beasley-Murray, R. W. N. Hoare, and J. K. Riches. 1971. Reprint, Eugene, OR: Wipf & Stock, 2014.

———. *The Johannine Epistles*. Translated by R. Philip O'Hara with Lane C. McGaughy and Robert W. Funk. Philadephia: Fortress, 1973.

Bunine, Alexis. "La date de la première visite de Paul à Jérusalem." *Revue Biblique* 113 (2006): 436–56, 601–22.

Cadwallader, Alan H. "Honouring the Repairer of the Baths: A New Inscription from Kolossai." *Antichthon* 46 (2012): 150–83.

———. "Honouring the Repairer of the Baths at Colossae." In *New Documents Illustrating Early Christianity*, edited by S. R. Llewelyn and J. R. Harrison, 10:110–13. Grand Rapids: Eerdmans, 2013.

———. "Refuting an Axiom of Scholarship on Colossae: Fresh Insights from New and Old Inscriptions." In *Colossae in Space and Time: Linking to an Ancient City*, edited by Alan H. Cadwallader and Michael Trainor, 151–79. Göttingen: Vandenhoeck & Ruprecht, 2011.

Campbell, Douglas A. "Anchor for Pauline Chronology: Paul's Flight from the 'Ethnarch of Aretas' (2 Corinthians 11:32–33)." *Journal of Biblical Literature* 121.2 (2002): 279–302.

———. *Framing Paul: An Epistolary Biography*. Grand Rapids: Eerdmans, 2014.

———. "Possible Inscriptional Attestation to Sergius Paul[l]us (Acts 13:6–12), and the Implications for Pauline Chronology." *Journal of Theological Studies*, n.s., 56.1 (2005): 1–29.

Campbell, William Sanger. "The Narrator as 'He,' 'Me,' and 'We': Grammatical Person in Ancient Histories and the Book of Acts." *Journal of Biblical Literature* 129.2 (2010): 385–407.

———. *The "We" Passages in the Acts of the Apostles: The Narrator as Narrative Character*. Atlanta: Society of Biblical Literature, 2007.

Carleton Paget, James. "The Definition of the Terms *Jewish Christian* and *Jewish Christianity* in the History of Research." In *Jewish Believers in Jesus: The Early Centuries*, edited by Oskar Skarsaune and Reidar Hvalvik, 22–52. Peabody, MA: Hendrickson, 2007.

———. "The *Epistle of Barnabas* and the Writings That Later Formed the New Testament." In *Reception of the New Testament in the Apostolic Fathers*, edited by Andrew F. Gregory and Christopher M. Tuckett, 229–49. Oxford: Oxford University Press, 2005.

———. *The Epistle of Barnabas: Outlook and Background*. Tübingen: Mohr Siebeck, 1994.

Carlson, Stephen C. "Clement of Alexandria and the 'Order' of the Gospels." *New Testament Studies* 47 (2001): 118–25.

———, ed. *Papias of Hierapolis, Exposition of Dominical Oracles: The Fragments, Testimonia, and Reception of a Second-Century Commentator*. Oxford Early Christian Texts. Oxford: Oxford University Press, 2021.

Casey, Maurice. *Aramaic Sources of Mark's Gospel*. Cambridge: Cambridge University Press, 1998.

———. *From Jewish Prophet to Gentile God: The Origins and Development of New Testament Christology.* Louisville: Westminster John Knox, 1991.

Charlesworth, James H. "Can One Recover Aramaic Sources behind Mark's Gospel?" *Review of Rabbinic Judaism* 5.2 (2002): 249–58.

Chilton, Bruce. "Maurice Casey's *Aramaic Sources of Mark's Gospel.*" *Journal of Biblical Literature* 120.1 (2001): 169–71.

Clark, Kenneth W. "Worship in the Jerusalem Temple after A.D. 70." *New Testament Studies* 6.4 (1960): 269–80.

Collingwood, R. G. *The Idea of History.* Edited by Jan van der Dussen. Rev. ed. Oxford: Oxford University Press, 1994.

Comfort, Philip Wesley, and David P. Barrett. *The Text of the Earliest New Testament Greek Manuscripts.* 3rd ed. 2 vols. Grand Rapids: Kregel, 2019.

Conzelmann, Hans. *Acts.* Translated by James Limburg, A. Thomas Kraabel, and Donald H. Juel. Minneapolis: Fortress, 1987.

———. *1 Corinthians.* Translated by James W. Leitch. Philadelphia: Fortress, 1975.

Cranfield, C. E. B. *Romans.* 2 vols. London: T&T Clark, 1975–79.

Crook, Zeba. "Collective Memory Distortion and the Quest for the Historical Jesus." *Journal for the Study of the Historical Jesus* 11.1 (2013): 53–76.

Crossley, James. *The Date of Mark's Gospel: Insight from the Law in Earliest Christianity.* London: T&T Clark, 2004.

Davies, W. D., and Dale C. Allison Jr. *Matthew.* 3 vols. London: T&T Clark, 1988–97.

Dibelius, Martin, and Hans Conzelmann. *The Pastoral Epistles.* Translated by Philip Buttolph and Adela Yarbro. Minneapolis: Fortress, 1972.

Dio Cassius. *Roman History.* Translated by Earnest Cary. LCL. Cambridge, MA: Harvard University Press, 1982–94.

Dodd, C. H. "The Fall of Jerusalem and the 'Abomination of Desolation.'" *Journal of Roman Studies* 37 (1947): 47–54.

Donahue, John R. Review of *Redating the New Testament,* by John A. T. Robinson. *Journal of the American Academy of Religion* 42.2 (1978): 212.

Donahue, John R., and Daniel J. Harrington. *Mark.* Collegeville, MN: Liturgical Press, 2002.

Draper, Jonathan A. "The *Didache* in Modern Research." In *The "Didache" in Modern Research,* edited by Jonathan A. Draper, 1–42. Leiden: Brill, 1996.

Dungan, David Laird. *The History of the Synoptic Problem: The Canon, the Text, the Composition, and the Interpretation of the Gospels.* New York: Doubleday, 1999.

Dunn, James D. G. *Christology in the Making: A New Testament Inquiry into the Origins of the Doctrine of the Incarnation.* 2nd ed. Grand Rapids: Eerdmans, 1996.

———. *Galatians.* London: A&C Black, 1993.

———. *The Theology of Paul the Apostle.* Grand Rapids: Eerdmans, 1998.

Dupont, Jacques. *The Sources of the Acts*. Translated by Kathleen Pond. London: Herder & Herder, 1964.

Duprez, André. *Jésus et les dieux guérisseurs: A propos de Jean, V*. Cahiers de la Revue biblique 12. Paris: Gabalda, 1970.

Eastman, David L. *The Ancient Martyrdom Accounts of Peter and Paul*. Atlanta: SBL Press, 2015.

———. *The Many Deaths of Peter and Paul*. Oxford: Oxford University Press, 2019.

Edmundson, George. *The Church in Rome in the First Century: An Examination of Various Controverted Questions Relating to Its History, Chronology, Literature and Traditions*. London: Longmans, Green, 1913.

Ehrman, Bart. *Forgery and Counterforgery: The Use of Literary Deceit in Early Christian Polemics*. Oxford: Oxford University Press, 2013.

Elliott, John H. *1 Peter*. Garden City, NY: Doubleday, 2000.

Ellis, E. Earle. "Dating the New Testament." *New Testament Studies* 26.4 (1980): 487–502.

———. *The Making of the New Testament Documents*. Atlanta: Scholars Press, 1999.

———. *Prophecy and Hermeneutic in Early Christianity*. Grand Rapids: Eerdmans, 1978.

Erlemann, K. "Die Datierung des ersten Klemensbriefes—Anfangen an eine Communis Opinio." *New Testament Studies* 44 (1998): 591–607.

Eusebius. *Ecclesiastical History*. Translated by Kirsopp Lake and J. E. L. Oulton. 2 vols. LCL. Cambridge, MA: Harvard University Press, 1926–32.

Evans, Craig A. *Mark 8:27–16:20*. Nashville: Thomas Nelson, 2001.

Eve, Eric. *Behind the Gospels: Understanding the Oral Tradition*. Minneapolis: Fortress, 2013.

Falls, Thomas B. *Saint Justin Martyr*. Washington, DC: Catholic University Press, 1948.

Fischer, David Hackett. *Historians' Fallacies: Toward a Logic of Historical Thought*. New York: Harper, 1970.

Fitzmyer, Joseph A. *Acts*. New York: Doubleday, 1988.

———. *First Corinthians*. New Haven: Yale University Press, 2008.

———. *Luke*. 2 vols. New York: Doubleday, 1970–85.

———. *Philemon*. Garden City, NY: Doubleday, 2000.

———. *Romans*. Garden City, NY: Doubleday, 1993.

———. "Two Views of New Testament Interpretation: Popular and Technical." Review of *Can We Trust the New Testament?* and *Redating the New Testament*, by John A. T. Robinson. *Interpretation* 32.3 (1978): 309–13.

Foster, Ora Delmer. "The Literary Relations of the First Epistle of Peter with Their Bearing on Date and Place of Authorship." *Transactions of the Connecticut Academy of Arts and Sciences* 17 (1913): 363–538.

Foster, Paul. *Colossians*. London: T&T Clark, 2016.

———. "The Epistles of Ignatius of Antioch and the Writings That Later Formed the New Testament." In *Reception of the New Testament in the Apostolic Fathers*, edited by Andrew F. Gregory and Christopher M. Tuckett, 159–86. Oxford: Oxford University Press, 2005.

———. "Q and James: A Source-Critical Conundrum." In *James, 1 and 2 Peter, and Early Jesus Traditions*, edited by Alicia J. Batten and John S. Kloppenborg, 3–34. London: T&T Clark, 2014.

Furnish, Victor Paul. *II Corinthians*. Garden City, NY: Doubleday, 1984.

Gamble, Harry Y. *Books and Readers in the Early Church: A History of Early Christian Texts*. New Haven: Yale University Press, 1995.

Garrow, Alan J. P. *The Gospel of Matthew's Dependence upon the Didache*. London: T&T Clark, 2004.

Gibson, Shimon. "The Pool of Bethesda in Jerusalem and Jewish Purification Practices of the Second Temple Period." *Proche-Orient Chrétien* 55 (2005): 270–93.

Goodacre, Mark. *The Case Against Q: Studies in Markan Priority and the Synoptic Problem*. Harrisburg, PA: Trinity Press International, 2002.

———. *Thomas and the Gospels: The Case for Thomas's Familiarity with the Synoptics*. Grand Rapids: Eerdmans, 2012.

Goulder, Michael D. "Did Peter Ever Go to Rome?" *Scottish Journal of Theology* 57.4 (2004): 376–96.

Grant, Robert M. Review of *Redating the New Testament*, by John A. T. Robinson. *Journal of Biblical Literature* 97.2 (1978): 294–96.

Green, Gene L. *Vox Petri: A Theology of Peter*. Eugene, OR: Wipf & Stock, 2019.

Gregory, Andrew F. "Disturbing Trajectories: 1 Clement, the Shepherd of Hermas and the Development of Early Roman Christianity." In *Rome in the Bible and the Early Church*, edited by Peter Oakes, 142–66. Grand Rapids: Baker Academic, 2002

———. "1 Clement and the Writings That Later Formed the New Testament." In *The Reception of the New Testament in the Apostolic Fathers*, edited by Andrew F. Gregory and Christopher M. Tuckett, 129–57. Oxford: Oxford University Press, 2005.

———. *The Reception of Luke and Acts in the Period before Irenaeus*. Tübingen: Mohr Siebeck, 2003.

Grenfell, Bernard P., and Arthur S. Hunt, eds. *The Oxyrhynchus Papyri*. Series 18. London: Egypt Exploration Society in Graeco-Roman Memoirs, 1922.

Guelich, Robert A. *Mark 1–8:26*. Dallas: Word, 1989.

Gundry, Robert H. *Mark: A Commentary on His Apology for the Cross*. Grand Rapids: Eerdmans, 1993.

———. *Matthew: A Commentary on His Handbook for a Mixed Church under Persecution*. 2nd ed. Grand Rapids: Eerdmans, 1994.

Hagner, Donald A. *Matthew*. 2 vols. Dallas: Word, 1993–95.

———. *The Use of the Old and New Testaments in Clement of Rome*. Leiden: Brill, 1973.

Hardy, E. R. Review of *Redating the New Testament*, by John A. T. Robinson. *Church History* 47.2 (1978): 215.

Hare, Douglas R. A. Introduction to *Chapters in a Life of Paul*, by John Knox. Rev. ed. London: SCM, 1990.

Harnack, Adolf von. *Acts of the Apostles*. Translated by J. R. Wilkinson. London: Williams & Norgate, 1909.

———. *The Date of the Acts and of the Synoptic Gospels*. Translated by J. R. Wilkinson. New York: Williams & Norgate, 1911.

———. *Die Chronologie der Litteratur bis Irenaeus*. Vol. 2, part 1, of *Geschichte der altchristlichen Litteratur bis Eusebius*. Leipzig: Hinrichs, 1897.

———. *Marcion: Gospel of the Alien God*. Translated by John E. Steely and Lyle D. Bierma. Durham, NC: Labyrinth, 1990.

Harrington, Daniel J. *1 Peter, Jude, 2 Peter*. Collegeville, MN: Liturgical Press, 2003.

———. *Matthew*. Collegeville, MN: Liturgical Press, 2007.

Harrington, Wilfrid J. *Revelation*. Collegeville, MN: Liturgical Press, 2008.

Harris, William V. *Ancient Literacy*. Cambridge, MA: Harvard University Press, 1989.

Harrison, P. N. *Polycarp's Two Epistles to the Philippians*. Cambridge: Cambridge University Press, 1936.

Hartin, Patrick J. *James*. Collegeville, MN: Liturgical Press, 2003.

Helm, Rudolf. *Die Chronik des Hieronymus*. Berlin: Akademie-Verlag, 1956.

Hemer, Colin J. *The Book of Acts in the Setting of Hellenistic History*. Edited by Conrad H. Gempf. Winona Lake, IN: Eisenbrauns, 1990.

Hendel, Ronald, and Jan Joosten. *How Old Is the Hebrew Bible? A Linguistic, Textual, and Historical Study*. New Haven: Yale University Press, 2018.

Hengel, Martin. *The Four Gospels and the One Gospel of Jesus Christ*. Translated by John Bowden. Harrisburg, PA: Trinity Press International, 2000.

———. *Judaism and Hellenism: Studies in Their Encounter in Palestine during the Early Hellenistic Period*. Translated by John Bowden. 2 vols. Philadelphia: Fortress, 1974.

———. *The Son of God: The Origin of Christology and the History of Jewish-Hellenistic Religion*. Philadelphia: Fortress, 1976.

———. *Studies in the Gospel of Mark*. Translated by John Bowden. London: SCM, 1985.

Herron, Thomas J. *Clement and the Early Church of Rome: The Dating of Clement's First Epistle to the Corinthians*. Steubenville, OH: Emmaus Road, 2008.

———. "The Most Probable Date of the First Epistle of Clement to the Corinthians." *Studia Patristica* 21 (1989): 106–21.

Hill, Charles E. *The Johannine Corpus in the Early Church*. Oxford: Oxford University Press, 2004.

Hill, Wesley. *Paul and the Trinity: Persons, Relations, and the Pauline Letters*. Grand Rapids: Eerdmans, 2015.

Holmes, Michael W. *The Apostolic Fathers: Greek Texts and English Translations*. 3rd ed. Grand Rapids: Baker Academic, 2007.

———. "Polycarp's *Letter to the Philippians* and the Writings That Later Formed the New Testament." In *The Reception of the New Testament in the Apostolic Fathers*, edited by Andrew F. Gregory and Christopher M. Tuckett, 187–228. Oxford: Oxford University Press, 2005.

Hooker, Morna D. *The Gospel according to Mark*. London: Continuum, 2001.

Hurtado, Larry W. *Lord Jesus Christ: Devotion to Jesus in Earliest Christianity*. Grand Rapids: Eerdmans, 2003.

———. *One God, One Lord: Early Christian Devotion and Ancient Jewish Monotheism*. 3rd ed. London: T&T Clark, 2015.

Huttner, Ulrich. *Early Christianity in the Lycus Valley*. Translated by David Green. Leiden: Brill, 2013.

Instone-Brewer, David. "The Eighteen Benedictions and the *Minim* before 70 C.E." *Journal of Theological Studies*, n.s., 54.1 (2003): 25–44.

Jefford, Clayton N. *The Sayings of Jesus in the Teachings of the Twelve Apostles*. Leiden: Brill, 1989.

———. "Tradition and Witness in Antioch: Acts 15 and Didache 6." *Perspectives in Religious Studies* 19.4 (1992): 409–19.

Jewett, Robert. *A Chronology of Paul's Life*. Philadelphia: Fortress, 1979.

———. *Romans*. Minneapolis: Fortress, 2007.

Johnson, Luke Timothy. *The First and Second Letters to Timothy*. Garden City, NY: Doubleday, 2001.

———. *The Gospel of Luke*. Collegeville, MN: Liturgical Press, 1991.

———. *The Letter of James*. Garden City, NY: Doubleday, 1995.

Jones, Christopher P. "The Historicity of the Neronian Persecution: A Response to Brent Shaw." *New Testament Studies* 63 (2017): 146–52.

Josephus. Translated by Henry St. J. Thackeray et al. 10 vols. LCL. Cambridge, MA: Harvard University Press, 1926–65.

Keener, Craig S. *Acts*. 4 vols. Grand Rapids: Baker Academic, 2012–15.

———. *Galatians*. Grand Rapids: Baker Academic, 2019.

———. *The Gospel of John*. 2 vols. Grand Rapids: Baker Academic, 2003.

Keith, Chris. *Jesus' Literacy: Scribal Culture and the Teacher from Galilee*. London: T&T Clark, 2011.

Kelly, J. N. D. *The Epistles of Peter and Jude*. London: A&C Black, 1969.

Kim, Young Kyu. "Paleographical Dating of P⁴⁶ to the Later First Century." *Biblica* 69.2 (1988): 248–57.

King, Karen L. "'The Gnostic Myth': How Does Its Demise Impact Twenty-First Century Historiography of Christianity's Second Century?" In *Christianity in the Second Century: Themes and Developments*, edited by Judith M. Lieu and James Carleton Paget, 122–36. Cambridge: Cambridge University Press, 2017.

Kinzig, Wolfgang. "The Nazoreans." In *Jewish Believers in Jesus: The Early Centuries*, edited by Oskar Skarsaune and Reidar Hvalvik, 463–87. Peabody, MA: Hendrickson, 2007.

Kitchen, Kenneth A. *On the Reliability of the Old Testament*. Grand Rapids: Eerdmans, 2003.

Klinghardt, Matthias. "The Marcionite Gospel and the Synoptic Problem." *Novum Testamentum* 50 (2008): 1–27.

Klink, Edward W., III, ed. *The Audience of the Gospels: The Origin and Function of the Gospels in Early Christianity*. London: T&T Clark, 2010.

———. *The Sheep of the Fold: The Audience and Origin of the Gospel of John*. Cambridge: Cambridge University Press, 2007.

Kloppenborg, John S. "Luke's Geography: Knowledge, Ignorance, Sources, and Spatial Conception." In *Luke on Jesus, Paul, and Earliest Christianity: What Did He Really Know?*, edited by Joseph Verheyden and John S. Kloppenborg, 101–43. Leuven: Peeters, 2017.

———. "The Reception of the Jesus Tradition in James." In *The Catholic Epistles and Apostolic Tradition*, edited by Karl-Wilhelm Niebuhr and Robert T. Wall, 71–100. Waco: Baylor University Press, 2009.

Kloppenborg Verbin, John S. *Excavating Q: The History and Setting of the Sayings Gospel*. Minneapolis: Fortress, 2000.

Knight, Jonathan. Preface to *Redrawing the Boundaries: The Date of Early Christian Literature*, by J. V. M. Sturdy. Edited by Jonathan Knight. London: Equinox, 2007.

Knox, John. *Chapters in a Life of Paul*. Rev. ed. London: SCM, 1990.

———. *Marcion and the New Testament*. Chicago: University of Chicago Press, 1942.

Koester, Craig R. *Hebrews*. Garden City, NY: Doubleday, 2001.

———. *Revelation*. Garden City, NY: Doubleday, 2008.

Kürzinger, Josef. *Papias von Hierapolis und die Evangelien des Neuen Testaments*. Regensburg: Friedrich Pustet, 1983.

Lambrecht, Jan. *Second Corinthians*. Collegeville, MN: Liturgical Press, 1999.

Lampe, Peter. *From Paul to Valentinus: Christians at Rome in the First Two Centuries*. Edited by Marshall D. Johnson. Translated by Michael Steinhauser. Minneapolis: Fortress, 2003.

Lane, William L. *Hebrews*. 2 vols. Dallas: Word, 1991.

Lange, John. "The Argument from Silence." *History and Theory* 5.3 (1966): 288–301.

Langer, Ruth. *Cursing the Christians? A History of the Birkat HaMinim.* Oxford: Oxford University Press, 2012.

Langlois, C. V., and C. Seignobos. *Introduction to the Study of History.* Translated by G. G. Berry. London: Duckworth, 1898.

Laws, Sophie. *The Epistle of James.* London: A&C Black, 1980.

Le Donne, Anthony. "The Problem of Selectivity in Memory Research: A Response to Zeba Crook." *Journal for the Study of the Historical Jesus* 11.1 (2013): 77–97.

Levine, Lee I. *The Ancient Synagogue: The First Thousand Years.* 2nd ed. New Haven: Yale University Press, 2005.

Lieu, Judith M. *Marcion and the Making of a Heretic: God and Scripture in the Second Century.* Cambridge: Cambridge University Press, 2015.

Lightfoot, J. B. *The Apostolic Fathers.* Part 1, *S. Clement of Rome.* 2 vols. London: MacMillan, 1890.

———. *Biblical Essays.* 2nd ed. London: MacMillan, 1904.

———. *The Epistles of 2 Corinthians and 1 Peter: Newly Discovered Commentaries.* Edited by Ben Witherington III and Todd D. Still. The Lightfoot Legacy Set 3. Downers Grove, IL: IVP Academic, 2016.

———. *The Gospel of St. John: A Newly Discovered Commentary.* Edited by Ben Witherington III and Todd D. Still. The Lightfoot Legacy Set 2. Downers Grove, IL: IVP Academic, 2015.

Lincoln, Andrew T. *Saint John.* London: Continuum, 2005.

Lohse, Eduard. *Colossians and Philemon.* Translated by William R. Poehlmann and Robert J. Karris. Philadelphia: Fortress, 1971.

Loke, Andrew Ter Ern. *The Origins of Divine Christology.* Cambridge: Cambridge University Press, 2017.

Lonergan, Bernard. *Method in Theology.* Edited by Robert M. Doran and John D. Dadosky. 3rd ed. Toronto: University of Toronto Press, 2017.

Lookadoo, Jonathon. "The Date and Authenticity of the Ignatian Letters: An Outline of Recent Discussions." *Currents in Biblical Research* 19.1 (2020): 88–114.

Lüdemann, Gerd. *Paul, Apostle to the Gentiles: Studies in Chronology.* Translated by F. Stanley Jones. London: SCM, 1984.

Luz, Ulrich. *Matthew.* Translated by James E. Crouch. 3 vols. Minneapolis: Fortress, 2001–7.

MacEwen, Robert K. *Matthean Posteriority: An Exploration of Matthew's Use of Mark and Luke as a Solution to the Synoptic Problem.* London: T&T Clark, 2015.

Magness, Jodi. "Sweet Memory: Archaeological Evidence of Jesus in Jerusalem." In *Memory in Ancient Rome and Early Christianity,* edited by Karl Galinsky, 324–43. Oxford: Oxford University Press, 2016.

Malherbe, Abraham J. *The Letters to the Thessalonians.* Garden City, NY: Doubleday, 2000.

Mangina, Joseph L. *Revelation*. Grand Rapids: Brazos, 2010.

Marcus, Joel. "*Birkat ha-Minim* Revisited." *New Testament Studies* 55 (2009): 523–51.

———. *Mark 1–8: A New Translation with Introduction and Commentary*. Anchor Bible 27. New York: Doubleday, 2000.

———. *Mark 8–16: A New Translation with Introduction and Commentary*. Anchor Yale Bible 27A. New Haven: Yale University Press, 2009.

Marshall, I. Howard. *The Pastoral Epistles*. London: T&T Clark, 1999.

Martin, Ralph P. *James*. Dallas: Word, 1988.

———. *2 Corinthians*. 2nd ed. Grand Rapids: Zondervan, 2014.

Martyn, J. Louis. *Galatians*. Garden City, NY: Doubleday, 1997.

———. *History and Theology in the Fourth Gospel*. 3rd ed. Louisville: Westminster John Knox, 2003.

Mason, Steve. *Josephus and the New Testament*. 2nd ed. Peabody, MA: Hendrickson, 2003.

Matson, Mark A. *In Dialogue with Another Gospel? The Influence of the Fourth Gospel on the Passion Narrative of the Gospel of Luke*. Atlanta: Society of Biblical Literature Press, 2001.

Méndez, Hugo. "Did the Johannine Community Exist?" *Journal of New Testament Studies* 42.3 (2020): 350–74.

Merrill, Elmer Truesdell. *Essays in Early Christian History*. London: MacMillan, 1924.

Meyer, Ben F. *The Aims of Jesus*. Eugene, OR: Pickwick, 2002.

———. *Critical Realism and the New Testament*. Allison Park, PA: Pickwick, 1989.

———. *Reality and Illusion in New Testament Scholarship: A Primer in Critical Realist Hermeneutics*. Collegeville, MN: Liturgical Press, 1994.

Michaels, J. Ramsey. *1 Peter*. Dallas: Word, 1988.

Milavec, Aaron. *The Didache: Faith, Hope, and Life of the Earliest Christian Communities, 50–70 C.E.* Mahwah, NY: Paulist Press, 2003.

Mitchell, Alan C. *Hebrews*. Collegeville, MN: Liturgical Press, 2007.

Moll, Sebastian. *The Arch-Heretic Marcion*. Tübingen: Mohr Siebeck, 2010.

Moloney, Francis J. *The Apocalypse of John: A Commentary*. Grand Rapids: Baker Academic, 2020.

———. *The Gospel of John*. Collegeville, MN: Liturgical Press, 1998.

Moody, Dale. Review of *Redating the New Testament*, by John A. T. Robinson. *Review and Expositor* 74.2 (1977): 234–36.

Muddiman, John. *The Letter to the Ephesians*. London: Continuum, 2001.

Murphy, Donald J. Review of *Redating the New Testament*, by John A. T. Robinson. *Theological Studies* 38.3 (1977): 563–64.

Murphy-O'Connor, Jerome. *Keys to Jerusalem: Collected Essays*. Oxford: Oxford University Press, 2012.

Neyrey, Jerome H. *2 Peter, Jude*. Garden City, NY: Doubleday, 1993.

Niederwimmer, Kurt. *The Didache*. Translated by Linda M. Mahoney. Minneapolis: Fortress, 1998.

Nolland, John. *Luke*. 3 vols. Waco: Word, 1989–93.

Nongbri, Brent. "The Limits of Paleographic Dating of Literary Papryi: Some Observations on the Date and Provenance of P. Bodmer II (P66)." *Museum Helveticum* 71.1 (2014): 1–35.

———. "P. Bodmer 2 as Possible Evidence for the Circulation of the Gospel according to John without Chapter 21." *Early Christianity* 9 (2018): 345–60.

———. "Reconsidering the Place of Papyrus Bodmer XIV–XV (P^{75}) in the Textual Criticism of the New Testament." *Journal of Biblical Literature* 135.2 (2016): 405–37.

———. "The Use and Abuse of P^{52}: Papyrological Pitfalls in the Dating of the Fourth Gospel." *Harvard Theological Review* 98.1 (2005): 23–48.

North, Wendy E. S. *What John Knew and What John Wrote: A Study in John and the Synoptics*. Lanham, MD: Lexington Books / Fortress Academic, 2020.

Orsini, Pasquale, and Willy Clarysse. "Early New Testament Manuscripts and Their Dates: A Critique of Theological Paleography." *Ephemerides Theologicae Lovanienses* 88.4 (2012): 443–74.

Osiek, Carolyn. *The Shepherd of Hermas*. Minneapolis: Fortress, 1999.

Pagels, Elaine. *The Johannine Gospel in Gnostic Exegesis: Heracleon's Commentary on John*. Nashville: Abingdon, 1973.

Painter, John. *1, 2, and 3 John*. Collegeville, MN: Liturgical Press, 2002.

Parker, Pierson. "John and John Mark." *Journal of Biblical Literature* 79.2 (1960): 97–110.

Pervo, Richard I. *Dating Acts: Between the Evangelists and the Apologists*. Santa Rosa, CA: Polebridge, 2006.

Pitkänen, Pekka. *Central Sanctuary and Centralization of Worship in Ancient Israel: From the Settlement to the Building of Solomon's Temple*. Piscataway, NJ: Gorgias, 2003.

Pitre, Brant. *Jesus and the Last Supper*. Grand Rapids: Eerdmans, 2015.

Plummer, Alfred. *A Critical and Exegetical Commentary on the Gospel according to St. Luke*. 4th ed. Edinburgh: T&T Clark, 1901.

Porter, Stanley E. *Verbal Aspect in the New Testament, with Reference to Tense and Mood*. New York: Lang, 1989.

Redman, Judith C. S. "How Accurate Are Eyewitnesses? Bauckham and the Eyewitnesses in the Light of Psychological Research." *Journal of Biblical Literature* 129.1 (2010): 177–97.

Reicke, Bo. *Re-examining Paul's Letters: The History of the Pauline Correspondence*. Edited by David P. Moessner and Ingalisa Reicke. Harrisburg, PA: Trinity Press International, 2001.

Reitzenstein, Richard. *Das iranische Erlösungsmysterium: Religionsgeschichtliche Untersuchungen.* Bonn: Marcus & Weber, 1921.

Rengstorf, K. H. "Der Stadt der Mörder (Mt. 22:7)." In *Judentum-Urchristentum-Kirche: Festschrift für Joachim Jeremias*, edited by Walther Eltester, 106–29. Berlin: Töpelmann, 1960.

Reumann, John. *Philippians.* New Haven: Yale University Press, 2008.

Richter, Sandra Lynn. "The Question of Provenance and the Economics of Deuteronomy." *Journal for the Study of the Old Testament* 42.1 (2017): 23–50.

———. "The Question of Provenance and the Economics of Deuteronomy: The Neo-Babylonian and Persian Periods." *Catholic Biblical Quarterly* 82.4 (2020): 547–66.

Riesner, Rainer. *Paul's Early Period: Chronology, Mission Strategy, Theology.* Translated by Doug Stott. Grand Rapids: Eerdmans, 1998.

Robbins, Vernon K. "By Land and by Sea: The We-Passages and Ancient Sea Voyages." In *Perspectives on Luke-Acts*, edited by Charles H. Talbert, 215–42. Edinburgh: T&T Clark, 1978.

———. "The We-Passages in Acts and Ancient Sea-Voyages." *Biblical Research* 20 (1975): 5–18.

Roberts, C. H. "An Unpublished Fragment of the Fourth Gospel in the John Rylands Library." *Bulletin of the John Rylands Library* 20.1 (1936): 45–55.

Robinson, John A. T. *Can We Trust the New Testament?* Grand Rapids: Eerdmans, 1977.

———. *Honest to God.* London: SCM, 1963.

———. *The Priority of John.* Edited by J. F. Coakley. London: SCM, 1985.

———. *Redating the New Testament.* London: SCM, 1976.

———. *Twelve New Testament Studies.* London: SCM, 1962.

Roth, Dieter T. "Marcion's Gospel and Luke: The History of Research in Current Debate." *Journal of Biblical Literature* 127.3 (2008): 513–27.

Rothschild, Clare K. *Hebrews as Pseudepigraphon: The History and Significance of the Pauline Attribution of Hebrews.* Tübingen: Mohr Siebeck, 2009.

Rowe, C. Kavin "History, Hermeneutics, and the Unity of Luke-Acts." In *Rethinking the Unity and Reception of Luke and Acts*, edited by Andrew F. Gregory and C. Kavin Rowe, 43–65. Columbia: University of South Carolina Press, 2010.

Ryan, Jordan J. "Jesus at the Crossroads of Inference and Imagination: The Relevance of R. G. Collingwood's Philosophy of History for Current Methodological Discussions in Historical Jesus Research." *Journal for the Study of the Historical Jesus* 13.1 (2015): 66–89.

Schechter, Solomon, and Israel Abrahams. "Genizah Specimens." *Jewish Quarterly Review* 10 (1898): 654–61.

Schmidt, Andreas. "Zwei Anmerkungen zu P.Ryl. III 457." *Archiv für Papyrusforschung* 35 (1989): 11–12.

Schmithals, Walter. Introduction to *The Gospel of John*, by Rudolf Bultmann, 3–12. Translated by G. R. Beasley-Murray, R. W. N. Hoare, and J. K. Riches. 1914. Reprint, Eugene, OR: Wipf & Stock, 2014.

Schnabel, Eckhard J. *Early Christian Mission*. 2 vols. Downers Grove, IL: InterVarsity, 2004.

Schneemelcher, Wilhelm. "The Acts of Peter." In *New Testament Apocrypha*, rev. ed, edited by Wilhelm Schneemelcher, 271–321. Translated by R. McL. Wilson. 2 vols. Louisville: Westminster John Knox, 2003.

Schoedel, William R. *Ignatius of Antioch*. Minneapolis: Fortress, 1985.

Schubert, Josef. *Dating Deuteronomy: The Wellhausen Fallacy*. Eugene, OR: Wipf & Stock, 2018.

Schwartz, Daniel, and Zeev Weiss, eds. *Was 70 CE a Watershed in Jewish History? On Jews and Judaism Before and After the Destruction of the Second Temple*. Leiden: Brill, 2012.

Shaw, Brent D. "The Myth of the Neronian Persecution." *Journal of Roman Studies* 105 (2015): 73–100.

———. "Response to Christopher Jones: The Historicity of the Neronian Persecution." *New Testament Studies* 64 (2018): 231–42.

Skarsaune, Oskar. "Jewish Believers in Jesus in Antiquity—Problems of Definition, Method, and Sources." In *Jewish Believers in Jesus: The Early Centuries*, edited by Oskar Skarsaune and Reidar Hvalvik, 1–21. Peabody, MA: Hendrickson, 2007.

Skarsaune, Oskar, and Reidar Hvalvik, eds. *Jewish Believers in Jesus: The Early Centuries*. Peabody, MA: Hendrickson, 2007.

Sloyan, Gerard S. Review of *Redating the New Testament*, by John A. T. Robinson. *Horizons* 5.1 (1978): 96–99.

Smalley, Stephen S. *1, 2, 3 John*. Dallas: Word, 1984.

Smith, D. Moody. *John among the Gospels*. 2nd ed. Columbia: University of South Carolina Press, 2001.

Snyder, Graydon F. Review of *Redating the New Testament*, by John A. T. Robinson. *Catholic Biblical Quarterly* 40.1 (1978): 134–36.

Steenberg, M. C. "Irenaeus on Scripture, *Graphe*, and the Status of *Hermas*." *St. Vladimir's Theological Quarterly* 53 (2009): 29–66.

Stevens, Luke J. "Did Eusebius Read Papias?" *Journal of Theological Studies* 70.1 (2019): 163–83.

Strange, James F. "Archaeological Evidence of Jewish Believers?" In *Jewish Believers in Jesus: The Early Centuries*, edited by Oskar Skarsaune and Reidar Hvalvik, 710–41. Peabody, MA: Hendrickson, 2007.

Strecker, Georg. *The Johannine Letters*. Translated by Linda M. Maloney. Minneapolis: Fortress, 1996.

Sturdy, J. V. M. *Redrawing the Boundaries: The Date of Early Christian Literature.* Edited by Jonathan Knight. London: Equinox, 2007.

———. Review of *Redating the New Testament*, by John A. T. Robinson. *Journal of Theological Studies*, n.s., 30.1 (1979): 255–62.

Suetonius. *The Lives of the Caesars and the Lives of Illustrious Men.* Translated by J. C. Rolfe. 2 vols. LCL. Cambridge, MA: Harvard University Press, 1914.

Tacitus. *The Histories and the Annals.* Translated by Clifford H. Moore and John Jackson. 4 vols. LCL. Cambridge, MA: Harvard University Press, 1937.

Tajra, Harry W. *The Martyrdom of St. Paul: Historical and Judicial Context, Traditions, and Legends.* Tübingen: Mohr Siebeck, 1994.

Thrall, Margaret E. *The Second Epistle to the Corinthians.* 2 vols. London: T&T Clark, 1994–2000.

Trobisch, David. *Paul's Letter Collection: Tracing the Origins.* Minneapolis: Fortress, 1994.

Troftgruben, Troy M. *A Conclusion Unhindered: A Study of the Ending of Acts within Its Literary Environment.* Tübingen: Mohr Siebeck, 2010.

Tuckett, Christopher M. "The *Didache* and the Writings That Later Formed the New Testament." In *The Reception of the New Testament in the Apostolic Fathers*, edited by Andrew F. Gregory and Christopher M. Tuckett, 83–127. Oxford: Oxford University Press, 2005.

Tyson, Joseph B. *Marcion and Luke-Acts: A Defining Struggle.* Columbia: University of South Carolina Press, 2006.

Verheyden, Joseph. "The *Shepherd of Hermas* and the Writings That Later Formed the New Testament." In *Reception of the New Testament in the Apostolic Fathers*, edited by Andrew F. Gregory and Christopher M. Tuckett, 292–329. Oxford: Oxford University Press, 2005.

von Wahlde, Urban C. "Archaeology and John's Gospel." In *Jesus and Archaeology*, edited by James H. Charlesworth, 523–86. Grand Rapids: Eerdmans, 2006.

———. "The Gospel of John and Archaeology." In *The Oxford Handbook of Johannine Studies*, edited by Judith M. Lieu and Martinus C. de Boer, 101–20. Oxford: Oxford University Press, 2018.

Wallace, Daniel B. "John 5,2 and the Date of the Fourth Gospel." *Biblica* 71.2 (1990): 177–205.

Watson, Francis. "Toward a Literal Reading of the Gospels." In *The Gospels for All Christians: Rethinking the Gospel Audiences*, edited by Richard Bauckham, 195–217. Grand Rapids: Eerdmans, 1998.

Welborn, L. L. "On the Date of First Clement." *Biblical Research* 29 (1984): 35–54.

Wenham, John. *Redating Matthew, Mark and Luke: A Fresh Assault on the Synoptic Problem.* London: Hodder & Stoughton, 1992.

Whittaker, Molly. *Der Hirt des Hermas.* Berlin: Akademie-Verlag, 1956.

Wilhelm-Hooijbergh, A. E. "A Different View of Clemens Romanus." *Heythrop Journal* 16 (1975): 266–88.

Wilhite, Shawn J. *The Didache: A Commentary*. Eugene, OR: Cascade Books, 2019.

———. "Thirty-Five Years Later: A Summary of Didache Scholarship Since 1983." *Currents in Biblical Research* 17.3 (2019): 266–305.

Wise, Michael Owen. *Language and Literacy in Roman Judea: A Study of the Bar Kokhba Documents*. New Haven: Yale University Press, 2015.

Wright, N. T. *Jesus and the Victory of God*. London: SPCK, 1996.

Yarbro Collins, Adela. *Mark*. Minneapolis: Fortress, 2007.

Author Index

Scripture and Ancient Writings Index

Subject Index